Holt Literature & Language Arts

Fifth Course

S0-AWW-860

UNIVERSAL ACCESS **Interactive Reading**

- **Word Analysis, Fluency, and Systematic Vocabulary Development**
- **Reading Comprehension**
- **Literary Response and Analysis**

HOLT, RINEHART AND WINSTON

A Harcourt Education Company

Austin • Orlando • Chicago • New York • Toronto • London • San Diego

Credits

Editorial

Project Directors: Kathleen Daniel, Juliana Koenig
Editor: Amy Fleming
Managing Editor: Mike Topp
Manager of Editorial Services: Abigail Winograd
Senior Product Manager: Don Wulbrecht
Editorial Staff: Victoria Moreland, Brenda Sanabria, Jan Watson-Collins
Project Administration: Elizabeth LaManna
Editorial Support: Renée Benitez, Louise Fernandez, Bret Isaacs, Laurie Muir
Editorial Permissions: David Smith, Carrie Jones

Art, Design, and Production

Director: Athena Blackorby
Senior Design Director: Betty Mintz
Series Design: Proof Positive/Farrowlyne Associates, Inc.
Design and Electronic Files: Kirchoff/Wohlberg, Inc.
Photo Research: Kirchoff/Wohlberg, Inc.
Production Manager: Catherine Gessner
Production Coordinator: Joseph Padial

Printed in the United States of America
ISBN 0-03-065093-3

16 17 082 12 11 10 09 08

Contents

• PART ONE •
LITERATURE AND INFORMATIONAL READINGS

CHAPTER 2 American Romanticism (1800–1860)

CHAPTER 3   American Masters: Whitman and Dickinson

CHAPTER 4   The Rise of Realism: The Civil War to 1914

CHAPTER 6   Contemporary Literature (1939 to Present)

• PART TWO •
CONSUMER, WORKPLACE, AND PUBLIC DOCUMENTS

To the Student

A Book for You

*Reading a book is like re-writing it for yourself. . . .
You bring to a novel, anything you read, all your experience of the world.
You bring your history and you read it in your own terms.*
—Angela Carter, English novelist and short-story writer

Imagine this: a book full of stories you want to read and informational articles that are really interesting. Make it a book that actually tells you to write in it, circling, underlining, and jotting down responses. Fill it with graphic organizers that encourage you to think in a different way. Make it a size that's easy to carry around. That's *Interactive Reading*—a book created especially for you.

A Book Designed for Your Success

Interactive Reading is designed to accompany *Holt Literature and Language Arts,* Fifth Course. Like *Holt Literature and Language Arts,* its purpose is to help you interact with the selections and master the California English–Language Arts Content Standards. The chart below shows you how your book is organized.

Part One Literature and Informational Readings	Part Two Consumer, Workplace, and Public Documents
Literary and informational selections from *Holt Literature and Language Arts*	New selections that help you learn how to read various kinds of documents

When you read documents such as technical directions or a Web site, you usually read to "get the facts." When you read literature, you need to go beyond "the facts" and read between the lines of a poem or story to discover the writer's meaning. No matter what kind of reading you do, *Interactive Reading* will help you practice the skills you need to become an active and successful reader. Here's how . . .

Part One   Literature and Informational Readings

Interactive Reading will help you respond to, analyze, evaluate, and interpret literature. These skills will increase your understanding of the literature you read, which is a major goal of the California language arts standards.

In Part One of *Interactive Reading,* here is what you will find in each chapter.

- Every chapter begins with a **historical essay** that provides highlights of the period. A more detailed version of this essay can be found in the corresponding chapter of *Holt Literature and Language Arts.* This historical introduction is divided into short, easy-to-read sections. The interactive notes in the side column will guide you through each section, so that you come to understand the people, events, and ideas that shaped the life and literature of that period.

- Following the historical essay are **literary and informational selections.** These pieces were selected from *Holt Literature and Language Arts,* Fifth Course. They are reprinted in a single column and in larger type to give you the room you need to mark up the text and respond to the interactive notes in the side column.

The following features appear with the selections in Part One:

- A **Before You Read** page that teaches a literary focus and provides you with a reading skill to help you read the selection successfully and master the standards
- **Interactive notes** in the side column to guide your reading and help you respond to the selection
- A **Practice and Review graphic organizer** that helps you understand the reading skill and literary focus for the selection
- A **Vocabulary Development** page that provides practice with selection vocabulary (in cases where selection vocabulary is taught)

Part Two   Consumer, Workplace, and Public Documents

Reading various kinds of documents is another important goal of the California language arts standards. To help you master how to read these kinds of materials, Part Two contains:

- A **Before You Read** page that introduces you to the special features of the type of document you will be reading and teaches you the informational focus for the selection
- **New selections** accompanied by notes in the side column (as in Part One) to guide your reading and help you respond to the text
- A **Standards Review** page that helps you practice test-taking skills while applying the standards

At the back of your book, following Part Two, you will find more special features to help you keep track of what you have read and what you have learned:

- A **Checklist for Standards Mastery** that helps you track your progress by checking off the skills you have acquired
- A **Vocabulary Development** guide that explains how to read the pronunciation respellings provided with vocabulary and word study notes

What is reading but silent conversation?
—*Walter Savage Landor, English poet and essayist*

Reading is an interactive process, like a conversation. This book is designed to help you interact with the selections you read by marking them up, asking your own questions, taking notes, recording your own ideas, and responding to the questions of others. The more you "talk" to the text in this way, the more you will make valuable connections between your reading and your own life.

A Walk Through the Book

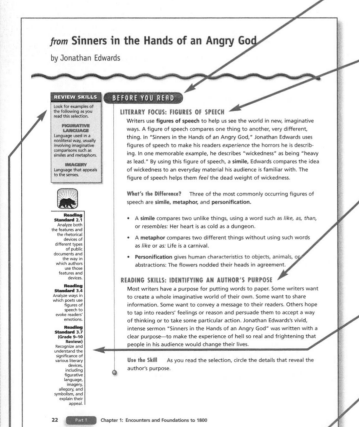

Historical Essay

This historical essay is a shortened version of the one that appears in *Holt Literature and Language Arts*. The short, easy-to-read sections will help you understand the political, religious, ethical, and social influences of the historical period.

Reading Standards

The California reading standards that are covered in the essay are listed here.

Side-column Notes

This essay, and each selection that follows, is accompanied by interactive notes in the side columns. The notes are designed to help you master the California standards that are listed with each selection. The notes guide your interaction with the text. Many notes ask you to circle or underline in the text itself. Others provide lines on which you can write your responses to questions.

Before You Read

This feature explains important elements of the selection you are about to read and sets the stage for reading.

Literary Focus

Here, you learn about the literary focus for the selection—the same focus that is covered in *Holt Literature and Language Arts*. Often, an activity is included to help you connect with and understand the literary focus.

Reading Skills

This feature provides a reading skill for you to apply to the selection. Each skill ties into and supports the literary focus so that you can make sense of the text while mastering the California standards.

Reading Standards

The California standards covered with the selection (both grade level and review) are listed here.

Review Skills

When a review standard is taught with a selection, definitions of key elements from the standard are given here.

A Walk Through the Book

from
Sinners in the Hands of an Angry God

Jonathan Edwards

So that, thus it is that natural men[1] are held in the hand of God, over the pit of hell; they have deserved the fiery pit, and are already sentenced to it; and God is dreadfully **provoked**, His anger is as great toward them as to those that are actually suffering the executions of the fierceness of His wrath in hell, and they have done nothing in the least to **appease** or abate[2] that anger, neither is God in the least bound by any promise to hold them up one moment: The devil is waiting for them, hell is gaping for them, the flames gather and flash about them, and would fain[3]
10 lay hold on them, and swallow them up; the fire pent up in their own hearts is struggling to break out: And they have no interest in any Mediator,[4] there are no means within reach that can be any security to them.

In short, they have no refuge, nothing to take hold of; all that preserves them every moment is the mere arbitrary will, and uncovenanted, unobliged forbearance[5] of an incensed[6] God.

The use of this awful subject may be for awakening unconverted persons in this congregation. This that you have heard is the case of every one of you that are out of Christ. That world
20 of misery, that lake of burning brimstone, is extended abroad under you. There is the dreadful pit of the glowing flames of the wrath of God; there is hell's wide gaping mouth open; and you

---

1. **natural men:** people who have not been "reborn."
2. **abate** v.: reduce in amount or intensity.
3. **fain** adv.: archaic word meaning "happily" or "gladly."
4. **Mediator:** Jesus Christ. In general, one who intervenes between two parties in conflict.
5. **forbearance** n.: tolerance or restraint.
6. **incensed** v. used as adj.: angered; enraged.

from Sinners in the Hands of an Angry God **23**

VOCABULARY

provoked (prə·vōkt') v.: used as adj.: angered.
appease (ə·pēz') v.: calm; satisfy.

IDENTIFY

Re-read lines 8–10. Circle the nouns, and underline the verbs and verb forms that create images of horror. *(Grade 9–10 Review)*

CLARIFY

Re-read lines 17–21. What does Edwards say is his **purpose** for discussing the subject of sinners and punishment? Underline the answer.

IDENTIFY

Underline the images in lines 19–22 that help you picture this "world of misery."

Interactive Selections from *Holt Literature and Language Arts*
The literary and informational selections in Part One also appear in *Holt Literature and Language Arts,* Fifth Course. The selections are reprinted in a single column and in larger type to give you the room you need to mark up the text.

Side-column Notes
Each selection is accompanied by notes in the side columns. They guide your interaction with the selection. Many notes ask you to circle or underline in the text itself. The notes will also help you—

- interpret, analyze, and evaluate the text
- understand literary elements
- build vocabulary
- develop word knowledge
- build fluency
- master the California grade-level and review standards

Footnotes
Difficult or unusual terms are defined in footnotes.

Practice and Review
After each selection, a **graphic organizer** gives you a visual way to organize, interpret, and understand the reading skill and literary focus of the selection.

PRACTICE AND REVIEW

from Sinners in the Hands of an Angry God

Reading Skills: Identifying an Author's Purpose   Most authors have a purpose, or reason, for writing. Jonathan Edwards's purpose for writing "Sinners in the Hands of an Angry God" is very clear, and his vivid details and frightening metaphors help him get his message across. Fill in the chart below with some details from the sermon that reveal Edwards's purpose for writing.

Author's Purpose
To scare his congregation into obeying the word of God

Passage 1

Passage 2

Passage 3

from Sinners in the Hands of an Angry God **27**

A Walk Through the Book

from Sinners in the Hands of an Angry God

VOCABULARY DEVELOPMENT

VOCABULARY IN CONTEXT

DIRECTIONS: Write vocabulary words from the Word Box on the correct blanks to complete the paragraph. Not all words will be used.

Word Box

provoked
appease
constitution
contrivance
inconceivable
omnipotent
abhors
abominable
ascribed
induce

Jonathan Edwards's emotional sermons described an all-powerful,

(1) _____ God. Edwards wanted to

(2) _____, or force, his listeners to obey God. His descrip-

tions of God were not meant to calm or (3) _____ the

fears of his audience. Instead, he wanted them to believe that God's anger was

(4) _____ by their sins. Many modern readers find

Edwards's scare tactics loathsome and (5) _____.

PREFIXES AND SUFFIXES

A **prefix** is a letter, syllable, or word part that is added to the beginning of a word. A **suffix** is a letter, syllable, or word part that is added to the end of a word. Both prefixes and suffixes change the meaning of the word.

DIRECTIONS: Using the information in the box, match each numbered word with its definition. Write the letters on the blanks.

Reading Standard 1.1 (Grade 9–10 Review) Identify and use the literal and figurative meanings of words and understand word derivations.

Common Prefixes and Suffixes	
con– means "with" or "together"	*–able* means "capable of"
omni– means "all"	*–ance* means "state of being"

____ 1. omnipresent   a. "come together"
____ 2. arguable   b. "able to be argued"
____ 3. attendance   c. "state of being; being present"
____ 4. converge   d. "able to be broken"
____ 5. breakable   e. "everywhere; present at all times"

✓ Check your Standards Mastery at the back of this book.

28   Part 1   Chapter 1: Encounters and Foundations to 1800

Vocabulary Development

After selections in which vocabulary words are taught, you will find this page of vocabulary development activities. These activities reinforce your understanding of the words' meanings and provide you with instruction and practice on a vocabulary skill.

Checklist for Standards Mastery

Each time you read, you learn something new. Track your growth as a reader and your progress toward success by checking off skills you have acquired. If you read all the selections in this book and complete the side-column note questions and activities, you will be able to check off all the standards for success listed below at least once.

✓	California Reading Standard (Grade 9–10 Review)	Selection/Author
☐	**1.1** Identify and use the literal and figurative meanings of words and understand word derivations.	
☐	**1.2** Distinguish between the denotative and connotative meanings of words and interpret the connotative power of words.	
☐	**1.3** Identify Greek, Roman, and Norse mythology and use the knowledge to understand the origin and meaning of new words (e.g., the word *narcissistic* drawn from the myth of Narcissis and Echo).	
☐	**2.1** Analyze the structure and format of functional workplace documents, including the graphics and headers, and explain how authors use the features to achieve their purposes.	
☐	**2.3** Generate relevant questions about readings on issues that can be researched.	
☐	**2.5** Extend ideas presented in primary or secondary sources through original analysis, evaluation, and elaboration.	
☐	**2.6** Demonstrate use of sophisticated learning tools by following technical directions (e.g., those found with graphic calculators and specialized software programs and in access guides to World Wide Web sites on the Internet).	
☐	**2.7** Critique the logic of functional documents by examining the sequence of information and procedures in anticipation of possible reader misunderstandings.	

376   Checklist for Standards Mastery

Checklist for Standards Mastery

Use this chart at the back of your book to track your progress as you acquire reading skills.

Part One

Literature and Informational Readings

Encounters and Foundations to 1800

Indian petroglyphs, or rock carvings, at Newspaper Rock,
Indian Creek State Park, Utah.

Reading Standard 3.5
Analyze recognized works of American literature representing a variety of genres and traditions.

Encounters and Foundations to 1800

Gary Q. Arpin

Highlights of the period are presented in the following historical essay.
For a more detailed version of this essay, see *Holt Literature and Language Arts,* pp. 6–19.

About five hundred years ago European explorers first set foot on land in our hemisphere. In some ways their voyages must have seemed as daring and ultimately triumphant as Neil Armstrong's first steps on the moon in 1969. However, European feet were not the first to tread on American soil. American Indians

10 had lived here for thousands of years before the first Europeans stumbled across what they called the New World.

Forming New Relationships

The first interactions between Europeans and American Indians largely involved trading near harbors and rivers of North America. As the English began to establish colonies on these new shores, they relied on American Indians to teach them survival skills, such as how to make canoes and shelters, how to fashion clothing from buckskin, and how to plant crops. At the same

20 time, American Indians were eager to acquire European firearms, textiles, and steel tools.

In the early years of European settlement, American Indians vastly outnumbered the colonists. Historians estimate that in 1600, the total American Indian population of New England

---

IDENTIFY

Review the historical introduction, noting the main headings. Underline the headings that relate to the Puritans. Circle the heading that indicates the next topic will be the Age of Reason.

IDENTIFY

Pause at line 12. Who lived in America before the Europeans arrived?

_____

_____

_____

_____

_____

_____

IDENTIFY

Re-read lines 14–21. What did the English rely on the American Indians for? Underline the details that give you this information.

Battling New Diseases

The arrival of the European settlers had a deadly impact on
Native Americans. When settlers made contact with American

30   Indians, they unknowingly exposed them to deadly diseases that
sometimes killed the population of an entire village. Against
enormous odds, some Native Americans managed to survive
the epidemics. Many of them, however, were eventually forced to
vacate their home and land by settlers who no longer needed the
American Indians' friendship and guidance. As the historian
Francis Jennings wrote, "The so-called settlement of America
was a resettlement, a reoccupation of a land made waste by the
diseases and demoralization introduced by the newcomers."

Explorers' Writings

40   The first detailed European observations of life on this continent
were recorded in Spanish and French by explorers of the fifteenth
and sixteenth centuries. Christopher Columbus (c. 1451–1506)
and many other explorers described the Americas in a flurry
of letters, journals, and books. Hoping to receive funding for
further expeditions, the explorers emphasized the Americas'
abundant resources, the peacefulness and hospitality of the
inhabitants, and the promise of unlimited wealth from fantastic
treasuries of gold.

The Puritan Legacy

50   The writings of the Puritans of New England have been central
to the development of the American literary tradition. *Puritan*
is a broad term, referring to a number of Protestant groups
that, beginning about 1560, sought to "purify" the Church of
England, which had been virtually inseparable from the
country's government since the time of Henry VIII (who

IDENTIFY CAUSE & EFFECT

What tragic effect did the European settlement have on American Indians (lines 28–38)?

_____

_____

_____

_____

_____

_____

_____

WORD STUDY

The word *demoralization* in line 38 is a noun referring to a state of corruption. Based on his use of the word *demoralization,* what can you infer about Jennings's attitude toward the American resettlement?

_____

_____

_____

_____

_____

_____

IDENTIFY

Re-read lines 44–48. Why did the explorers write home about the Americas' abundant resources? Underline the answer.

reigned from 1509 to 1547). English Puritans wished to return
to a simpler form of worship. For them, religion was first of all a
personal, inner experience. They did not believe that the clergy
or government should act as an intermediary between the indi-
60 vidual and God.

    Many Puritans suffered persecution in England. Some were
put in jail and whipped, their noses slit and their ears chopped
off. Some fled England for Holland and later for what was
advertised as the New World.

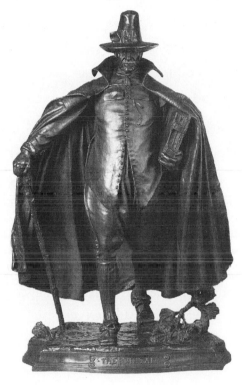

*The Puritan Deacon
Samuel Chapin*
(1899) by Augustus
Saint-Gaudens.
Bronze model.
James Graham & Sons, Inc.,
New York.

Puritan Beliefs: Sinners All?

At the center of Puritan theology was an uneasy mixture of certainty and doubt. The certainty was that because of Adam's and
Eve's disobedience, most of humanity would be damned for all
eternity. However, the Puritans were also certain that God in his
70 mercy had sent his son Jesus Christ to earth to save particular
people. The doubt centered on knowing if you were saved or
damned. People hoping to be among the saved examined their
inner lives closely for signs of grace and tried to live lives that
were free of sin. They came to value self-reliance, industriousness,

IDENTIFY

Pause at line 60. Who were
the Puritans?

_____

_____

_____

_____

IDENTIFY

Why did the Puritans flee
their country (lines 61–64)?
Circle the details that give
you this information.

IDENTIFY

Re-read lines 66–71. What
were the Puritans certain of?
Circle the answer.

CLARIFY

What were the Puritans'
beliefs about human nature
(lines 66–74)?

_____

_____

_____

_____

_____

_____

_____

_____

_____

_____

temperance, and simplicity. These were, coincidentally, the ideal qualities needed to carve out a new society in a strange land.

The examination of Sarah Good at the Salem witchcraft trials.

Puritan Politics: Government by Contract

In the Puritan view, a covenant, or contract, existed between
80 God and humanity. This spiritual covenant was a useful model for social organization as well: Puritans believed that people should enter freely into arguments concerning their government. On the *Mayflower,* for example, in 1620, the Puritans composed and signed the Mayflower Compact, which outlined how they would be governed once they landed. In this use of a contractual agreement, they prepared the ground for American constitutional democracy.

On the other hand, the Puritans' political views tended to be undemocratic because they believed that a few "saved"
90 persons should control the government. In 1692, the witchcraft hysteria in Salem, Massachusetts, resulted in part from fear that the community's moral foundation was threatened, and therefore its political unity was also in danger.

WORD STUDY

The word *covenant* in line 79 is defined in context. Underline the context clue.

CLARIFY

What was the Mayflower Compact (lines 83–87)?

_____

_____

_____

_____

_____

_____

_____

_____

_____

_____

_____

CLARIFY

Re-read lines 88–90. Why were Puritans' political views undemocratic?

_____

_____

_____

_____

_____

_____

_____

_____

_____

The Bible in America

The Puritans believed that the Bible was the literal word of God. Reading the Bible was a necessity for all Puritans, as was the ability to understand theological, or religious, debates. For these reasons the Puritans placed great emphasis on education. Harvard College, originally intended to train Puritan ministers, was founded in 1636, only sixteen years after the first Pilgrims had landed.

Their beliefs required the Puritans to keep a close watch on both their spiritual and their public lives. Diaries and histories were important forms of Puritan literature because they were viewed as records of the workings of God.

The Age of Reason: Tinkerers and Experimenters

By the end of the seventeenth century, new ideas from Europe began to challenge the unshakable faith of the Puritans. The Age of Reason, or the Enlightenment, began in Europe with the philosophers and scientists of the seventeenth and eighteenth centuries who called themselves rationalists. **Rationalism** is the belief that human beings can arrive at truth by using reason.

The Puritans saw God as actively and mysteriously involved in the workings of the universe; the rationalists saw God differently. The great English rationalist Sir Isaac Newton (1642–1727) compared God to a clockmaker. Having created the perfect mechanism of this universe, God then left his creation to run on its own, like a clock. The rationalists believed that God's special gift to humanity is reason—the ability to think in an ordered, logical manner. This gift of reason enables people to discover both scientific and spiritual truth. According to the rationalists, everyone has the capacity to regulate and improve his or her own life.

While the background for the Age of Reason took place in Europe, a homegrown practicality and interest in scientific

IDENTIFY CAUSE & EFFECT

Re-read lines 103–105. Why did the Puritans think that diaries and histories were important? Underline the reason.

WORD STUDY

The word *rationalism* in line 111 is based on the word *rational,* which means "based on reason."

COMPARE & CONTRAST

Re-read lines 113–123. How is rationalism different from Puritanism?

IDENTIFY

Pause at line 129. Why did Americans become interested in tinkering? Circle the details that give you this information.

WORD STUDY

Inoculation (line 141) involves the injection of a disease agent into a person. Inoculation usually causes a mild form of the disease, which then helps the person develop immunity to the disease.

FLUENCY

Read the boxed passage aloud twice. During your first reading, watch for marks of punctuation that indicate where you should pause or come to a full stop. During your second reading, focus on improving your reading speed.

_____

_____

_____

_____

_____

_____

_____

IDENTIFY

Re-read lines 151–161. What two interesting points about early American life are made? Underline them.

tinkering or experimenting already was taking place in America. From the earliest Colonial days, Americans had no choice but to be tinkerers; they had to make do with what was on hand, and they had to achieve results.

The Smallpox Plague

130

In 1721, a ship from the West Indies docked in Boston Harbor. In addition to its usual cargo of sugar and molasses, the West Indian ship carried smallpox—a disease as deadly to early American life as AIDS and the Ebola virus are today. The outbreak in Boston in 1721 was a major health problem. What was to be done?

■ An Unlikely Cure

At the time of the smallpox epidemic, Cotton Mather was working on what would be the first scholarly essay on medicine written in America. He had heard of a method for dealing with smallpox. It was called inoculation. In June 1721, as the smallpox epidemic spread throughout Boston, Mather began a public campaign for inoculation. Boston's medical community was violently opposed to such an experiment, and controversy erupted into violence. In November, Mather's house was bombed.

140

Despite such fierce opposition, Mather succeeded in inoculating nearly 300 people. By the time the epidemic was over, in March of the following year, only six of these people had died. The evidence, according to Mather's figures, was clear: Whether or not inoculation made much sense to scientists, it worked.

150

■ A Practical Approach to Change

The smallpox controversy illustrates two interesting points about American life in the early eighteenth century. First, it shows that Puritan thinking was not limited to a rigid and narrow interpretation of the Bible; a devout Puritan like Mather could also be a practical scientist.

Mather's experiment also reveals that a practical approach to social change and scientific research was necessary in America. American thought had to be thought in action: Improving the public welfare required a willingness to experiment, no matter what the authorities might say.

Deism: Are People Basically Good?

Like the Puritans, the rationalists discovered God through the natural world, but in a different way. Rationalists thought it unlikely that God would choose to reveal himself only at particular times to particular people. It seemed much more reasonable to believe that God had made it possible for *all* people at *all* times to discover natural laws through their God-given power of reason.

This outlook, called **deism** (dē′iz′əm), was shared by many eighteenth-century thinkers. In contrast to the Puritans, deists stressed humanity's goodness. God's objective, in the deist view, was the happiness of his creatures. Therefore, the best form of worship was to do good for others. There already existed in America an impulse to improve people's lives. Deism raised this impulse to one of the nation's highest goals. To this day, social welfare is still a political priority and still the subject of fierce debate.

Self-made Americans

The unquestioned masterpiece of the American Age of Reason is *The Autobiography* by Benjamin Franklin (page 47). Franklin (1706–1790) used the autobiographical narrative, a form common in Puritan writing. Written in clear, witty prose, this account of the development of the self-made American provided the model for a story that would be told again and again. In the twentieth century, it appeared in F. Scott Fitzgerald's novel *The Great Gatsby* (1925). It is still found in the countless biographies and autobiographies of self-made men and women on the bestseller lists today.

COMPARE & CONTRAST

How were the deists' views of humanity different from the Puritans' views (lines 169–177)?

IDENTIFY

Why is Benjamin Franklin's *Autobiography* considered a masterpiece of the American Age of Reason (lines 179–188)?

Coyote Finishes His Work, *retold by* Barry Lopez

REVIEW SKILLS

As you read "Coyote Finishes His Work," think about the following literary element:

THEME
The insight about human life revealed in a literary work.

LITERARY FOCUS: ARCHETYPES

An **archetype** (är′kə·tīp′) is an old imaginative pattern that appears across cultures and is repeated through the ages. An archetype can be a character, a plot, or an image. The **trickster** is an archetype that is especially important in the Native American storytelling tradition. For Native Americans, the trickster is often a coyote, but he can also be a fox, badger, raven, or rabbit. Sometimes the trickster is just naughty; sometimes he is creative and even helpful to a group of people. Tricksters can be masters at lying, and they often rebel against authority.

Tricky Types   Think of some characters or people from literature, film, television, or comics who get what they want through clever scheming. On the left-hand side of the chart below, list their names. In the right-hand column, write the qualities that make them tricksters.

What Makes a Trickster a Trickster?	
A List of Tricksters	**Qualities of Tricksters**

READING SKILLS: UNDERSTANDING CULTURAL CHARACTERISTICS

Literature written in a time period or culture different from your own helps you learn what it's like to live in that time and place. "Coyote Finishes His Work" contains several revealing details about the American Indian way of life. These details provide insights into Nez Perce religion, customs, views on nature, and beliefs about the way the universe works.

Use the Skill   As you read the selection, underline or highlight the descriptions or details that shed light on the Nez Perce culture.

Reading Standard 3.6
Analyze the way in which authors through the centuries have used archetypes from myth and tradition in literature, film, political speeches, and religious writings.

Reading Standard 3.12 (Grade 9–10 Review)
Analyze the way in which a work of literature is related to themes and issues of its historical period.

COYOTE FINISHES HIS WORK

retold by **Barry Lopez**

BACKGROUND

"Coyote Finishes His Work" is an oral tale handed down by the Nez Perce, a Native American people. The French coined the term *nez percé,* meaning "pierced nose," because some of them wore nose pendants. Following the establishment of the Oregon Trail and fueled by the frenzy of the nineteenth-century gold rush, conflicts erupted over the Nez Perce land. In 1877, the Nez Perce leader, Chief Joseph, surrendered to federal troops with the immortal words "I will fight no more forever."

From the very beginning, Coyote was traveling around all over the earth. He did many wonderful things when he went along. He killed the monsters and the evil spirits that preyed on the people. He made the Indians, and put them out in tribes all over the world because Old Man Above wanted the earth to be inhabited all over, not just in one or two places.

He gave all the people different names and taught them different languages. This is why Indians live all over the country now and speak in different ways.

10 He taught the people how to eat and how to hunt the buffalo and catch eagles. He taught them what roots to eat and how to make a good lodge and what to wear. He taught them how to dance. Sometimes he made mistakes, and even though he was wise and powerful, he did many foolish things. But that was his way.

Coyote liked to play tricks. He thought about himself all the time, and told everyone he was a great warrior, but he was not. Sometimes he would go too far with some trick and get

IDENTIFY

In the first paragraph, circle two or three things that Coyote does as he travels the earth. How would you describe Coyote's personality, from his actions?

_____

_____

ANALYZE

Re-read lines 10–14. Circle the things that Coyote taught his people to do. What do these teachings reveal about Nez Perce culture?

_____

_____

_____

INFER

What can you infer about the Nez Perce's views on mortality (lines 19–20)? *(Grade 9–10 Review)*

_____

_____

_____

ANALYZE

Re-read lines 15–25. What **archetypal** trickster qualities does Coyote demonstrate?

_____

_____

_____

_____

_____

INTERPRET

Pause at line 46. Why does Coyote say, "Now I know you are the Chief"?

_____

_____

_____

_____

_____

_____

_____

someone killed. Other times, he would have a trick played on himself by someone else. He got killed this way so many times that Fox and the birds got tired of bringing him back to life. Another way he got in trouble was trying to do what someone else did. This is how he came to be called Imitator.

Coyote was ugly too. The girls did not like him. But he was smart. He could change himself around and trick the women. Coyote got the girls when he wanted.

One time, Coyote had done everything he could think of and was traveling from one place to another place, looking for other things that needed to be done. Old Man saw him going along and said to himself, "Coyote has now done almost everything he is capable of doing. His work is almost done. It is time to bring him back to the place where he started."

So Great Spirit came down and traveled in the shape of an old man. He met Coyote. Coyote said, "I am Coyote. Who are you?"

Old Man said, "I am Chief of the earth. It was I who sent you to set the world right."

"No," Coyote said, "you never sent me. I don't know you. If you are the Chief, take that lake over there and move it to the side of that mountain."

"No. If you are Coyote, let me see you do it."

Coyote did it.

"Now, move it back."

Coyote tried, but he could not do it. He thought this was strange. He tried again, but he could not do it.

Chief moved the lake back.

Coyote said, "Now I know you are the Chief."

Old Man said, "Your work is finished, Coyote. You have traveled far and done much good. Now you will go to where I have prepared a home for you."

50   Then Coyote disappeared. Now no one knows where he is anymore.

        Old Man got ready to leave, too. He said to the Indians, "I will send messages to the earth by the spirits of the people who reach me but whose time to die has not yet come. They will carry messages to you from time to time. When their spirits come back into their bodies, they will revive and tell you their experiences.

        "Coyote and myself, we will not be seen again until Earth-woman is very old. Then we shall return to earth, for it will
60   require a change by that time. Coyote will come along first, and when you see him, you will know I am coming. When I come along, all the spirits of the dead will be with me. There will be no more Other Side Camp. All the people will live together. Earthmother will go back to her first shape and live as a mother among her children. Then things will be made right."

        Now they are waiting for Coyote.

INTERPRET

Old Man is also an **archetype.** Based on the evidence in the text, what kind of archetype do you think he is?

_____

_____

_____

_____

_____

_____

_____

INFER

Based on the details in lines 58–65, what do you think Other Side Camp might be?

_____

_____

_____

_____

_____

THEME

A common theme found in this myth could be stated as follows: "People all over the world hope that in the future a hero will come and usher in a time of peace and happiness." Underline details at the end of this myth that reflect that theme.

Coyote Finishes His Work

Reading Skills: Understanding Cultural Characteristics   Look back over the details you highlighted or underlined that reveal characteristics of Nez Perce culture. The chart below contains a list of different aspects of Nez Perce life. Fill in the right-hand column with details from "Coyote Finishes His Work" that tell you about each aspect.

Aspect of Nez Perce Life	Details from the Story
religious beliefs	
customs (what they are, how they are followed)	
social life	

 Check your Standards Mastery at the back of this book.

World, in hounding me . . . by Sor Juana Inés de la Cruz

BEFORE YOU READ

LITERARY FOCUS: SONNET

A **sonnet** is a fourteen-line poem that follows a strict structure. The writer Petrarch (1304–1374) created the model for what is now referred to as the **Petrarchan,** or Italian, sonnet. Here are the characteristics of a Petrarchan sonnet:

- The first eight lines, or **octave,** ask a question or pose a problem.

- The rhyme scheme of the octave is *abba abba.* (The first and fourth lines rhyme, as do the second and third, and so on.)

- The last six lines, or the **sestet,** respond to the question or problem.

- The sestet may contain the rhyme scheme *cde cde* or *cdc dcd.*

Sor Juana's "World, in hounding me . . ." is a Petrarchan sonnet. Note that some of the rhymes are approximate, because of the translation from Spanish to English.

READING SKILLS: FINDING UNITS OF MEANING

In many poems the speaker's ideas do not end at the ends of lines. Instead, those ideas may fill up two, three, four, or even more lines. When you read poetry, look for punctuation clues like commas, periods, and question marks to help you identify units of meaning.

Look at the following example from "World, in hounding me . . .". The end punctuation clues are circled. The other marks are underlined. This passage from the poem contains two complete thoughts over four lines of poetry.

World, in hounding me, what do you gain?

How can it harm you if I choose, astutely,

rather to stock my mind with things of beauty,

than waste its stock on every beauty's claim?

Use the Skill   As you read "World, in hounding me . . .," look for capitalization and punctuation clues that indicate the beginning and ending of the speaker's ideas.

Reading Standard 3.1
Analyze characteristics of subgenres (e.g., satire, parody, allegory, pastoral) that are used in poetry, prose, plays, novels, short stories, essays, and other basic genres.

Reading Standard 3.7
Analyze recognized works of world literature from a variety of authors.

World, in hounding me . . .

Sor Juana Inés de la Cruz
translated by Alan S. Trueblood

INTERPRET

What idea is expressed in line 5?

_____

_____

_____

_____

CLARIFY

Underline what Sor Juana describes as her "only happiness" (lines 6–7). What does she mean?

_____

_____

_____

_____

ANALYZE

Re-read the last six lines, or sestet, of the **sonnet**. What belief does Sor Juana express?

_____

_____

_____

_____

_____

_____

    World, in hounding me, what do you gain?

How can it harm you if I choose, astutely,

rather to stock my mind with things of beauty,

than waste its stock on every beauty's claim?

5   Costliness and wealth bring me no pleasure;

the only happiness I care to find

derives from setting treasure in my mind,

and not from mind that's set on winning treasure.

     I prize no comeliness.° All fair things pay

10   to time, the victor, their appointed fee

and treasure cheats even the practiced eye.

     Mine is the better and the truer way:

to leave the vanities of life aside,

not throw my life away on vanity.

_____

°**comeliness:** beauty.

World, in hounding me . . .

Reading Skills: Finding Units of Meaning   In a Petrarchan sonnet, the octave poses a question or problem, and the sestet answers the question or solves the problem. Sor Juana's "World, in hounding me . . ." is reprinted below. Examine each section of the sonnet, and complete the right-hand column with details from the poem.

Octave	Problems or Questions Posed
World, in hounding me, what do you gain? How can it harm you if I choose, astutely, rather to stock my mind with things of beauty, than waste its stock on every beauty's claim? Costliness and wealth bring me no pleasure; the only happiness I care to find derives from setting treasure in my mind, and not from mind that's set on winning treasure.	

Sestet	Conclusion or Answers to Problem
I prize no comeliness. All fair things pay to time, the victor, their appointed fee and treasure cheats even the practiced eye. Mine is the better and the truer way: to leave the vanities of life aside, not throw my life away on vanity.	

☑ Check your Standards Mastery at the back of this book.

from Sinners in the Hands of an Angry God

by Jonathan Edwards

REVIEW SKILLS

Look for examples of the following as you read this selection.

FIGURATIVE LANGUAGE
Language used in a nonliteral way, usually involving imaginative comparisons such as similes and metaphors.

IMAGERY
Language that appeals to the senses.

Reading Standard 2.1
Analyze both the features and the rhetorical devices of different types of public documents and the way in which authors use those features and devices.

Reading Standard 3.4
Analyze ways in which poets use figures of speech to evoke readers' emotions.

Reading Standard 3.7 (Grade 9–10 Review)
Recognize and understand the significance of various literary devices, including figurative language, imagery, allegory, and symbolism, and explain their appeal.

BEFORE YOU READ

LITERARY FOCUS: FIGURES OF SPEECH

Writers use **figures of speech** to help us see the world in new, imaginative ways. A figure of speech compares one thing to another, very different, thing. In "Sinners in the Hands of an Angry God," Jonathan Edwards uses figures of speech to make his readers *experience* the horrors he is describing. In one memorable example, he describes "wickedness" as being "heavy as lead." By using this figure of speech, a **simile,** Edwards compares the idea of wickedness to an everyday material his audience is familiar with. The figure of speech helps them *feel* the dead weight of wickedness.

What's the Difference?   Three of the most commonly occurring figures of speech are **simile, metaphor,** and **personification.**

- A **simile** compares two unlike things, using a word such as *like, as, than,* or *resembles:* Her heart is as cold as a dungeon.

- A **metaphor** compares two different things without using such words as *like* or *as:* Life is a carnival.

- **Personification** gives human characteristics to objects, animals, or abstractions: The flowers nodded their heads in agreement.

READING SKILLS: IDENTIFYING AN AUTHOR'S PURPOSE

Most writers have a purpose for putting words to paper. Some writers want to create a whole imaginative world of their own. Some want to share information. Some want to convey a message to their readers. Others hope to tap into readers' feelings or reason and persuade them to accept a way of thinking or to take some particular action. Jonathan Edwards's vivid, intense sermon "Sinners in the Hands of an Angry God" was written with a clear purpose—to make the experience of hell so real and frightening that people in his audience would change their lives.

Use the Skill   As you read the selection, circle the details that reveal the author's purpose.

But alas! ere long it was my fate to be thus attacked and to be carried off when none of the grown people were nigh. One day, when all our people were gone out to their works as usual and only I and my dear sister were left to mind the house, two men and a woman got over our walls, and in a moment seized us both, and without giving us time to cry out or make resistance they stopped our mouths and ran off with us into the nearest wood. Here they tied our hands and continued to carry us as far as they could till night came on, when we reached a small house where the robbers halted for refreshment and spent the night. We were then unbound but were unable to take any food, and being quite overpowered by fatigue and grief, our only relief was some sleep, which allayed our misfortune for a short time. The next morning we left the house and continued traveling all the day. For a long time we had kept to the woods, but at last we came into a road which I believed I knew. I had now some hopes of being delivered, for we had advanced but a little way before I discovered some people at a distance, on which I began to cry out for assistance: But my cries had no other effect than to make them tie me faster and stop my mouth, and then they put me into a large sack. They also stopped my sister's mouth and tied her hands, and in this manner we proceeded till we were out of the sight of these people.

When we went to rest the following night they offered us some victuals, but we refused it, and the only comfort we had was in being in one another's arms all that night and bathing each other with our tears. But alas! we were soon deprived of even the small comfort of weeping together. The next day proved a day of greater sorrow than I had yet experienced, for my sister and I were then separated while we lay clasped in each other's arms. It was in vain that we besought them not to part us; she was torn from me and immediately carried away, while I was left in a state of **distraction** not to be described. I cried and grieved continually, and for several days I did not eat anything but what they forced into my mouth. At length, after many days' traveling, during which I had often changed masters, I got into

---

WORD STUDY

Alas, ere, and *nigh* (lines 25–26) are words that are no longer in common use. Use context clues to figure out their meanings, and write their definitions below.

_____

_____

_____

_____

CLARIFY

Pause at line 47. What has happened to Equiano and his sister?

_____

_____

IDENTIFY CAUSE & EFFECT

Why do the kidnappers gag Equiano and put him in a sack (lines 39–48)?

_____

_____

_____

WORD STUDY

Victuals (vit'lz) in line 49 is a regional term for "food."

VOCABULARY

distraction (di·strak'shən) n.: mental disturbance or distress.

IDENTIFY

Re-read lines 61–76. Circle
the details that describe
Equiano's first master. What
was Equiano's job while
working for him?

_____

_____

_____

_____

_____

INFER

Pause at line 81. Why does
Equiano's master sell him?

_____

_____

_____

_____

_____

_____

_____

_____

_____

IDENTIFY

Re-read lines 83–89. Circle
the passage that describes
how Equiano is treated by
his new owners.

the hands of a chieftain in a very pleasant country. This man
had two wives and some children, and they all used me extremely well and did all they could to comfort me, particularly
the first wife, who was something like my mother. Although I
was a great many days' journey from my father's house, yet these
people spoke exactly the same language with us. This first
master of mine, as I may call him, was a smith, and my principal
employment was working his bellows,[2] which were the same
kind as I had seen in my vicinity. They were in some respects

70 not unlike the stoves here in gentlemen's kitchens, and were
covered over with leather; and in the middle of that leather a
stick was fixed, and a person stood up and worked it in the same
manner as is done to pump water out of a cask with a hand
pump. I believe it was gold he worked, for it was of a lovely
bright yellow color and was worn by the women on their wrists
and ankles. . . .

Soon after this my master's only daughter and child by his
first wife sickened and died, which affected him so much that
for some time he was almost frantic, and really would have

80 killed himself had he not been watched and prevented. However,
in a small time afterward he recovered and I was again sold. I
was now carried to the left of the sun's rising, through many different countries and a number of large woods. The people I was
sold to used to carry me very often when I was tired either on
their shoulders or on their backs. I saw many convenient well-
built sheds along the roads at proper distances, to accommodate
the merchants and travelers who lay in those buildings along
with their wives, who often accompany them; and they always
go well armed.

90 From the time I left my own nation I always found somebody that understood me till I came to the seacoast. The languages of different nations did not totally differ, nor were they

_____

2. **bellows** *n.:* device that produces a strong air current, used for
   blowing fires.

Slave Deck of the Albanoz (1843–1847) by Lt. Francis Meynell.
Watercolor on paper.
National Maritime Museum, Greenwich, England.

ANALYZE

In lines 95–102, what personal information does Equiano give that a biographer would probably not be able to give?

CLARIFY

Who are the "sable destroyers of human rights"? What point is the writer making in lines 102–106?

so copious[3] as those of the Europeans, particularly the English. They were therefore easily learned, and while I was journeying thus through Africa I acquired two or three different tongues. In this manner I had been traveling for a considerable time, when one evening, to my great surprise, whom should I see brought to the house where I was but my dear sister! As soon as she saw me she gave a loud shriek and ran into my arms—I was quite over-
100 powered: Neither of us could speak, but for a considerable time clung to each other in mutual embraces, unable to do anything but weep. Our meeting affected all who saw us, and indeed I must acknowledge, in honor of those sable destroyers of human rights, that I never met with any ill-treatment or saw any offered to their slaves except tying them, when necessary, to keep them from running away.

---

3. **copious** *adj.:* here, wordy.

IDENTIFY

Pause at line 114. What has happened to Equiano's sister?

_____

_____

_____

_____

_____

_____

_____

_____

_____

_____

WORD STUDY

Find and circle the context clues that help you figure out the meaning of _rivulets_ (line 124).

VOCABULARY

apprehensions (ap′rē·hen′shənz) _n.:_ feelings of anxiety or dread.

alleviate (ə·lē′vē·āt′) _v.:_ relieve; reduce.

interspersed (in′tər·spʉrst′) _v._ used as _adj.:_ placed at intervals; scattered.

commodious (kə·mō′dē·əs) _adj.:_ roomy; spacious.

When these people knew we were brother and sister they indulged us to be together, and the man to whom I supposed we belonged lay with us, he in the middle while she and I held one
110 another by the hands across his breast all night; and thus for a while we forgot our misfortunes in the joy of being together: But even this small comfort was soon to have an end, for scarcely had the fatal morning appeared when she was again torn from me forever! I was now more miserable, if possible, than before. The small relief which her presence gave me from pain was gone, and the wretchedness of my situation was redoubled by my anxiety after her fate and my **apprehensions** lest her sufferings should be greater than mine, when I could not be with her to **alleviate** them. . . .

120   I did not long remain after my sister. I was again sold and carried through a number of places till, after traveling a considerable time, I came to a town called Tinmah in the most beautiful country I had yet seen in Africa. It was extremely rich, and there were many rivulets which flowed through it and supplied a large pond in the center of town, where the people washed. Here I first saw and tasted coconuts, which I thought superior to any nuts I had ever tasted before; and the trees, which were loaded, were also **interspersed** amongst the houses, which had **commodious** shades adjoining and were in the same manner as
130 ours, the insides being neatly plastered and whitewashed. Here I also saw and tasted for the first time sugar cane. Their money consisted of little white shells the size of the fingernail. I was sold here for 172 of them by a merchant who lived and brought me there. I had been about two or three days at his house when a wealthy widow, a neighbor of his, came there one evening, and brought with her an only son, a young gentleman about my own age and size. Here they saw me; and, having taken a fancy to me, I was bought of the merchant, and went home with them. Her house and premises were situated close to one of
140 those rivulets I have mentioned, and were the finest I ever saw

in Africa: They were very extensive, and she had a number of slaves to attend her. The next day I was washed and perfumed, and when mealtime came I was led into the presence of my mistress, and ate and drank before her with her son. This filled me with astonishment; and I could scarce help expressing my surprise that the young gentleman should suffer me, who was bound, to eat with him who was free; and not only so, but that he would not at any time either eat or drink till I had taken first, because I was the eldest, which was agreeable to our cus-

150 tom. Indeed everything here, and all their treatment of me, made me forget that I was a slave. The language of these people resembled ours so nearly that we understood each other perfectly. They had also the very same customs as we. There were likewise slaves daily to attend us, while my young master and I with other boys sported with our darts and bows and arrows, as I had been used to do at home. In this resemblance to my former happy state I passed about two months; and I now began to think I was to be adopted into the family, and was beginning to be reconciled to my situation, and to forget by degrees my

160 misfortunes, when all at once the delusion vanished; for without the least previous knowledge, one morning early, while my dear master and companion was still asleep, I was wakened out of my reverie to fresh sorrow, and hurried away even amongst the uncircumcised.

Thus at the very moment I dreamed of the greatest happiness, I found myself most miserable; and it seemed as if fortune wished to give me this taste of joy only to render the reverse more poignant. The change I now experienced was as painful as it was sudden and unexpected. It was a change indeed from a

170 state of bliss to a scene which is inexpressible by me, as it discovered to me an element I had never before beheld and till then had no idea of, and wherein such instances of hardship and cruelty continually occurred as I can never reflect on but with horror. . . .

WORD STUDY

In line 147, Equiano refers to himself as "bound." Locate and circle the nearby context clue that describes a state opposite of being bound.

DRAW CONCLUSIONS

Here, Equiano is sold again (lines 156–164). What value do you suppose slave owners placed on slaves' lives? *(Grade 9–10 Review)*

WORD STUDY

The word *poignant* (line 168) (poin'yənt) can be defined by surrounding context clues. Find and circle these clues. What does *poignant* mean?

INTERPRET

Pause at line 174. What has happened to Equiano? What are his feelings about his situation?

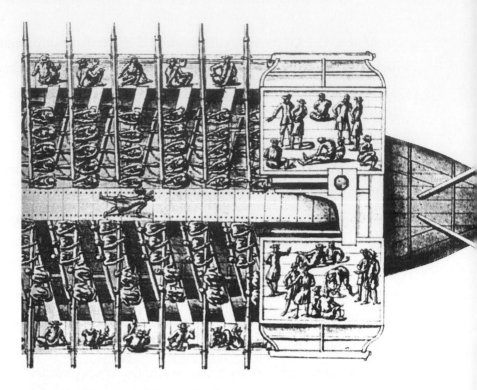

A slave ship manned by captives.

The Slave Ship

The first object which saluted[4] my eyes when I arrived on the
coast was the sea, and a slave ship which was then riding at
anchor and waiting for its cargo. These filled me with astonishment, which was soon converted into terror when I was carried
180   on board. I was immediately handled and tossed up to see if I
were sound by some of the crew, and I was now persuaded that I
had gotten into a world of bad spirits and that they were going to
kill me. Their complexions too differing so much from ours,
their long hair and the language they spoke (which was very different from any I had ever heard) united to confirm me in this
belief. Indeed such were the horrors of my views and fears at the
moment that, if ten thousand worlds had been my own, I would
have freely parted with them all to have exchanged my condition
with that of the meanest[5] slave in my own country. When I
190   looked round the ship too and saw a large furnace or copper

---

4. **saluted** *v.:* met.
5. **meanest** *adj.:* lowest.

PREDICT

Re-read lines 175–180. What
do you think Equiano will
write about next?

_____

IDENTIFY
CAUSE & EFFECT

Re-read lines 180–189. Why is
Equiano so filled with terror?

_____

boiling and a multitude of black people of every description chained together, every one of their countenances[6] expressing dejection and sorrow, I no longer doubted of my fate; and quite overpowered with horror and anguish, I fell motionless on the deck and fainted. When I recovered a little I found some black people about me, who I believed were some of those who had brought me on board and had been receiving their pay; they talked to me in order to cheer me, but all in vain. I asked them if we were not to be eaten by those white men with horrible looks, red faces, and loose hair. They told me I was not, and one of the crew brought me a small portion of spirituous liquor in a wineglass, but being afraid of him I would not take it out of his hand. One of the blacks therefore took it from him and gave it to me, and I took a little down my palate, which instead of reviving me, as they thought it would, threw me into the greatest **consternation** at the strange feeling it produced, having never tasted such any liquor before. Soon after this the blacks who brought me on board went off, and left me abandoned to despair.

I now saw myself deprived of all chance of returning to my native country or even the least glimpse of hope of gaining the shore, which I now considered as friendly; and I even wished for my former slavery in preference to my present situation, which was filled with horrors of every kind, still heightened by my ignorance of what I was to undergo. I was not long suffered to indulge my grief; I was soon put down under the decks, and there I received such a salutation in my nostrils as I had never experienced in my life: So that with the loathsomeness of the stench and crying together, I became so sick and low that I was not able to eat, nor had I the least desire to taste anything. I now wished for the last friend, death, to relieve me; but soon, to my grief, two of the white men offered me eatables, and on my refusing to eat, one of them held me fast by the hands and laid me across, I think, the windlass,[7] and tied my feet while the other

200

210

220

6. **countenances** *n. pl.:* faces.
7. **windlass** (wind′ləs) *n.:* device used to raise and lower heavy objects, like a ship's anchor.

from **The Interesting Narrative of the Life of Olaudah Equiano**   **37**

CLARIFY

Pause at line 209. Who tries to comfort Equiano after he faints? What is ironic, or surprising, about this?

_____

_____

_____

_____

_____

_____

_____

VOCABULARY

consternation
(kän′stər·nā′·shən) *n.:* confusion resulting from fear or shock.

IDENTIFY CAUSE & EFFECT

Read on to line 225. Why do the white men beat Equiano?

_____

_____

_____

_____

_____

_____

_____

_____

CLARIFY

How does Equiano finally find out what is going to happen to him (lines 234–238)?

_____

_____

_____

_____

CLARIFY

Pause at line 249. What event confirms Equiano's idea that the white men are brutal?

_____

_____

_____

_____

INFER

What do you learn about Equiano from the series of questions he asked (lines 251–258)? Underline the questions.

_____

_____

_____

_____

_____

flogged[8] me severely. I had never experienced anything of this kind before, and although, not being used to the water, I naturally feared that element the first time I saw it, yet nevertheless could I have got over the nettings I would have jumped over the side, but I could not; and besides, the crew used to watch us very

230 closely who were not chained down to the decks, lest we should leap into the water: And I have seen some of these poor African prisoners most severely cut for attempting to do so, and hourly whipped for not eating. This indeed was often the case with myself. In a little time after, amongst the poor chained men I found some of my own nation, which in a small degree gave ease to my mind. I inquired of these what was to be done with us; they gave me to understand we were to be carried to these white people's country to work for them. I then was a little revived, and thought if it were no worse than working, my situation was not

240 so desperate: But still I feared I should be put to death, the white people looked and acted, as I thought, in so savage a manner; for I had never seen among my people such instances of brutal cruelty, and this not only shown toward us blacks but also to some of the whites themselves. One white man in particular I saw, when we were permitted to be on deck, flogged so unmercifully with a large rope near the foremast[9] that he died in consequence of it; and they tossed him over the side as they would have done a brute. This made me fear these people the more, and I expected nothing less than to be treated in the same manner. I could not

250 help expressing my fears and apprehensions to some of my countrymen: I asked them if these people had no country but lived in this hollow place (the ship): They told me they did not, but came from a distant one. "Then," said I, "how comes it in all our country we never heard of them?" They told me because they lived so very far off. I then asked where were their women? Had they any like themselves? I was told they had: "And why," said I, "do we not see them?" They answered, because they were left

---

8. **flogged** _v._: beat with a rod or whip.
9. **foremast** _n._: mast closest to the bow, or front, of a ship.

behind. I asked how the vessel could go? They told me they could not tell, but that there were cloths put upon the masts by the help of the ropes I saw, and then the vessel went on; and the white men had some spell or magic they put in the water when they liked in order to stop the vessel. I was exceedingly amazed at this account and really thought they were spirits. I therefore wished much to be from amongst them for I expected they would sacrifice me: But my wishes were vain, for we were so quartered that it was impossible for any of us to make our escape.

While we stayed on the coast I was mostly on deck, and one day, to my great astonishment, I saw one of these vessels coming in with the sails up. As soon as the whites saw it they gave a great shout, at which we were amazed; and the more so as the vessel appeared larger by approaching nearer. At last she came to an anchor in my sight, and when the anchor was let go I and my countrymen who saw it were lost in astonishment to observe the vessel stop, and were now convinced it was done by magic. Soon after this the other ship got her boats out, and they came on board of us, and the people of both ships seemed very glad to see each other. Several of the strangers also shook hands with us black people, and made motions with their hands, signifying I suppose we were to go to their country; but we did not understand them. At last, when the ship we were in had got in all her cargo, they made ready with many fearful noises, and we were all put under deck so that we could not see how they managed the vessel.

But this disappointment was the least of my sorrow. The stench of the hold[10] while we were on the coast was so intolerably loathsome that it was dangerous to remain there for any time, and some of us had been permitted to stay on the deck for the fresh air; but now that the whole ship's cargo were confined together it became absolutely pestilential.[11] The closeness of the place and the heat of the climate, added to the number in the

---

10. **hold** *n.:* enclosed area below a ship's deck, where cargo is usually stored.
11. **pestilential** *adj.:* deadly; harmful.

IDENTIFY

According to Equiano's countrymen, how do the white men make the ship stop (lines 258–262)?

_____

_____

CLARIFY

Summarize what happens in lines 267–283.

_____

_____

_____

_____

_____

_____

_____

_____

_____

IDENTIFY CAUSE & EFFECT

Pause at line 289. What makes the conditions in the hold of the ship even worse than they were before?

_____

_____

_____

_____

IDENTIFY

Underline the words and phrases that describe conditions in the hold (lines 289–296).

VOCABULARY

improvident
(im·präv′ə·dənt) *adj.:* careless; not providing for the future.

avarice (av′ə·ris) *n.:* extreme greed.

IDENTIFY CAUSE & EFFECT

Why is Equiano permitted to stay on deck (lines 302–304)?

_____

_____

_____

_____

_____

CLARIFY

Re-read lines 308–311. Whose freedom does Equiano envy?

_____

_____

_____

_____

_____

_____

ship, which was so crowded that each had scarcely room to turn himself, almost suffocated us. This produced copious perspirations, so that the air soon became unfit for respiration from a variety of loathsome smells, and brought on a sickness among the slaves, of which many died, thus falling victims to the **improvident avarice**, as I may call it, of their purchasers. This wretched situation was again aggravated by the galling of the chains, now become insupportable, and the filth of the necessary tubs,[12] into which the children often fell and were almost suffo-

300 cated. The shrieks of the women and the groans of the dying rendered the whole a scene of horror almost inconceivable. Happily perhaps for myself I was soon reduced so low here that it was thought necessary to keep me almost always on deck, and from my extreme youth I was not put in fetters.[13] In this situation I expected every hour to share the fate of my companions, some of whom were almost daily brought upon deck at the point of death, which I began to hope would soon put an end to my miseries. Often did I think many of the inhabitants of the deep much more happy than myself. I envied them the freedom

310 they enjoyed, and as often wished I could change my condition for theirs. Every circumstance I met with served only to render my state more painful, and heighten my apprehensions and my opinion of the cruelty of the whites. One day they had taken a number of fishes, and when they had killed and satisfied themselves with as many as they thought fit, to our astonishment who were on the deck, rather than give any of them to us to eat as we expected, they tossed the remaining fish into the sea again, although we begged and prayed for some as well as we could, but in vain; and some of my countrymen, being pressed by

320 hunger, took an opportunity when they thought no one saw them of trying to get a little privately; but they were discovered, and the attempt procured them some very severe floggings.

---

12. **necessary tubs:** toilets.
13. **fetters** *n. pl.:* shackles or chains for the feet.

One day, when we had a smooth sea and moderate wind, two of my wearied countrymen who were chained together (I was near them at the time), preferring death to such a life of misery, somehow made through the nettings and jumped into the sea: Immediately another quite dejected fellow, who on account of his illness was suffered to be out of irons, also followed their example; and I believe many more would very soon have done the same if they had not been prevented by the ship's crew, who were instantly alarmed. Those of us that were the most active were in a moment put down under the deck, and there was such a noise and confusion amongst the people of the ship as I never heard before, to stop her and get the boat out to go after the slaves. However two of the wretches were drowned, but they got the other and afterward flogged him unmercifully for thus attempting to prefer death to slavery. In this manner we continued to undergo more hardships than I can now relate, hardships which are inseparable from this accursed trade. Many a time we were near suffocation from the want of fresh air, which we were often without for whole days together. This and the stench of the necessary tubs carried off many.

During our passage I first saw flying fishes, which surprised me very much: They used frequently to fly across the ship and many of them fell on the deck. I also now first saw the use of the quadrant; I had often with astonishment seen the mariners make observations with it, and I could not think what it meant. They at last took notice of my surprise, and one of them, willing to increase it as well as to gratify my curiosity, made me one day look through it. The clouds appeared to me to be land, which disappeared as they passed along. This heightened my wonder, and I was now more persuaded than ever that I was in another world and that everything about me was magic. At last we came in sight of the island of Barbados, at which the whites on board gave a great shout and made many signs of joy to us. We did not know what to think of this, but as the vessel drew nearer we plainly saw the harbor and other ships of different kinds and

330

340

350

IDENTIFY

What events are described in lines 323–331?

_____

_____

_____

_____

_____

_____

IDENTIFY
CAUSE & EFFECT

Pause at line 342. What effect does the prisoners' attempts at suicide or escape have on the slavers' behavior toward the prisoners?

_____

_____

_____

_____

_____

_____

_____

_____

WORD STUDY

What context clues help you figure out the meaning of the word quadrant in line 346? Circle the clues you find.

from **The Interesting Narrative of the Life of Olaudah Equiano** 41

CLARIFY

Pause at line 368. Where has the ship docked? What do the prisoners believe will happen next?

_____

_____

_____

_____

_____

_____

_____

IDENTIFY
CAUSE & EFFECT

Why are older slaves brought onboard the ship (lines 368–372)?

_____

_____

_____

_____

_____

_____

_____

_____

IDENTIFY

What two sights surprise Equiano (lines 375–379)? Underline the details that tell you.

sizes, and we soon anchored amongst them off Bridgetown. Many merchants and planters now came on board, though it was in the evening. They put us in separate parcels and examined us attentively. They also made us jump, and pointed to the land, signifying we were to go there. We thought by this we should be eaten by these ugly men, as they appeared to us; and when soon after we were all put down under the deck again, there was much dread and trembling among us, and nothing but bitter cries to be heard all the night from these apprehensions, insomuch that at last the white people got some old slaves from the land to pacify us. They told us we were not to be eaten but to work, and were soon to go on land where we should see many of our countrypeople. This report eased us much; and sure enough soon after we were landed there came to us Africans of all languages.

We were conducted immediately to the merchant's yard, where we were all pent up together like so many sheep in a fold without regard to sex or age. As every object was new to me everything I saw filled me with surprise. What struck me first was that the houses were built with stories, and in every other respect different from those in Africa: But I was still more astonished on seeing people on horseback. I did not know what this could mean, and indeed I thought these people were full of nothing but magical arts. While I was in this astonishment one of my fellow prisoners spoke to a countryman of his about the horses, who said they were the same kind they had in their country. I understood them though they were from a distant part of Africa, and I thought it odd I had not seen any horses there; but afterward when I came to converse with different Africans I found they had many horses amongst them, and much larger than those I then saw.

We were not many days in the merchant's custody before we were sold after their usual manner, which is this: On a signal given (as the beat of a drum) the buyers rush at once into the yard where the slaves are confined, and make choice of that parcel they like best. The noise and clamor with which this is attended and the eagerness visible in the countenances of the buyers serve not a little to increase the apprehensions of the terrified Africans, who may well be supposed to consider them as the ministers of that destruction to which they think themselves devoted. In this manner, without scruple,[14] are relations and friends separated, most of them never to see each other again. I remember in the vessel in which I was brought over, in the men's apartment there were several brothers who, in the sale, were sold in different lots; and it was very moving on this occasion to see and hear their cries at parting. O, ye nominal Christians! might not an African ask you, Learned you this from your God who says unto you, Do unto all men as you would men should do unto you? Is it not enough that we are torn from our country and friends to toil for your luxury and lust of gain? Must every tender feeling be likewise sacrificed to your avarice? Are the dearest friends and relations, now rendered more dear by their separation from their kindred, still to be parted from each other and thus prevented from cheering the gloom of slavery with the small comfort of being together and mingling their sufferings and sorrows? Why are parents to lose their children, brothers their sisters, or husbands their wives? Surely this is a new refinement in cruelty which, while it has no advantage to atone for it, thus aggravates distress and adds fresh horrors even to the wretchedness of slavery.

---

14. **scruple** *n.*: unease or doubt arising from difficulty in determining what is right.

CLARIFY

What is a "nominal" Christian (lines 403–404)? Whom is Equiano addressing here?

_____

_____

_____

_____

ANALYZE

Re-read lines 406–417. Underline the details that reveal what slaves had to endure. What do these details tell you about Equiano's beliefs?

_____

_____

_____

_____

_____

_____

_____

_____

_____

FLUENCY

Read the boxed passage aloud twice. On your first reading, go slowly and strive for clarity. The second time you read, try to increase your pace without sacrificing clarity.

from The Interesting Narrative of the Life of Olaudah Equiano

Reading Skills: Making Inferences About an Author's Beliefs   Look back over the details you highlighted or underlined. Which passages helped you make inferences about Equiano's beliefs? The chart below contains some passages from the autobiography. In column two, write what you can infer from each passage.

What Equiano Said	Inference About Equiano's Belief
". . . I must acknowledge, in honor of those sable destroyers of human rights, that I never met with any ill-treatment or saw any offered to their slaves except tying them, when necessary, to keep them from running away." (lines 102–106)	
". . . instances of hardship and cruelty continually occurred as I can never reflect on but with horror. . . ." (lines 172–174)	
"Often did I think many of the inhabitants of the deep much more happy than myself. I envied them the freedom they enjoyed . . ." (lines 308–310)	
"O, ye nominal Christians! might not an African ask you, Learned you this from your God who says unto you, Do unto all men as you would men should do unto you?" (lines 403–406)	

from The Interesting Narrative of the Life of Olaudah Equiano

VOCABULARY DEVELOPMENT

VOCABULARY IN CONTEXT

DIRECTIONS: Write words from the Word Box in the blanks to complete the passage. Not all words will be used.

Word Box

assailant

distraction

apprehensions

alleviate

interspersed

commodious

consternation

improvident

avarice

The Interesting Narrative of the Life of Olaudah Equiano is one of the most famous first-person accounts by a former slave. Readers all over the world learned about the cruelty of the slave traders who were driven by pure (1) _____. Equiano describes the slaves' great (2) _____, their feelings of anxiety during the Atlantic passage. Nothing could be done to (3) _____ their fears. Equiano also describes conditions aboard the slave ships. These vessels, which were not (4) _____, were packed with hundreds of humans. Any slave who protested was attacked by an (5) _____ and flogged or tossed overboard.

CONTEXT CLUES

When you encounter unfamiliar words, look at **context clues**—the words surrounding the unfamiliar word. Context clues might help you figure out the meanings of the unfamiliar words.

DIRECTIONS: Practice identifying context clues. Read each of the following sentences. Then, underline the context clue provided for each boldface word.

1. Equiano's **consternation** rose when he saw the slave ships in the harbor; his anxiety became even worse when he encountered the slavers.

2. In the town of Tinmah, Equiano marveled at the trees, which were **interspersed** among the houses. This scattering of the trees among the houses made the town look very neat.

3. The slavers' actions were motivated by **avarice;** they were simply greedy for money.

4. The slaves meant money for the traders. Therefore, Equiano wonders why they were so **improvident**—so careless of their precious cargo—that they would not provide adequate food and water for their investments.

Reading Standard 1.1 (Grade 9–10 Review) Identify and use the literal and figurative meanings of words and understand word derivations.

 Check your Standards Mastery at the back of this book.

from **The Autobiography** by Benjamin Franklin

BEFORE YOU READ

LITERARY FOCUS: AUTOBIOGRAPHY

An **autobiography** is an account of a person's life, written by that person. Generally, the events in an autobiography are described in the order in which they take place. Readers learn about specific episodes that take place during the writer's life and what these events mean to him or her. Autobiographers not only provide information; they also express their personal thoughts and feelings. After reading an autobiography, you often feel that you know the writer personally.

Autobiography Wish List   Whose autobiography would you like to read? List your ideas in the left-hand column below. Then, in the right-hand column, write what you'd like to learn about each person.

Subject of Autobiography	What I'd Like to Learn About Him or Her

READING SKILLS: MAKING INFERENCES

One of the best things about reading an autobiography is getting to know the writer's likes and dislikes, philosophical beliefs and attitudes, even biases. Writers don't always reveal these things directly. At times you must guess what the writer thinks or believes.

Use the Skill   As you read this excerpt from *The Autobiography,* combine clues from the text and your own experiences to make inferences about Franklin's ideas or beliefs that he doesn't state directly.

Reading Standard 2.5
Analyze an author's implicit and explicit philosophical assumptions and beliefs about a subject.

from
The Autobiography
Benjamin Franklin

Arrival in Philadelphia

I have been the more particular in this description of my journey, and shall be so of my first entry into that city, that you may in your mind compare such unlikely beginnings with the figure I have since made there. I was in my working dress, my best clothes being to come round by sea. I was dirty from my journey; my pockets were stuffed out with shirts and stockings, and I knew no soul nor where to look for lodging. I was fatigued with traveling, rowing, and want of rest, I was very hungry; and my

10 whole stock of cash consisted of a Dutch dollar, and about a shilling in copper. The latter I gave the people of the boat for my passage, who at first refused it, on account of my rowing; but I insisted on their taking it. A man being sometimes more generous when he has but a little money than when he has plenty, perhaps through fear of being thought to have but little.

Then I walked up the street, gazing about till near the market house I met a boy with bread. I had made many a meal on bread, and, inquiring where he got it, I went immediately to the baker's he directed me to, in Second Street, and asked for biscuit,

20 intending such as we had in Boston; but they, it seems, were not made in Philadelphia. Then I asked for a three-penny loaf, and was told they had none such. So not considering or knowing the difference of money, and the greater cheapness nor the names of his bread, I bade him give me three-penny worth of any sort. He gave me, accordingly, three great puffy rolls. I was surprised at the quantity, but took it, and, having no room in my pockets, walked off with a roll under each arm, and eating the other. Thus I went up Market Street as far as Fourth Street, passing by the door of Mr. Read, my future wife's father; when she,

ANALYZE

Re-read lines 2–11. Underline the details that describe Franklin's arrival in Philadelphia. Why is he telling us this?

_____

_____

_____

_____

_____

CLARIFY

Re-read lines 11–15. What lesson is Franklin teaching us with this anecdote?

_____

_____

_____

_____

_____

WORD STUDY

What might *bade* mean (line 24)? Use **context clues** to help you.

_____

_____

Why did Franklin's future wife think he looked "awkward" and "ridiculous" (line 31) when she first saw him walk past her father's door?

_____

_____

_____

_____

_____

_____

_____

_____

INFER

Re-read lines 31–37. Circle the phrase describing what Franklin does with the extra rolls. What can you infer about his character from this detail?

_____

_____

_____

_____

_____

_____

_____

_____

Second Street, North from Market Street, with Christ Church, Philadelphia (1799) by W. Birch & Son. Colored line engraving.
The Granger Collection, New York.

30   standing at the door, saw me, and thought I made, as I certainly did, a most awkward, ridiculous appearance. Then I turned and went down Chestnut Street and part of Walnut Street, eating my roll all the way, and, coming round, found myself again at Market Street wharf, near the boat I came in, to which I went for a draft[1] of the river water; and, being filled with one of my rolls, gave the other two to a woman and her child that came down the river in the boat with us, and were waiting to go farther.

    Thus refreshed, I walked again up the street, which by this time had many clean-dressed people in it, who were all walking 40   the same way. I joined them, and thereby was led into the great meetinghouse of the Quakers[2] near the market. I sat down

---

1. **draft** *n.:* gulp or swallow.
2. **Quakers:** members of the Religious Society of Friends, a Christian group founded in the seventeenth century.

among them, and, after looking round awhile and hearing nothing said, being very drowsy through labor and want of rest the preceding night, I fell fast asleep, and continued so till the meeting broke up, when one was kind enough to rouse me. This was, therefore, the first house I was in, or slept in, in Philadelphia. . . .

Arriving at Moral Perfection

It was about this time I conceived the bold and **arduous** project of arriving at moral perfection. I wished to live without committing any fault at any time; I would conquer all that either natural inclination, custom, or company might lead me into. As I knew, or thought I knew, what was right and wrong, I did not see why I might not always do the one and avoid the other. But I soon found I had undertaken a task of more difficulty than I had imagined. While my care was employed in guarding against one fault, I was often surprised by another; habit took the advantage of inattention; inclination was sometimes too strong for reason. I concluded, at length, that the mere speculative conviction that it was our interest to be completely virtuous,[3] was not sufficient to prevent our slipping; and that the contrary habits must be broken, and good ones acquired and established, before we can have any dependence on a steady, uniform **rectitude** of conduct. For this purpose I therefore contrived the following method.

In the various enumerations of the moral virtues I had met with in my reading, I found the catalog more or less numerous, as different writers included more or fewer ideas under the same name. Temperance, for example, was by some confined to eating and drinking, while by others it was extended to mean the moderating every other pleasure, appetite, inclination, or passion, bodily or mental, even to our avarice and ambition. I proposed to myself, for the sake of clearness, to use rather more names, with fewer ideas annexed to each, than a few names with more ideas; and I included under thirteen names of virtues all that at

50

60

70

---

3. **virtuous** *adj.:* morally excellent; pure.

arduous (är′jo͞o·əs) *adj.:* difficult.

rectitude (rek′tə·to͞od′) *n.:* correctness.

IDENTIFY

Re-read lines 48–51. What project does Franklin plan to undertake? Underline the phrase that tells you so.

CLARIFY

What difficulty does Franklin discover as he tries to become morally perfect (lines 53–57)?

_____

_____

_____

_____

_____

_____

_____

CLARIFY

Pause at line 62. According to Franklin, what has to happen before a person's conduct can become steadily or uniformly good?

_____

_____

_____

from The Autobiography   **49**

that time occurred to me as necessary or desirable, and annexed to each a short precept,[4] which fully expressed the extent I gave to its meaning.

These names of virtues, with their precepts, were:

> 1. **Temperance.** *Eat not to dullness; drink not to elevation.*
> 2. **Silence.** *Speak not but what may benefit others or*
> 80 *yourself; avoid trifling[5] conversation.*
> 3. **Order.** *Let all your things have their places; let each part of your business have its time.*
> 4. **Resolution.** *Resolve to perform what you ought; perform without fail what you resolve.*
> 5. **Frugality.** *Make no expense but to do good to others or yourself; i.e., waste nothing.*

6. **Industry.** *Lose no time; be always employed in something useful; cut off all unnecessary actions.*
7. **Sincerity.** *Use no hurtful deceit; think innocently and*
90 *justly, and, if you speak, speak accordingly.*
8. **Justice.** *Wrong none by doing injuries, or omitting the benefits that are your duty.*
9. **Moderation.** *Avoid extremes; forbear resenting injuries so much as you think they deserve.*
10. **Cleanliness.** *Tolerate no uncleanliness in body, clothes, or habitation.*
11. **Tranquility.** *Be not disturbed at trifles, or at accidents common or unavoidable.*
12. **Chastity.** *Rarely use venery[6] but for health or offspring,*
100 *never to dullness, weakness, or the injury of your own or another's peace or reputation.*
13. **Humility.** *Imitate Jesus and Socrates.[7]*

My intention being to acquire the habitude of all these virtues, I judged it would be well not to distract my attention by

---

4. **precept** *n.:* rule of moral conduct; principle.
5. **trifling** *adj.:* unimportant; shallow.
6. **venery** (ven′ər · ē) *n.:* sex.
7. **Socrates** (säk′rə · tēz′) (470?–399 B.C.): Greek philosopher who is said to have lived a simple, virtuous life.

FLUENCY

Read the boxed passage aloud twice. On your second reading, try to stress the most important words or phrases in the list.

CLARIFY

Before Franklin begins his project, he decides on a plan. Read lines 103–110 carefully, and summarize his intentions.

attempting the whole at once, but to fix it on one of them at a time; and, when I should be master of that, then to proceed to another, and so on, till I should have gone through the thirteen; and, as the previous acquisition of some might **facilitate** the acquisition of certain others, I arranged them with that view, as they stand above. *Temperance* first, as it tends to procure that coolness and clearness of head, which is so necessary where constant vigilance was to be kept up, and guard maintained against the unremitting[8] attraction of ancient habits, and the force of perpetual temptations. This being acquired and established, *silence* would be more easy; and my desire being to gain knowledge at the same time that I improved in virtue, and considering that in conversation it was obtained rather by the use of the ears than of the tongue, and therefore wishing to break a habit I was getting into of prattling, punning, and joking, which only made me acceptable to trifling company, I gave *silence* the second place. This and the next, order, I expected would allow me more time for attending to my project and my studies. *Resolution,* once become habitual, would keep me firm in my endeavors to obtain all the **subsequent** virtues; *frugality* and *industry* freeing me from my remaining debt, and producing affluence and independence, would make more easy the practice of *sincerity* and *justice,* etc., etc. Conceiving then, that, agreeably to the advice of Pythagoras[9] in his Golden Verses, daily examination would be necessary, I contrived the following method for conducting that examination.

I made a little book, in which I allotted a page for each of the virtues. I ruled each page with red ink, so as to have seven columns, one for each day of the week, marking each column with a letter for the day. I crossed these columns with thirteen red lines, marking the beginning of each line with the first letter of one of the virtues, on which line, and in its proper column,

---

8. **unremitting** *adj.:* not stopping; persistent.
9. **Pythagoras** (pi·thag'ə·rəs): Greek philosopher and mathematician of the sixth century B.C.

INFER

Re-read lines 140–150. What can you infer about Franklin from his approach to arriving at moral perfection?

_____

_____

_____

_____

_____

_____

CLARIFY

Franklin plans to begin working on the virtue of temperance. At what point will Franklin begin working on the second virtue (lines 144–148)?

_____

_____

_____

_____

_____

_____

_____

VOCABULARY

eradicate (ē·rad′i·kāt′) v.: eliminate.

I might mark, by a little black spot, every fault I found upon examination to have been committed respecting that virtue upon that day.

140   I determined to give a week's strict attention to each of the virtues successively. Thus, in the first week, my great guard was to avoid every[10] the least offense against *temperance,* leaving the other virtues to their ordinary chance, only marking every evening the faults of the day. Thus, if in the first week I could keep my first line, marked T, clear of spots, I supposed the habit of that virtue so much strengthened, and its opposite weakened, that I might venture extending my attention to include the next, and for the following week keep both lines clear of spots. Proceeding thus to the last, I could go through a course com-
150   plete in thirteen weeks, and four courses in a year. And like him who, having a garden to weed, does not attempt to **eradicate** all the bad herbs at once, which would exceed his reach and his strength, but works on one of the beds at a time, and, having accomplished the first, proceeds to a second, so I should have, I hoped, the encouraging pleasure of seeing on my pages the progress I made in virtue, by clearing successively my lines of their spots, till in the end, by a number of courses, I should be happy in viewing a clean book, after a thirteen weeks' daily examination. . . .

---

10. every: archaic for "even."

from The Autobiography

Reading Skills: Making Inferences The left-hand column of the chart below lists details from Franklin's autobiography. In the right-hand column, write an inference you can make about Franklin's character or beliefs, based on these details.

Details from *The Autobiography*	My Inferences about Franklin's Character or Beliefs
". . . my whole stock of cash consisted of a Dutch dollar, and about a shilling in copper. The latter I gave the people of the boat for my passage, who at first refused it, on account of my rowing; but I insisted on their taking it." (lines 9–13)	
". . . Thus I went up Market Street . . . passing by the door of Mr. Read, my future wife's father; when she, standing at the door, saw me, and thought I made, as I certainly did, a most awkward, ridiculous appearance." (lines 28–31)	
"I wished to live without committing any fault at any time; I would conquer all that either natural inclination, custom, or company might lead me into." (lines 49–51)	
"My intention being to acquire the habitude of all these virtues, I judged it would be well not to distract my attention by attempting the whole at once, but to fix it on one of them at a time . . ." (lines 103–106)	

from The Autobiography

VOCABULARY IN CONTEXT

DIRECTIONS: Write vocabulary words from the Word Box to complete the paragraph below. Use each vocabulary word only once.

Word Box

- arduous
- rectitude
- facilitate
- subsequent
- eradicate

As a young man, Franklin traveled from Boston to Philadelphia to make a new life for himself. Although his trip was long and (1) _____, Franklin arrived in Philadelphia in a good frame of mind. Soon after his arrival, Franklin decided to improve himself, so he set out to (2) _____ his faults. (3) _____ steps Franklin took were geared toward achieving a measure of correctness, or (4) _____. To (5) _____ his difficult task, Franklin created a chart and a scientific system for tracking his progress.

MATHEMATICAL AND SCIENTIFIC ROOTS AND AFFIXES

In his *Autobiography,* Franklin describes a project he approached in a scientific and mathematical way. In the box below are some mathematical prefixes and suffixes Franklin would have known.

DIRECTIONS: Using the information provided in the box, write definitions of the numbered items below.

uni– means "one"	*–meter* means "something that measures"
bi– means "two"	*–ology* means "the study of"
tri– means "three"	

Reading Standard 1.2
Apply knowledge of Greek, Latin, and Anglo-Saxon roots and affixes to draw inferences concerning the meaning of scientific and mathematical terminology.

1. *uniform* means _____

2. *biweekly* means _____

3. *tricolored* means _____

4. *thermometer* means _____

5. *psychology* means _____

   (Note: *Psych*– means "mind.")

 Check your Standards Mastery at the back of this book.

Speech to the Virginia Convention by Patrick Henry

LITERARY FOCUS: PERSUASION

Persuasion is a form of writing or speech that aims to change the way a person thinks or feels. Some forms of persuasion also contain a call to action—they call on people to take action to solve a problem. To be persuasive, a writer or speaker must provide good reasons that support an opinion or course of action. Persuasive speakers can appeal to the audience's emotions or to their logic, or reason. Listed below are two examples.

Emotional Appeal: How could you leave your homeland, the country of your ancestors?

Appeal to Reason: If you leave the country, you will have to give up your citizenship.

READING SKILLS: RECOGNIZING METHODS OF PERSUASION

In this speech to the Virginia Convention, Patrick Henry uses persuasive techniques. He appeals to his audience's **reason** by presenting logical arguments in support of war. He also appeals to their **emotions** to win their support for his political position. Notice that this speech also contains another persuasive technique: a call to action.

Use the Skill As you read, underline passages that Patrick Henry uses to appeal to his audience's reason and emotions. Keep track of the number of appeals and their type by keeping a tally sheet like this one:

Appeals to Logic	Appeals to Emotion
ЖЖ	|||

REVIEW SKILLS

Refresh your ability to evaluate as you read "Speech to the Virginia Convention."

EVALUATION
Judgment of the worth or quality of a text or speech.

Reading Standard 2.1
Analyze both the features and the rhetorical devices of different types of public documents and the way in which authors use those features and devices.

Reading Standard 2.5 (Grade 9–10 Review)
Extend ideas presented in primary and secondary sources through original analysis, evaluation, and elaboration.

Reading Standard 2.6
Critique the power, validity, and truthfulness of arguments set forth in public documents; their appeal to both friendly and hostile audiences; and the extent to which the arguments anticipate and address reader concerns and counterclaims.

Patrick Henry Arguing the Parson's Cause (c. 1830), attributed to George Cooke. Oil on canvas.
Virginia Historical Society, Richmond, Virginia.

Speech to the Virginia Convention

Patrick Henry

Mr. President:[1] No man thinks more highly than I do of the patriotism, as well as abilities, of the very worthy gentlemen who have just addressed the House. But different men often see the same subject in different lights; and, therefore, I hope that it will not be thought disrespectful to those gentlemen, if, entertaining[2] as I do, opinions of a character very opposite to theirs, I shall speak forth my sentiments freely and without reserve. This is no time for ceremony. The question before the House is one of awful moment[3] to this country. For my own part I consider it as nothing less than a question of freedom or slavery; and in proportion to the magnitude of the subject ought to be the freedom of the debate. It is only in this way that we can hope to arrive at truth, and fulfill the great responsibility which we hold to God and our country. Should I keep back my opinions at such a time, through fear of giving offense, I should consider myself as guilty of treason toward my country, and of an act of disloyalty toward the majesty of heaven, which I revere above all earthly kings.

Mr. President, it is natural to man to indulge in the illusions of hope. We are apt to shut our eyes against a painful truth, and listen to the song of that siren, till she transforms us into beasts.[4] Is this the part of wise men, engaged in a great and arduous struggle for liberty? Are we disposed to be of the number of those who, having eyes, see not, and having ears, hear not, the things which so nearly concern their temporal salvation? For my part, whatever anguish of spirit it may cost, I am willing to know the whole truth; to know the worst and to provide for it.

10

20

---

1. **Mr. President:** Peyton Randolph (1721–1775), president of the Virginia Convention.
2. **entertaining** *v.:* having in mind; considering.
3. **awful moment:** great importance.
4. **listen . . . beasts:** In Greek mythology, the sirens are sea maidens whose seductive singing lures men to wreck their boats on coastal rocks. In the *Odyssey*, Circe, an enchanter, transforms Odysseus's men into swine after they arrive at her island home. Henry's allusion combines these two stories.

IDENTIFY

Re-read lines 1–3. Whom is Patrick Henry addressing?

IDENTIFY

Re-read lines 8–18. Underline what Patrick Henry sees as the nature of the question before the house.

CLARIFY

What reason does Henry give for speaking his mind (lines 14–18)?

IDENTIFY

Re-read lines 19–22. What does Henry say people usually do when faced with a painful truth?

VOCABULARY

solace (säl′is) *v.:* comfort.
insidious (in · sid′ē · əs) *adj.:*
sly; sneaky.
martial (mär′shəl) *adj.:*
warlike.
supplication (sup′lə · kā′shən)
n.: plea; prayer.

IDENTIFY

Rhetorical questions are
persuasive devices. They
pose questions to which no
answers are necessary, and
they point out obvious
truths. Locate and underline
two rhetorical questions in
lines 39–43.

CLARIFY

Re-read lines 44–51. According to Henry, why has the
army of Great Britain been
sent? Underline the answer.

I have but one lamp by which my feet are guided; and that
is the lamp of experience. I know of no way of judging of the
30 future but by the past. And judging by the past, I wish to know
what there has been in the conduct of the British ministry for
the last ten years, to justify those hopes with which gentlemen
have been pleased to **solace** themselves and the House? Is it that
insidious smile with which our petition[5] has been lately
received? Trust it not, sir; it will prove a snare to your feet. Suffer
not yourselves to be betrayed with a kiss. Ask yourselves how
this gracious reception of our petition comports[6] with these
warlike preparations which cover our waters and darken our
land. Are fleets and armies necessary to a work of love and rec-
40 onciliation? Have we shown ourselves so unwilling to be reconciled, that force must be called in to win back our love? Let us
not deceive ourselves, sir. These are the implements of war and
subjugation;[7] the last arguments to which kings resort.

I ask gentlemen, sir, what means this **martial** array, if its
purpose be not to force us to submission? Can gentlemen assign
any other possible motives for it? Has Great Britain any enemy,
in this quarter of the world, to call for all this accumulation of
navies and armies? No, sir, she has none. They are meant for us;
they can be meant for no other. They are sent over to bind and
50 rivet upon us those chains which the British ministry have been
so long forging. And what have we to oppose to them? Shall we
try argument? Sir, we have been trying that for the last ten years.
Have we anything new to offer on the subject? Nothing. We have
held the subject up in every light of which it is capable; but it
has been all in vain. Shall we resort to entreaty and humble
supplication? What terms shall we find which have not been
already exhausted? Let us not, I beseech you, sir, deceive ourselves longer. Sir, we have done everything that could be done, to

---

5. **our petition:** The First Continental Congress had recently protested
   against new tax laws. King George III had withdrawn the laws condi-
   tionally, but the colonists were unwilling to accept his conditions.
6. **comports** *v.:* agrees.
7. **subjugation** *n.:* conquest; domination.

avert the storm which is now coming on. We have petitioned;
60 we have remonstrated;[8] we have supplicated; we have prostrated
ourselves before the throne, and have implored its interposition[9]
to arrest the tyrannical hands of the ministry and Parliament.
Our petitions have been slighted; our remonstrances have produced additional violence and insult; our supplications have
been disregarded; and we have been **spurned,** with contempt,
from the foot of the throne. In vain, after these things, may we
indulge the fond[10] hope of peace and reconciliation. There is no
longer any room for hope. If we wish to be free—if we mean to
preserve **inviolate** those inestimable privileges for which we
70 have been so long contending—if we mean not basely to abandon the noble struggle in which we have been so long engaged,
and which we have pledged ourselves never to abandon until the
glorious object of our contest shall be obtained, we must fight!
I repeat it, sir, we must fight! An appeal to arms and to the God
of Hosts is all that is left us!

They tell us, sir, that we are weak; unable to cope with so
formidable[11] an **adversary.** But when shall we be stronger? Will
it be the next week, or the next year? Will it be when we are
totally disarmed, and when a British guard shall be stationed in
80 every house? Shall we gather strength by irresolution and inac-
tion? Shall we acquire the means of effectual resistance, by lying
supinely on our backs, and hugging the delusive[12] phantom of
hope, until our enemies shall have bound us hand and foot? Sir,
we are not weak, if we make a proper use of the means which
the God of nature hath placed in our power. Three millions of
people, armed in the holy cause of liberty, and in such a country
as that which we possess, are invincible by any force which our
enemy can send against us. Besides, sir, we shall not fight our

---

8. **remonstrated** *v.:* objected; complained.
9. **interposition** *n.:* intervention; stepping in to try to solve the
   problem.
10. **fond** *adj.:* foolishly optimistic.
11. **formidable** *adj.:* powerful; difficult to defeat.
12. **delusive** *adj.:* deceptive; misleading.

VOCABULARY

avert (ə·vʉrt′) *v.:* prevent;
turn away.
spurned (spʉrnd) *v.:* rejected.
inviolate (in·vī′ə·lit) *adj.:*
uncorrupted.
adversary (ad′vər·ser′ē) *n.:*
opponent.

IDENTIFY

Henry uses parallel structures
(repeated words and phrases)
to hammer his point home.
Locate and underline examples of parallel structures
in lines 59–66.

IDENTIFY

In lines 68–75, Henry repeats
the main point of his persuasive argument. Find
and circle his main point.

CLARIFY

Re-read lines 76–85. What
counterargument is Henry
preparing to tear down?

_____

_____

_____

_____

_____

_____

_____

IDENTIFY

Pause at line 91. According to Henry's **argument,** what two strengths do the colonists have?

_____

_____

_____

_____

VOCABULARY

vigilant (vij′ə·lənt) *adj.* used as *n.:* those who are watchful.

inevitable (in·ev′i·tə·bəl) *adj.:* not avoidable.

IDENTIFY CAUSE & EFFECT

According to Henry in lines 92–97, what will happen if the war is not fought?

_____

_____

_____

_____

INTERPRET

Underline the famous ending of Henry's speech (line 106). What does Henry say he is willing to die for?

_____

_____

_____

_____

90 battles alone. There is a just God who presides over the destinies of nations; and who will raise up friends to fight our battles for us. The battle, sir, is not to the strong alone; it is to the **vigilant,** the active, the brave. Besides, sir, we have no election.[13] If we were base[14] enough to desire it, it is now too late to retire from the contest. There is no retreat, but in submission and slavery! Our chains are forged! Their clanking may be heard on the plains of Boston! The war is **inevitable**—and let it come! I repeat it, sir, let it come!

It is in vain, sir, to extenuate[15] the matter. Gentlemen may cry peace, peace—but there is no peace. The war is actually

100 begun! The next gale that sweeps from the north will bring to our ears the clash of resounding arms! Our brethren are already in the field! Why stand we here idle? What is it that gentlemen wish? What would they have? Is life so dear, or peace so sweet, as to be purchased at the price of chains and slavery? Forbid it, Almighty God! I know not what course others may take; but as for me, give me liberty, or give me death!

---

13. **election** *n.:* choice.
14. **base** *adj.:* showing little courage, honor, or decency.
15. **extenuate** *v.:* weaken.

Speech to the Virginia Convention

Reading Skills: Recognizing Modes of Persuasion   The chart below contains details from Patrick Henry's "Speech to the Virginia Convention." Each detail is a persuasive appeal. Read each appeal. Then, in column two, identify what it appeals to—a listener's logic or emotion. Then, evaluate the effectiveness of the speech in the space provided. Give reasons for your evaluation.

Example of Persuasive Appeal	Type of Persuasive Appeal
"Ask yourselves how this gracious reception of our petition comports with these warlike preparations which cover our waters and darken our land." (lines 36–39)	
"Shall we gather strength by irresolution and inaction? Shall we acquire the means of effectual resistance, by lying supinely on our backs, and hugging the delusive phantom of hope, until our enemies shall have bound us hand and foot?" (lines 80–83)	
"There is no retreat, but in submission and slavery! Our chains are forged! Their clanking may be heard on the plains of Boston!" (lines 94–96)	

Evaluate the Speech   Review the persuasive appeals in the chart above as well as others you identified while reading "Speech to the Virginia Convention." How well do you think Patrick Henry presented his case? Explain, giving reasons for your answers.

_____

_____

_____

_____

Speech to the Virginia Convention

VOCABULARY IN CONTEXT

DIRECTIONS: Write words from the Word Box to complete this paragraph. Use each vocabulary word only once. Not all words will be used.

Word Box

solace

insidious

martial

supplication

avert

spurned

inviolate

adversary

vigilant

inevitable

Patrick Henry was one of the most famous leaders in the struggle for independence. He was well-known for his speeches in which he attacked Great Britain, a powerful (1) _____. Patrick Henry considered England a sly, or (2) _____ foe. Henry was among the (3) _____, a patriot who was always on the lookout for any political act that threatened the colonies. Colonists protested England's new laws, which treated them unfairly. Despite some people's wishes to stay out of war, Patrick Henry knew that war with Great Britain was (4) _____. For this reason he encouraged his listeners to fight, not to try to (5) _____ the conflict.

WORDS FROM POLITICS

Patrick Henry was actively involved in the politics of early America. Many of the political words he used in his famous speech are also in common use today. The words listed below all spring from Latin words and roots.

DIRECTIONS: Match each word on the left with its Latin origin on the right. Write the correct letters on the numbered lines.

POLITICAL TERM

_____ 1. patriot

_____ 2. martial

_____ 3. treason

_____ 4. liberty

_____ 5. nation

LATIN ORIGIN AND MEANING

a. *tradere*, meaning "to give over or up"

b. *natus*, meaning "born"

c. *liber*, meaning "free"

d. *patris*, meaning "fatherland"

e. *martialis*, meaning "of Mars, god of war"

Reading Standard 1.1
Trace the etymology of significant terms used in political science and history.

 Check your Standards Mastery at the back of this book.

Letter to John Adams by Abigail Adams

LITERARY FOCUS: AUTHOR'S PURPOSE

In reading Abigail Adams's letter to her husband John, you will want to identify the author's **purpose,** or reason, for writing this letter. There are three major purposes for writing:

- **To inform:** The writer's purpose is to present and explain facts.

- **To persuade:** The writer's purpose is to persuade a reader to do something or to behave in a certain way.

- **To entertain:** The writer's purpose is to tell a good story or to share an experience or emotion.

To identify Abigail Adams's purpose, look for a direct statement of why she is writing this letter. Examine other details to evaluate the letter: Does she achieve her purpose?

READING SKILLS: PARAPHRASING

Texts that were written a long time ago usually contain old-fashioned language and inverted sentence structure. If you have difficulty understanding such texts, try paraphrasing sections of the text that give you difficulty.

When you **paraphrase,** you restate the text using your own words. Here are some points to remember when you paraphrase:

1. Find simpler words to replace difficult or archaic words (words no longer in use).

2. Rewrite inverted sentences so that they follow standard subject-verb-complement order.

3. Restate figures of speech to be sure you understand what is being compared with what.

Here is a paraphrase of two lines from Anne Bradstreet's poem on page 16:

Bradstreet: "Then straight I 'gin my heart to chide,
And did thy wealth on earth abide?"

Paraphrase: Then right away I began to scold my heart, and I asked my heart: Is your wealth to be found on earth?

Reading Standard 3.8 Analyze the clarity and consistency of political assumptions in a selection of literary works or essays on a topic (e.g., suffrage, women's role in organized labor).

Letter to John Adams

Abigail Adams

IDENTIFY

Re-read lines 1–8. Underline the words that identify Abigail Adams's **purpose** for writing to her husband.

IDENTIFY

Re-read lines 8–11. Underline the passage that tells what will happen if women are not recognized under the new laws. What is Adams's point of view about giving legal rights and representation to women?

_____

_____

_____

_____

_____

CLARIFY

Whom does Adams refer to as "vicious" and "lawless" (line 16)?

_____

_____

IDENTIFY

How does Adams say men should regard women? Underline the detail that tells you so (lines 19–21).

March 31, 1776

I long to hear that you have declared an independency—and by the way in the new Code of Laws which I suppose it will be necessary for you to make I desire you would Remember the Ladies, and be more generous and favorable to them than your ancestors. Do not put such unlimited power into the hands of the Husbands. Remember all Men would be tyrants if they could. If particular care and attention is not paid to the Ladies we are determined to foment[1] a Rebellion, and will not hold
10 ourselves bound by any Laws in which we have no voice, or Representation.

That your Sex are Naturally Tyrannical[2] is a Truth so thoroughly established as to admit of no dispute, but such of you as wish to be happy willingly give up the harsh title of Master for the more tender and endearing one of Friend. Why then, not put it out of the power of the vicious and the Lawless to use us with cruelty and indignity with impunity.[3] Men of Sense in all Ages abhor[4] those customs which treat us only as the vassals[5] of your Sex. Regard us then as Beings placed by providence under
20 your protection and in imitation of the Supreme Being make use of that power only for our happiness.

A Adams

---

1. **foment** *v.:* stir up.
2. **tyrannical** *adv.:* harsh; cruel; unjust.
3. **impunity** *n.:* freedom from punishment or harm.
4. **abhor** *v.:* turn away from in disgust; detest.
5. **vassals** *n. pl.:* servants; subjects.

Letter to John Adams

Reading Skills: Paraphrasing   Abigail Adams's letter was written well over two hundred years ago. Many of her words are archaic—that is, they are no longer in common use. Some of her sentences are very long and complex, and some sentences do not follow traditional subject-verb-complement order.

To be sure you understand the content of Adams's letter, paraphrase the following passages. Remember that when you paraphrase, you restate all the details of a text using your own words. Replace archaic words with modern words. Restate inverted sentences so that they follow traditional subject-verb-complement format. Rephrase long complex sentences into shorter sentences. Reword any figures of speech, explaining what is compared with what.

Use the right-hand column below to paraphrase the passages from Adams's letter, at the left.

Passage from "Letter to John Adams"	Paraphrase
". . . I desire you would Remember the Ladies, and be more generous and favorable to them than your ancestors." (lines 4–6)	
". . . such of you as wish to be happy willingly give up the harsh title of Master for the more tender and endearing one of Friend." (lines 13–15)	
"Why then, not put it out of the power of the vicious and the Lawless to use us with cruelty and indignity?" (lines 15–17)	

Check your Standards Mastery at the back of this book.

Chapter 2

American Romanticism (1800–1860)

Illustration by Wilfred Satty for Edgar Allan Poe's short story "The Fall of the House of Usher."

American Romanticism 1800-1860

Reading Standard 3.5a–c
Analyze recognized works of American literature representing a variety of genres and traditions.

Gary Q. Arpin

The following essay provides highlights of the historical period. For a more detailed version of this essay, see *Holt Literature and Language Arts,* pages 138–149.

The Romantic Sensibility: Celebrating Imagination

In general, Romanticism is the name given to those schools of thought that value feeling and intuition over reason. The first rumblings of Romanticism were felt in Germany in the second half of the eighteenth century. Romanticism had a strong influence on literature, music, and painting in Europe and England well into the nineteenth century. When it finally arrived in America, it took different forms.

10   Romanticism, especially in Europe, developed as part of a reaction against **rationalism.** The Romantics came to believe that, through the imagination, you could discover truths that the rational mind could not reach. To the Romantics, the imagination, individual feelings, and wild nature were of greater value than reason and logic.

    Poetry was considered the highest embodiment of the Romantic imagination. Romantic artists often contrasted poetry with science, which they saw as destroying the very truth it claimed to seek. Edgar Allan Poe, for example, called science a "vulture"
20 with wings of "dull realities," preying on the hearts of poets.

Notes _____

_____

_____

_____

_____

_____

IDENTIFY

What did the Romantics value (lines 3–4)? Circle the details that give you that information.

WORD STUDY

The word *rationalism* in line 11 refers to the practice of accepting reason as the only authority in forming one's opinions or choosing a course of action. It comes from the word *rational,* which means "based on reason."

IDENTIFY

What was considered to be the highest embodiment of the Romantic imagination (lines 16–17)? Circle the answer.

Underline the two ways in which the Romantics sought a higher truth (lines 25–30). Restate these characteristics of Romanticism in your own words.

_____

_____

_____

_____

_____

_____

_____

Re-read lines 36–40. How did the Puritan view of nature differ from the Romantic view?

_____

_____

_____

_____

_____

_____

Romantic Escapism: From Dull Realities to Higher Truths

The Romantics wanted to rise above the "dull realities" to a realm of higher truth. They did this in two principal ways. First, the Romantics searched for exotic settings in the more "natural" past, far from the grimy and noisy industrial age. Sometimes they found this world in the supernatural realm or in old legends and folklore. Second, the Romantics tried to reflect on the natural world until dull reality fell away to reveal

30 underlying truth and beauty. This second Romantic approach is evident in many lyric poems. In a typical Romantic poem, the speaker sees an ordinary object or scene. A flower found by a stream or a bird flying overhead brings the speaker to some important, deeply felt insight, which is then recorded in the poem. This process is similar to the way the Puritans drew moral lessons from nature. The Puritans' lessons were defined by their religion. The Romantics, on the other hand, found a less clearly defined divinity in nature. Their contemplation of the natural world led to a more generalized emotional and

40 intellectual awakening.

The American Novel and the Wilderness Experience

The development of the American novel coincided with west-ward expansion, with the growth of nationalist spirit, and with the rapid spread of cities. A geography of the imagination developed, in which town, country and frontier would play a powerful role in American life and literature—as they continue to do today.

We can see how the novel developed by looking at the

50 career of James Fenimore Cooper (1789–1851). Cooper explored uniquely American settings and characters: frontier communities, American Indians, and the wilderness of western New York and Pennsylvania. Most of all, he created the first American heroic

figure: Natty Bumppo (also known as Hawkeye, Deerslayer, and Leatherstocking), a skilled frontiersman whose simple morality and almost superhuman resourcefulness mark him as a true Romantic hero.

■ A New Kind of Hero

Cooper's Natty Bumppo is a triumph of American innocence
60 and an example of one of the most important outgrowths of the early American novel: the American Romantic hero. Here was a new kind of heroic figure, one quite different from the hero of the Age of Reason. The rationalist hero was worldly, educated, sophisticated, and bent on making a place for himself in civilization. The typical hero of American Romantic fiction, on the other hand, was youthful, innocent, intuitive, and close to nature.

Today, Americans still create Romantic heroes; the twentieth- and twenty-first-century descendants of Natty Bumppo are all around us. They can be found in dozens of pop-culture
70 heroes: the Lone Ranger, Superman, Luke Skywalker, Indiana Jones, and any number of western, detective, and fantasy heroes.

Daniel Day-Lewis as Natty Bumppo in the movie
The Last of the Mohicans (1992).

IDENTIFY

Re-read lines 59–66. Underline the characteristics of the typical hero of Romantic fiction.

IDENTIFY

Re-read the last paragraph on this page. Underline the pop-culture heroes that are descendants of Natty Bumppo.

Notes _____

_____

_____

_____

_____

_____

_____

_____

_____

_____

_____

_____

_____

_____

_____

_____

_____

INTERPRET

Re-read lines 74–81. Why didn't Romantic poets try to craft a unique American voice?

_____

_____

_____

_____

IDENTIFY

Pause at line 88. How did the Fireside Poets get their name? Underline the answer.

IDENTIFY

Who were the Transcendentalists (lines 98–103)?

_____

_____

_____

_____

_____

_____

_____

_____

_____

_____

_____

_____

American Romantic Poetry: Read at Every Fireside

The American Romantic novelists looked for new subject matter and new themes, but the opposite tendency appears in the works of the Romantic poets. They attempted to prove their sophistication by working solidly within European literary traditions rather than crafting a unique American voice. Even when they constructed poems with American settings and subject matter,

80 the American Romantic poets used typically English themes, meter, and imagery.

The Fireside Poets—as the Boston group of Henry Wadsworth Longfellow (page 73), John Greenleaf Whittier, Oliver Wendell Holmes, and James Russell Lowell was called— were, in their own time and for many decades afterward, the most popular poets America had ever produced. They were called Fireside Poets because their poems were often read aloud at the fireside as family entertainment.

The Fireside Poets were unable to recognize the poetry of

90 the future, which was being written right under their noses. Whittier's response in 1855 to the first volume of a certain poet's work was to throw the book into the fire. Ralph Waldo Emerson's response was much more farsighted. "I greet you," Emerson wrote to this maverick new poet Walt Whitman, "at the beginning of a great career."

The Transcendentalists: True Reality Is Spiritual

At the heart of America's coming-of-age were the Transcendentalists, who were led by Massachusetts writer and lecturer

100 Ralph Waldo Emerson (page 76). **Transcendental** refers to the idea that in determining the ultimate reality of God, the universe, the self, and other important matters, one must transcend, or go beyond, everyday human experience in the physical world.

For Emerson, Transcendentalism was not a new philosophy but "the very oldest of thoughts cast into the mold of these new times." That "oldest of thoughts" was idealism. Idealists said that true reality was found in ideas rather than in the world as perceived by the senses.

110 Idealists sought the permanent reality that underlies physical appearances. The Americans who called themselves Transcendentalists were idealists but in a broader, more practical sense. Like many Americans today, they also believed in human perfectibility, and they worked to achieve this goal.

Ralph Waldo Emerson.
Drawing by David Levine.
Reprinted with permission from
The New York Review of Books.
Copyright ©1968 NYREV, Inc.

■ Emerson and Transcendentalism:
120   The American Roots

Emerson was the most influential and best-known member of the Transcendentalist group. His writing and that of his friend Henry David Thoreau (1817–1862) clearly and forcefully expressed Transcendentalist ideas. As developed by Emerson, Transcendentalism grafted ideas from Europe and Asia onto a homegrown American philosophical stem. Its American roots included Puritan thought and Romantic tradition. "Every natural fact," Emerson wrote, "is a symbol of some spiritual fact."

■ Emerson's Optimistic Outlook

130 Emerson's view of the world sprang not from logic but from intuition. Intuition is our capacity to know things spontaneously and immediately through our emotions rather than through our reasoning abilities. Intuitive thought—the kind Emerson believed in—contrasts with the rational thinking of someone like Benjamin Franklin. Franklin did not gaze on nature and feel the presence of a Divine Soul; he looked at nature and saw something to be examined scientifically and used to help humanity.

An intense feeling of optimism was one product of Emerson's belief that we can find God directly in nature. God is good, and God works through nature, Emerson believed. If we
140

INTERPRET

Re-read lines 144–150. Why was Emerson's optimism appealing to the audiences of his day?

_____

_____

_____

_____

_____

FLUENCY

Read the boxed passage aloud twice. In your second reading, try to improve your speed as well as your comprehension.

CLARIFY

Pause at line 174. Why are Hawthorne, Melville, and Poe called Dark Romantics?

_____

_____

_____

_____

_____

_____

_____

_____

_____

can simply trust ourselves—that is, trust in the power each of us has to know God directly—then we will realize that each of us is also part of the Divine Soul, the source of all good.

Emerson's sense of optimism and hope appealed to audiences who lived in a period of economic downturns, regional strife, and conflict over slavery. Your condition today, Emerson seemed to tell his readers and his listeners, may seem dull and disheartening, but it need not be. If you discover the God within you, he suggested, your lives will become a part of the grandeur
150 of the universe.

The Dark Romantics

Emerson's idealism was exciting for his audiences, but not all the writers and thinkers of the time agreed with Transcendentalist thought. "To one who has weathered Cape Horn as a common sailor," Herman Melville wrote scornfully of Emerson's ideas, "what stuff all this is."

Some people think of Nathaniel Hawthorne, Herman Melville, and Edgar Allan Poe as anti-Transcendentalists, because their views of the world seem opposed to the optimistic views of Emerson and his followers. But these Dark Romantics, as they
160 are known, had much in common with the Transcendentalists. Both groups valued intuition over logic and reason. Both groups, like the Puritans before them, saw signs and symbols in all events—as Anne Bradstreet found spiritual significance in the fire that destroyed her house (page 15).

In contrast to Emerson, however, the Dark Romantics did not believe that nature is necessarily good or harmless. Their view of existence developed from both the mystical and melancholy features of Puritan thought. In their works they explored
170 the conflict between good and evil, the psychological effects of guilt and sin, and even madness. Behind the pasteboard masks of social respectability, the Dark Romantics saw the blankness and the horror of evil. From this imaginative, unflinching vision they shaped a uniquely American literature.

The Tide Rises, the Tide Falls by Henry Wadsworth Longfellow

BEFORE YOU READ

LITERARY FOCUS: METER

Meter is a pattern of stressed and unstressed syllables in poetry. Meter gives poetry rhythm. You can hear the meter of a poem when you read it aloud. Stressed syllables are emphasized more than unstressed syllables.

Analyzing the meter of a poem is called **scanning.** You can use special marks to scan a poem. The stress mark (ˈ) is placed over each stressed syllable. The "short" mark (˘) is placed over each unstressed syllable. Read aloud this line from "The Tides Rises, the Tide Falls," emphasizing the syllables marked with a "ˈ" symbol.

˘ ˈ / ˘ ˈ / ˘ ˈ / ˘ ˘ ˈ
Along / the sea- / sands damp / and brown

Why Does Meter Matter? Think of a line from a poem or song. Write it in the space below. Read the line aloud several times, marking the stressed syllables with a "ˈ" symbol and the unstressed syllables with a "˘." Then, use your symbols to read the line aloud once more, emphasizing the meter.

> ˈ ˘ / ˈ ˘ / ˈ ˘ / ˈ ˘
> **Example:** Happy birthday to you.

READING SKILLS: PARAPHRASING

One way to better understand the meaning of a text is to **paraphrase,** or restate its ideas in your own words. Here is an example of how a line from "The Tide Rises, the Tide Falls" can be paraphrased.

Original Line	Possible Paraphrase
The twilight darkens, the curlew calls	Night is falling. A shorebird cries out.

Use the Skill As you read the poem, pause after each stanza. Paraphrase each line in the stanza, using your own words. Your paraphrase should include the important details expressed in each stanza.

Reading Standard 3.3 Analyze the ways in which irony, tone, mood, the author's style, and the "sound" of language achieve specific rhetorical or aesthetic purposes or both.

Reading Standard 3.4 Analyze ways in which poets use imagery, personification, figures of speech, and sounds to evoke readers' emotions.

The Tide Rises, the Tide Falls

Henry Wadsworth Longfellow

IDENTIFY

Scan the **meter** of lines 1–5. Mark stressed syllables with (′) and unstressed syllables with (˘).

ANALYZE

Circle the title of the poem each time it appears. In what way does its **rhythm** help convey meaning?

_____

_____

_____

_____

_____

_____

_____

_____

_____

FLUENCY

Read the boxed stanza aloud. Pause only when you come to a semicolon or comma. Read once to emphasize the **meter**. Then read again to emphasize meaning and **mood**.

The tide rises, the tide falls,
The twilight darkens, the curlew[1] calls;
Along the sea-sands damp and brown
The traveler hastens toward the town,
5   And the tide rises, the tide falls.

Darkness settles on roofs and walls,
But the sea, the sea in the darkness calls;
The little waves, with their soft, white hands,
Efface[2] the footprints in the sands,
10   And the tide rises, the tide falls.

The morning breaks; the steeds in their stalls
Stamp and neigh, as the hostler[3] calls;
The day returns, but nevermore
Returns the traveler to the shore,
15   And the tide rises, the tide falls.

---

1. **curlew** (kur′lōō′) *n.:* large, brownish shorebird with long legs.
2. **efface** (ə·fās′) *v.:* wipe out; erase.
3. **hostler** (häs′lər) *n.:* person who takes care of horses.

The Tide Rises, the Tide Falls

Reading Skills: Paraphrasing   Use this chart to paraphrase the poem. Remember, in a paraphrase, you must restate the poem using your own words, line by line. You must explain figures of speech to be sure you understand what is being compared with what. After you complete your paraphrase, complete the activity below the chart.

Stanzas from the Poem	Paraphrase
The tide rises, the tide falls, The twilight darkens, the curlew calls; Along the sea-sands damp and brown The traveler hastens toward the town, And the tide rises, the tide falls.	

Darkness settles on roofs and walls,
But the sea, the sea in the darkness
    calls;
The little waves, with their soft, white
    hands,
Efface the footprints in the sands,
    And the tide rises, the tide falls.	

The morning breaks; the steeds in
    their stalls
Stamp and neigh, as the hostler calls;
The day returns, but nevermore
Returns the traveler to the shore,
    And the tide rises, the tide falls.	

Compare and Contrast   Read your paraphrase aloud. Then read the original poem. Compare the two versions. Your paraphrase has the same ideas, but no meter. What does the meter add to the poem?

_____

_____

_____

 Check your Standards Mastery at the back of this book.

from **Self-Reliance** by Ralph Waldo Emerson

LITERARY FOCUS: FIGURES OF SPEECH

"Self-Reliance" is an essay that includes some striking figures of speech. **Figures of speech** are based on unusual comparisons; they are not meant to be taken literally. For example, when Emerson says "Society is a joint-stock company," he is comparing society to a business. In a joint-stock company, all of the owners share the company's profits and losses equally. Emerson's comparison points out that society is interested in money and success. Figures of speech include **similes, metaphors,** and **personification.**

READING SKILLS: UNDERSTANDING FIGURES OF SPEECH

A **figure of speech** can help us see something in a new, imaginative way. When you come across a figure of speech, ask yourself these questions:

- What two things are being compared?

- What do these two things have in common?

- Why does the writer create this comparison? How does it affect the text?

Reading Standard 2.4
Make warranted and reasonable assertions about the author's arguments by using elements of the text to defend and clarify interpretations.

Reading Standard 3.4
Analyze ways in which poets use imagery, personification, figures of speech and sounds to evoke readers' emotions.

Reading Standard 3.11 (Grade 9–10 Review):
Evaluate the aesthetic qualities of style, including the impact of diction and figurative language on tone, mood, and theme.

Use the Skill   As you read the selection, pause whenever you notice an unusual comparison. Such comparisons may be figures of speech. Underline each figure of speech you find. Ask the questions above to help you understand each comparison.

Caricature of Emerson by Christopher Pearce Cranch from *Illustrations of the New Philosophy.*

from Self-Reliance

Ralph Waldo Emerson

There is a time in every man's education when he arrives at the
conviction that envy is ignorance; that imitation is suicide; that
he must take himself for better, for worse, as his portion; that
though the wide universe is full of good, no kernel of nourish-
ing corn can come to him but through his toil bestowed on that
plot of ground which is given to him to till. The power which
resides in him is new in nature, and none but he knows what
that is which he can do, nor does he know until he has tried.
Not for nothing one face, one character, one fact makes much
10 impression on him, and another none. This sculpture in the
memory is not without preestablished harmony. The eye was
placed where one ray should fall, that it might testify of that particular ray. We but half express ourselves, and are ashamed of
that divine idea which each of us represents. It may be safely
trusted as proportionate[1] and of good issues, so it be faithfully
imparted, but God will not have his work made **manifest** by
cowards. A man is relieved and gay when he has put his heart
into his work and done his best; but what he has said or done
otherwise, shall give him no peace. It is a deliverance which does
20 not deliver. In the attempt his genius deserts him; no muse
befriends; no invention, no hope.

    Trust thyself: Every heart vibrates to that iron string. Accept
the place the divine Providence has found for you; the society of
your contemporaries, the connection of events. Great men have
always done so and confided themselves childlike to the genius
of their age, betraying their perception that the absolutely trust-
worthy was seated at their heart, working through their hands,
predominating[2] in all their being. And we are now men, and
must accept in the highest mind the same **transcendent** destiny;

---

1. **proportionate** adj.: having a correct relationship between parts;
balanced.
2. **predominating** v. used as adj.: having influence or power.

INTERPRET

Re-read lines 40–41. What is the opposite of or the "aversion to" self-reliance?

_____

_____

_____

_____

VOCABULARY

integrity (in·teg′rə·tē) *n.:* sound moral principles; honesty.

IDENTIFY

What is "sacred" to Emerson (lines 44–45)?

_____

_____

_____

_____

_____

_____

INTERPRET

What is the **theme,** or message of this essay? *(Grade 9–10 Review)*

_____

_____

_____

_____

_____

30 and not minors and invalids in a protected corner, not cowards fleeing before a revolution, but guides, redeemers, and benefactors, obeying the Almighty effort, and advancing on Chaos and the Dark. . . .

These are the voices which we hear in solitude, but they grow faint and inaudible as we enter into the world. Society everywhere is in conspiracy against the manhood of every one of its members. Society is a joint-stock company in which the members agree for the better securing of his bread to each shareholder, to surrender the liberty and culture of the eater.

40 The virtue in most request is conformity. Self-reliance is its aversion.[3] It loves not realities and creators, but names and customs.

Whoso would be a man must be a non-conformist. He who would gather immortal palms[4] must not be hindered by the name of goodness, but must explore if it be goodness. Nothing is at last sacred but the **integrity** of your own mind. Absolve[5] you to yourself, and you shall have the suffrage of the world. . . .

A foolish consistency is the hobgoblin of little minds, adored by little statesmen and philosophers and divines. With consistency a great soul has simply nothing to do. He may as

50 well concern himself with his shadow on the wall. Speak what you think now in hard words, and tomorrow speak what tomorrow thinks in hard words again, though it contradict everything you said today—"Ah, so you shall be sure to be misunderstood"—Is it so bad then to be misunderstood? Pythagoras was misunderstood, and Socrates, and Jesus, and Luther, and Copernicus, and Galileo, and Newton,[6] and every pure and wise spirit that ever took flesh. To be great is to be misunderstood. . . .

---

3. **aversion** *n.:* object of intense dislike or opposition.
4. **he who . . . immortal palms:** he who would win fame. In ancient times, palm leaves were carried as a symbol of victory or triumph.
5. **absolve** *v.:* pronounce free from guilt or blame.
6. **Pythagoras . . . Newton:** people whose contributions to scientific, philosophical, and religious thought were ignored or suppressed during their lifetimes.

from **Self-Reliance**

Reading Skills: Understanding Figures of Speech   The following chart lists passages from "Self-Reliance." Within each passage are boldface words and phrases that are figures of speech. Interpret and explain each figure of speech in the space provided to the right.

Figure of Speech	Interpretation
"Trust thyself: Every heart vibrates to that **iron string.**" (line 22)	
"[We are] guides, redeemers, and benefactors, obeying the Almighty effort, and advancing on **chaos and the Dark . . . .**" (lines 31–33)	
"A foolish consistency is the **hobgoblin of little minds.**" (lines 47–48)	

from Self-Reliance

VOCABULARY IN CONTEXT

DIRECTIONS: Write words from the Word Box to complete the paragraph below.

Word Box

conviction

imparted

manifest

transcendent

integrity

Emerson held the strong (1) _____ that ideas should be shared and discussed in public. In addition to this belief, he felt that a speaker showed (2) _____ by being honest and straight-forward with an audience. Emerson was well-known for his truthful speeches, which made his ideas (3) _____ and easy to understand. His fascinating thoughts were (4) _____ in the elegant language of his lectures. Some readers found Emerson's words (5) _____, taking them out of their own world and beyond to a new and better one.

ANALOGIES: USING SYNONYMS AND ANTONYMS

In an **analogy** the words in one pair should relate to each other in the same way as the words in a second pair. The colon (:) should be read as "is to"; the double colon (::) should be read as "as."

> ENGINE : AUTOMOBILE :: propeller : airplane

To understand an analogy, think of the relationships between the words. This analogy is accurate because both sets of words have the same relationship. An engine is part of an automobile just as a propeller is part of an airplane.

DIRECTIONS: Complete each analogy below by circling the letter of the correct entry.

Reading Standard 1.3 Discern the meaning of analogies encountered, analyzing specific comparisons as well as relationships and inferences.

1. BOOK : SCHOLAR :: tool : _____

   A   mechanic   C   teacher

   B   metal   D   implement

2. HONESTY : DECEIT :: courage : _____

   F   conviction   H   cowardice

   G   loyalty   J   intelligence

3. ACORN : TREE :: infant :_____

   A   baby   C   crying

   B   adult   D   offspring

4. HOPE : DESIRE :: plead : _____

   F   braid   H   yell

   G   divide   J   beg

 Check your Standards Mastery at the back of this book.

from **Resistance to Civil Government** by Henry David Thoreau

LITERARY FOCUS: PARADOX

A **paradox** is a statement that appears to contradict itself but that actually holds a kind of truth. For example, you might say that "the most beautiful sound is silence." This statement seems contradictory because silence is not a sound. However, the statement also makes sense, because sometimes silence is what people want to "hear."

Paradoxes grab your attention because they seem to state a contradiction. Once you think about them, however, the truths you find in them stay in your memory. Thoreau was fond of using paradoxes to reveal truths. Look for them as you read.

Sense or Nonsense? Explain the truths within the paradoxes below.

Paradox	Truth Revealed
Sometimes the fastest way to finish a job is to slow down.	
You can't be happy without being sad.	

READING SKILLS: RECOGNIZING PERSUASIVE TECHNIQUES

Many writers want to persuade their readers to think, feel, or act in a certain way. To do so, they might use the following persuasive techniques:

- **Logical appeals** use facts, examples, and careful arguments.
  School taxes should be cut because 85 percent of the taxpayers are senior citizens and do not have children.

- **Ethical appeals** are arguments based on values or moral beliefs.
  Even taxpayers without children should invest in the future of our country.

- **Emotional appeals** use language and details that play on our feelings.
  Senior taxpayers are sick and tired of seeing their taxes used to pay for expensive and unnecessary school programs.

Use the Skill As you read the selection, look for the techniques Thoreau uses to persuade you.

REVIEW SKILLS

As you read this excerpt from "Resistance to Civil Government," identify and evaluate Thoreau's argument.

ARGUMENT
Reasons for or against something.

Reading Standard 2.4
Make warranted and reasonable assertions about the author's arguments by using elements of the text to defend and clarify interpretations.

Reading Standard 2.8 (Grade 9–10 Review)
Evaluate the credibility of an author's argument or defense of a claim.

Reading Standard 3.8
Analyze the clarity and consistency of political assumptions in a selection of literary works or essays on a topic.

from Resistance to Civil Government

Henry David Thoreau

IDENTIFY

Underline the phrase in the second sentence that contains a bold **paradox**. Why is this statement a paradox?

_____

_____

_____

_____

_____

_____

_____

_____

VOCABULARY

expedient (ek·spē'dē·ənt) *n.:* means to an end; something that is convenient.

I heartily accept the motto— "That government is best which governs least";[1] and I should like to see it acted up to more rapidly and systematically. Carried out, it finally amounts to this, which also I believe—"That government is best which governs not at all"; and when men are prepared for

10   it, that will be the kind of government which they will have. Government is at best but an **expedient;** but most governments are usually, and all governments are sometimes, inexpedient. The objections which have been brought against a standing army, and they are many and weighty, and deserve to prevail,

Henry David Thoreau (1856).
Photograph by Benjamin D. Maxham.

---

1. **That . . . least:** This statement, attributed to Thomas Jefferson, was the motto of the New York *Democratic Review,* which had published two of Thoreau's essays.

may also at last be brought against a standing government. The standing army is only an arm of the standing government. The government itself, which is only the mode which the people have chosen to execute their will, is equally liable to be abused and **perverted** before the people can act through it. Witness the present Mexican war, the work of comparatively a few individuals using the standing government as their tool; for, in the outset, the people would not have consented to this measure.[2]

This American government—what is it but a tradition, though a recent one, endeavoring to transmit itself unimpaired to **posterity,** but each instant losing some of its integrity? It has not the vitality and force of a single living man; for a single man can bend it to his will. It is a sort of wooden gun to the people themselves; and, if ever they should use it in earnest as a real one against each other, it will surely split. But it is not the less necessary for this; for the people must have some complicated machinery or other, and hear its din, to satisfy that idea of government which they have. Governments show thus how successfully men can be imposed on, even impose on themselves, for their own advantage. It is excellent, we must all allow; yet this government never of itself furthered any enterprise, but by the **alacrity** with which it got out of its way. It does not keep the country free. It does not settle the West. It does not educate. The character **inherent** in the American people has done all that has been accomplished; and it would have done somewhat more, if the government had not sometimes got in its way. For government is an expedient by which men would fain[3] succeed in letting one another alone; and, as has been said, when it is most expedient, the governed are most let alone by it. Trade and commerce, if they were not made of India rubber, would never manage to bounce over the obstacles which legislators are continually

---

2. **this measure:** On May 9, 1846, President James K. Polk received word that Mexico had attacked U.S. troops. He then asked Congress to declare war, which it did on May 13. Some Americans, including Thoreau, thought the war was unjustified. Because Thoreau would not pay taxes to support the war, he went to jail.
3. **fain** adv.: archaic for "gladly; willingly."

IDENTIFY

Re-read lines 52–54. Locate and underline what Thoreau wants.

IDENTIFY CAUSE & EFFECT

According to Thoreau, when power is in the hands of the people, why does the majority rule (lines 57–61)?

_____

_____

_____

INTERPRET

Underline Thoreau's idea about being a man versus being a subject (lines 69–70). What does he mean by this statement?

_____

_____

_____

_____

_____

_____

CLARIFY

Does Thoreau believe it's a person's duty to fight against wrongs? Underline the statements in lines 73–77 that support your answer.

_____

putting in their way; and, if one were to judge these men wholly by the effects of their actions, and not partly by their intentions,
50 they would deserve to be classed and punished with those mischievous persons who put obstructions on the railroads.

But, to speak practically and as a citizen, unlike those who call themselves no-government men, I ask for, not at once no government, but *at once* a better government. Let every man make known what kind of government would command his respect, and that will be one step toward obtaining it.

After all, the practical reason why, when the power is once in the hands of the people, a majority are permitted, and for a long period continue, to rule, is not because they are most likely
60 to be in the right, nor because this seems fairest to the minority, but because they are physically the strongest. But a government in which the majority rule in all cases cannot be based on justice, even as far as men understand it. Can there not be a government in which majorities do not virtually decide right and wrong, but conscience?—in which majorities decide only those questions to which the rule of expediency is applicable? Must the citizen ever for a moment, or in the least degree, resign his conscience to the legislator? Why has every man a conscience, then? I think that we should be men first, and subjects after-
70 ward. It is not desirable to cultivate a respect for the law, so much as for the right. The only obligation which I have a right to assume, is to do at any time what I think right. . . .

It is not a man's duty, as a matter of course, to devote himself to the **eradication** of any, even the most enormous wrong; he may still properly have other concerns to engage him; but it is his duty, at least, to wash his hands of it, and, if he gives it no thought longer, not to give it practically his support. If I devote myself to other pursuits and contemplations, I must first see, at least, that I do not pursue them sitting upon another man's
80 shoulders. I must get off him first, that he may pursue his contemplations too. See what gross inconsistency is tolerated. I have heard some of my townsmen say, "I should like to have them

order me out to help put down an **insurrection** of the slaves, or to march to Mexico—see if I would go"; and yet these very men have each, directly by their allegiance, and so indirectly, at least, by their money, furnished a substitute. The soldier is applauded who refuses to serve in an unjust war by those who do not refuse to sustain the unjust government which makes the war; is applauded by those whose own act and authority he disregards and sets at nought; as if the State were **penitent** to that degree that it hired one to scourge it while it sinned, but not to that degree that it left off sinning for a moment. Thus, under the name of order and civil government, we are all made at last to pay homage to and support our own meanness. After the first blush of sin, comes its indifference and from immoral it becomes, as it were, *un*moral, and not quite unnecessary to that life which we have made. . . .

I meet this American government, or its representative the State government, directly, and face to face, once a year, no more, in the person of its tax gatherer; this is the only mode in which a man situated as I am necessarily meets it; and it then says distinctly, Recognize me; and the simplest, the most **effectual,** and, in the present posture of affairs, the indispensablest mode of treating with it on this head, of expressing your little satisfaction with and love for it, is to deny it then. My civil neighbor, the tax gatherer, is the very man I have to deal with—for it is, after all, with men and not with parchment that I quarrel—and he has voluntarily chosen to be an agent of the government. How shall he ever know well what he is and does as an officer of the government, or as a man, until he is obliged to consider whether he shall treat me, his neighbor, for whom he has respect, as a neighbor and well-disposed man, or as a maniac and disturber of the peace, and see if he can get over this obstruction to his neighborliness without a ruder and more **impetuous** thought or speech corresponding with his action? I know this well, that if one thousand, if one hundred, if ten men whom I could name—if ten *honest* men only—aye, if *one*

90

100

110

VOCABULARY

eradication (ē · rad′i · kā′shən) *n.:* utter destruction; obliteration.
insurrection (in′sə · rek′shən) *n.:* rebellion; revolt.
penitent (pen′i · tənt) *adj.:* sorry for doing wrong.
effectual (e · fek′chŏŏ · əl) *adj.:* productive; efficient.
impetuous (im · pech′ŏŏ · əs) *adj.:* impulsive.

CLARIFY

Re-read lines 86–92. According to Thoreau, how do men who refuse to fight for causes they do not support end up supporting those very causes?

_____

_____

_____

_____

_____

_____

_____

_____

IDENTIFY

Who is the representative of the government that Thoreau meets once and only once a year (lines 98–101)?

_____

_____

ANALYZE

Why does Thoreau think that it is foolish for him to be put in jail (lines 123–131)?

_____

_____

_____

_____

_____

_____

INTERPRET

Re-read lines 140–146. Thoreau says that locking up his body does nothing to lock up his mind. To what does he compare his jailers? Locate and underline the comparison.

IDENTIFY CAUSE & EFFECT

What three reasons does Thoreau give for his loss of respect for the government (lines 146–149)?

_____

_____

_____

_____

_____

_____

_____

_____

HONEST man, in this State of Massachusetts, *ceasing to hold slaves*, were actually to withdraw from this copartnership, and be 120 locked up in the county jail therefor, it would be the abolition of slavery in America. For it matters not how small the beginning may seem to be: What is once well done is done forever. . . .

I have paid no poll tax[4] for six years. I was put into a jail once on this account, for one night; and, as I stood considering the walls of solid stone, two or three feet thick, the door of wood and iron, a foot thick, and the iron grating which strained the light, I could not help being struck with the foolishness of that institution which treated me as if I were mere flesh and blood and bones, to be locked up. I wondered that it should have con- 130 cluded at length that this was the best use it could put me to, and had never thought to avail itself of my services in some way. I saw that, if there was a wall of stone between me and my townsmen, there was a still more difficult one to climb or break through, before they could get to be as free as I was. I did not for a moment feel confined, and the walls seemed a great waste of stone and mortar. I felt as if I alone of all my townsmen had paid my tax. They plainly did not know how to treat me, but behaved like persons who are underbred. In every threat and in every compliment there was a blunder; for they thought that my 140 chief desire was to stand the other side of that stone wall. I could not but smile to see how industriously they locked the door on my meditations, which followed them out again without let or hindrance, and *they* were really all that was dangerous. As they could not reach me, they had resolved to punish my body; just as boys, if they cannot come at some person against whom they have a spite, will abuse his dog. I saw that the State was half-witted, that it was timid as a lone woman with her silver spoons, and that it did not know its friends from its foes, and I lost all my remaining respect for it, and pitied it. . . .

---

4. **poll tax:** fee some states and localities required from each citizen as a qualification for voting. It is now considered unconstitutional in the United States to charge such a tax.

150   The night in prison was novel and interesting enough. The
prisoners in their shirt sleeves were enjoying a chat and the
evening air in the doorway, when I entered. But the jailer said,
"Come, boys, it is time to lock up"; and so they dispersed, and I
heard the sound of their steps returning into the hollow apart-
ments. My roommate was introduced to me by the jailer, as "a
first-rate fellow and a clever man." When the door was locked, he
showed me where to hang my hat, and how he managed matters
there. The rooms were whitewashed once a month; and this one,
at least, was the whitest, most simply furnished, and probably the
160   neatest apartment in the town. He naturally wanted to know
where I came from, and what brought me there; and, when I had
told him, I asked him in my turn how he came there, presuming
him to be an honest man, of course; and, as the world goes, I
believe he was. "Why," said he, "they accuse me of burning a
barn; but I never did it." As near as I could discover, he had probably gone to bed in a barn when drunk, and smoked his pipe
there; and so a barn was burnt. He had the reputation of being a
clever man, had been there some three months waiting for his
trial to come on, and would have to wait as much longer; but he
170   was quite domesticated and contented, since he got his board for
nothing, and thought that he was well treated.

He occupied one window, and I the other; and I saw, that, if
one stayed there long, his principal business would be to look
out the window. I had soon read all the tracts that were left
there, and examined where former prisoners had broken out,
and where a grate had been sawed off, and heard the history of
the various occupants of that room; for I found that even here
there was a history and a gossip which never circulated beyond
the walls of the jail. Probably this is the only house in the town
180   where verses are composed, which are afterward printed in a
circular form, but not published. I was shown quite a long list of
verses which were composed by some young men who had been
detected in an attempt to escape, who avenged themselves by
singing them.

WORD STUDY

Tracts (line 174) are persuasive writings on political or religious subjects. Circle the context clue that helps you figure out the meaning of this word.

WORD STUDY

Circular (line 181) is a word with many meanings. Here, it is used as an adjective meaning "intended for circulation (distribution) among the people." *Circular* is also a noun that refers to newspapers, magazines, or other writings that are sent out to a wide reading audience.

_____

_____

_____

_____

_____

_____

_____

_____

_____

_____

_____

_____

_____

I pumped my fellow prisoner as dry as I could, for fear I should never see him again; but at length he showed me which was my bed, and left me to blow out the lamp.

It was like traveling into a far country, such as I had never expected to behold, to lie there for one night. It seemed to me
190 that I never had heard the town clock strike before, nor the evening sounds of the village; for we slept with the windows open, which were inside the grating. It was to see my native village in the light of the middle ages, and our Concord was turned into a Rhine stream, and visions of knights and castles passed before me. They were the voices of old burghers that I heard in the streets. I was an involuntary spectator and auditor of whatever was done and said in the kitchen of the adjacent village inn—a wholly new and rare experience to me. It was a closer view of my native town. I was fairly inside of it. I never had seen
200 its institutions before. This is one of its peculiar institutions; for it is a shire town.[5] I began to comprehend what its inhabitants were about.

In the morning, our breakfasts were put through the hole in the door, in small oblong square tin pans, made to fit, and holding a pint of chocolate, with brown bread, and an iron spoon. When they called for the vessels again, I was green enough to return what bread I had left; but my comrade seized it, and said that I should lay that up for lunch or dinner. Soon after, he was let out to work at haying in a neighboring field,
210 whither he went every day, and would not be back till noon; so he bade me good day, saying that he doubted if he should see me again.

When I came out of prison—for someone interfered, and paid the tax—I did not perceive that great changes had taken place on the common, such as he observed who went in a youth, and emerged a tottering and gray-headed man; and yet a change had to my eyes come over the scene—the town, and State, and

---

5. **shire town:** town where a court sits, like a county seat.

country—greater than any that mere time could effect. I saw yet more distinctly the State in which I lived. I saw to what extent the people among whom I lived could be trusted as good neighbors and friends; that their friendship was for summer weather only; that they did not greatly purpose to do right; that they were a distinct race from me by their prejudices and superstitions, as the Chinamen and Malays are; that, in their sacrifices to humanity, they ran no risks, not even to their property; that, after all, they were not so noble but they treated the thief as he had treated them, and hoped, by a certain outward observance and a few prayers, and by walking in a particular straight though useless path from time to time, to save their souls. This may be to judge my neighbors harshly; for I believe that most of them are not aware that they have such an institution as the jail in their village.

It was formerly the custom in our village, when a poor debtor came out of jail, for his acquaintances to salute him, looking through their fingers, which were crossed to represent the grating of a jail window, "How do ye do?" My neighbors did not thus salute me, but first looked at me, and then at one another, as if I had returned from a long journey. I was put into jail as I was going to the shoemaker's to get a shoe which was mended. When I was let out the next morning, I proceeded to finish my errand, and, having put on my mended shoe, joined a huckleberry party, who were impatient to put themselves under my conduct; and in half an hour—for the horse was soon tackled[6]—was in the midst of a huckleberry field, on one of our highest hills, two miles off; and then the State was nowhere to be seen.

This is the whole history of "My Prisons." . . .

The authority of government, even such as I am willing to submit to—for I will cheerfully obey those who know and can do better than I, and in many things even those who neither know nor can do so well—is still an impure one: To be strictly

---

6. **tackled** v.: harnessed.

IDENTIFY

Thoreau has a harsh opinion of his "neighbors," his fellow citizens. Re-read lines 219–232, and underline his description of them.

CLARIFY

Re-read lines 238–245. What is the first thing Thoreau does when he gets out of jail?

_____

_____

_____

_____

_____

INTERPRET

What does Thoreau mean when he says "the State was nowhere to be seen" (line 245)?

_____

_____

_____

_____

_____

_____

_____

_____

_____

_____

_____

_____

_____

_____

_____

_____

_____

_____

_____

_____

_____

_____

_____

_____

Read the boxed passage aloud two times. Focus on its marks of punctuation and its basic meaning the first time you read. On your second read, adjust your tone of voice and reading rate to express Thoreau's feelings.

just, it must have the sanction and consent of the governed. It can have no pure right over my person and property but what I concede to it. The progress from an absolute to a limited monarchy, from a limited monarchy to a democracy, is a progress toward a true respect for the individual. Is a democracy, such as we know it, the last improvement possible in government? Is it not possible to take a step further toward recognizing and organizing the rights of man? There will never be a really free and enlightened State, until the State comes to recognize the individual as a higher and independent power, from which all its own power and authority are derived, and treats him accordingly. I please myself with imagining a State at last which can afford to be just to all men, and to treat the individual with respect as a neighbor; which even would not think it inconsistent with its own repose, if a few were to live aloof from it, not meddling with it, nor embraced by it, who fulfilled all the duties of neighbors and fellow men. A State which bore this kind of fruit, and suffered it to drop off as fast as it ripened, would prepare the way for a still more perfect and glorious State, which also I have imagined, but not yet anywhere seen.

Thoreau's journals and a writing box.

from Resistance to Civil Government

Reading Skills: Recognizing Persuasive Techniques   Review the persuasive details that are part of Thoreau's **argument**. Then, in the right-hand column, identify the kind of appeal that is being used in each case—logical, ethical, or emotional. You may find more than one appeal being made.

Persuasive Detail from Argument	Type of Appeal
"The objections which have been brought against a standing army . . . may also at last be brought against a standing government. . . . Witness the present Mexican war, the work of comparatively a few individuals using the standing government as their tool; for, in the outset, the people would not have consented to this measure." (lines 15–24)	
"Thus, under the name of order and civil government, we are all made at last to pay homage to and support [the State's] own meanness. After the first blush of sin, comes its indifference and from immoral it becomes, as it were, *un*moral. . . ." (lines 92–96)	
"I know this well, that if one thousand, if one hundred, if ten men whom I could name—if ten *honest* men only—aye, if *one* HONEST man, in this State of Massachusetts, *ceasing to hold slaves*, were actually to withdraw from this copartnership, and be locked up in the county jail therefor, it would be the abolition of slavery in America." (lines 116–121)	
"As they could not reach me, they had resolved to punish my body; just as boys, if they cannot come at some person against whom they have a spite, will abuse his dog." (lines 143–146)	

from **Resistance to Civil Government**

VOCABULARY IN CONTEXT

DIRECTIONS: Write words from the Word Box to complete the paragraph below. Not all words will be used.

Word Box

expedient

perverted

posterity

alacrity

inherent

eradication

insurrection

penitent

effectual

impetuous

In order to be fair and (1) _____, a government needs to balance action with care. An ideal government will respond with (2) _____ to any new problem or challenge. Wasted time can cost money or even lives. Nonetheless, major decisions must not be rushed or (3) _____. For example, any sudden and violent (4) _____ must be stopped immediately. The (5) _____ of rebellion is the primary goal.

POLITICAL TERMINOLOGY

Etymology is the history of a word. This chart contains etymologies and definitions of some political terms.

DIRECTIONS: Read the incomplete sentences below, and then fill in each blank with the appropriate political term from the chart.

Political Words and Etymologies
government: "an accepted system of political authority or rule," from the Latin *gubernares*, "to steer"
monarchy: "government headed by one person," from the Greek *monos*, "alone," and *archein*, "to rule"
congress: "the highest legislative body of a country," from the Latin *com–*, "together," and *gradus*, "a step"

Reading Standard 1.1
Trace the etymology of significant terms used in political science and history.

1. Britain is a _____, which means that a king or queen is head of government.

2. Thoreau wrote about a _____ that he viewed as imperfect.

3. Only the _____ had the power to decide whether the proposed law should be passed.

 Check your Standards Mastery at the back of this book.

from **Letter from Birmingham City Jail** by Martin Luther King, Jr.

BEFORE YOU READ

LITERARY FOCUS: PERSUASION

Persuasive writers have one goal: to get you to embrace certain beliefs and ideas or to get you to take some sort of action. To achieve this goal, writers use various types of details to support their positions. These details may include examples from real life or literature, statistics, definitions, and quotations. Following are examples:

Example from real life: The garbage strike should be stopped because I saw a rat in the piles of garbage outside my home.

Statistics: Nine out of ten city politicians say that the strike is just.

Definitions: "Liberty" includes the right to strike for better working conditions.

Quotations: Yesterday the mayor said, "This strike will eventually lead to violence."

As you read "Letter from Birmingham City Jail," look for the details Dr. Martin Luther King, Jr., uses to make his ideas clear and persuasive.

READING SKILLS: ANALYZING POLITICAL ASSUMPTIONS

In this selection, Martin Luther King, Jr., discusses his **political assumptions,** or beliefs, about unjust laws. As you read this letter, identify and carefully examine King's ideas about nonviolent resistance. Most of King's beliefs are directly stated, but you'll have to make inferences about some of them.

Use the Skill As you read the selection, underline or highlight details that reveal the writer's beliefs.

Martin Luther King, Jr., in Birmingham City Jail, November 3, 1963.

REVIEW SKILLS

As you read this excerpt, analyze the ideas Martin Luther King, Jr., expresses.

ANALYSIS
Close examination of a piece of literature.

Reading Standard 3.8 Analyze the clarity and consistency of political assumptions in a selection of literary works or essays on a topic. (Political approach)

Reading Standard 2.5 (Grade 9–10 Review): Extend ideas presented in primary and secondary sources through original analysis, evaluation, and elaboration.

from Letter from Birmingham City Jail

Martin Luther King, Jr.

BACKGROUND

The Reverend Dr. Martin Luther King, Jr., was a leader of the United States civil rights movement in the 1960s. He wrote this open letter on April 16, 1963, while serving a sentence for participating in a civil rights demonstration. Note how King's ideas relate to those of Henry David Thoreau in "Resistance to Civil Government" (page 81).

IDENTIFY

Pause at line 5. Why does King say it's "strange and paradoxical" for him to be breaking laws? Underline the reason.

CLARIFY

Re-read lines 7–8. What two kinds of laws does King believe exist?

_____

_____

_____

COMPARE & CONTRAST

King defines "just laws" and "unjust laws" in lines 10–13. Circle the definition of a "just law." Underline the definition of an "unjust law."

You express a great deal of anxiety over our willingness to break laws. This is certainly a legitimate concern. Since we so diligently urge people to obey the Supreme Court's decision of 1954 outlawing segregation in the public schools, it is rather strange and paradoxical to find us consciously breaking laws. One may well ask, "How can you advocate breaking some laws and obeying others?" The answer is found in the fact that there are two types of laws: there are just and there are unjust laws. I would agree with Saint Augustine that "An unjust law is no law at all."

10   Now what is the difference between the two? How does one determine when a law is just or unjust? A just law is a man-made code that squares with the moral law or the law of God. An unjust law is a code that is out of harmony with the moral law. . . .

An unjust law is a code inflicted upon a minority which that minority had no part in enacting or creating because they did not have the unhampered right to vote. Who can say that the legislature of Alabama which set up the segregation laws was democratically elected? Throughout the state of Alabama all types of conniving methods are used to prevent Negroes from

Martin Luther King, Jr., being booked for loitering as his stunned wife, Coretta, looks on (1958).

IDENTIFY

What does King believe is the real reason for his arrest (lines 26–31)? Underline details that support your answer.

20 becoming registered voters and there are some counties without a single Negro registered to vote despite the fact that the Negro constitutes a majority of the population. Can any law set up in such a state be considered democratically structured?

These are just a few examples of unjust and just laws. There are some instances when a law is just on its face and unjust in its application. For instance, I was arrested Friday on a charge of parading without a permit. Now there is nothing wrong with an ordinance which requires a permit for a parade, but when the ordinance is used to preserve segregation and to deny citizens
30 the First Amendment privilege of peaceful assembly and peaceful protest, then it becomes unjust.

I hope you can see the distinction I am trying to point out. In no sense do I advocate evading or defying the law as the rabid segregationist would do. This would lead to anarchy. One who breaks an unjust law must do it *openly, lovingly* (not hatefully as the white mothers did in New Orleans when they were seen on television screaming, "nigger, nigger, nigger"), and with a willingness to accept the penalty. I submit that an individual who breaks a law that conscience tells him is unjust, and willingly
40 accepts the penalty by staying in jail to arouse the conscience of the community over its injustice, is in reality expressing the very highest respect for law.

WORD STUDY

Anarchy (an'ər·kē), In line 34, refers to a state of disorder and violence in which laws are routinely disregarded and disobeyed.

CLARIFY

Re-read lines 38–42. Why is acceptance of the penalty for breaking the laws so important to King's method of protest?

from Letter from Birmingham City Jail

Reading Skills: Analyzing Political Beliefs   Persuasive details from Martin Luther King, Jr.'s "Letter from Birmingham City Jail" are listed in the chart below. In the right-hand column, next to each detail, identify the type of detail: example, statistic, definition, or quotation. Then, review the details from the selection, and write a summary of King's political beliefs, based on those details.

Selection Detail	Kind of Persuasive Detail
"I would agree with Saint Augustine that 'An unjust law is no law at all.'" (lines 8–9)	
"A just law is a man-made code that squares with the moral law or the law of God." (lines 11–12)	
"... there are some counties without a single Negro registered to vote despite the fact that the Negro constitutes a majority of the population." (lines 20–22)	
"For instance, I was arrested Friday on a charge of parading without a permit." (lines 26–27)	
King's Political Beliefs	

Check your Standards Mastery at the back of this book.

The Minister's Black Veil by Nathaniel Hawthorne

LITERARY FOCUS: SYMBOL

Many public buildings throughout our country proudly display the American flag, which is a symbol of the United States. A **symbol** is a person, a place, a thing, or an event that has meaning in itself but also stands for something beyond itself. Writers use symbols to create layers of meanings in their work. As you read "The Minister's Black Veil," pay attention to that black veil. What could it symbolize?

Recognizing Symbols   Universal symbols are symbols that are widely used and recognized. In the left-hand column of the chart below are listed some universal symbols. Write what they stand for in the space provided.

Universal Symbol	Meaning
white flag	
dove	
rainbow	

READING SKILLS: DRAWING INFERENCES

Writers do not come out and directly state what their symbols mean. Instead, they will provide clues that lead you to infer the wider significance of a particular thing, or place, or event in a story or poem. In fact, you will find that some writers say they do not consciously put symbols in their work at all. It is readers who discover the symbols and who make educated guesses about their broader meanings. You will find that different readers might even have different opinions about the meaning of a symbol—all of which makes reading a special pleasure.

Use the Skill   As you read the story, underline or highlight the details that help you make inferences about the black veil.

REVIEW SKILLS

As you read "The Minister's Black Veil," look for ways in which the use of symbolism makes the story rich and memorable.

SYMBOLISM
The use of a literary device in which a person, place, thing, or event has meaning in itself and also stands for something more than itself.

Reading Standard 3.1
Analyze characteristics of subgenres (e.g., satire, parody, allegory, pastoral) that are used in poetry, prose, plays, novels, short stories, essays, and other basic genres.

Reading Standard 3.7 (Grade 9–10 Review)
Recognize and understand the significance of various literary devices, including figurative language, imagery, allegory, and symbolism, and explain their appeal.

The Minister's BLACK VEIL

A Parable

Nathaniel Hawthorne

WORD STUDY

"The Minister's Black Veil" is subtitled "A Parable." A **parable** is a short story that teaches a moral lesson.

IDENTIFY

Pause at line 11. Who is Mr. Hooper?

_____

_____

_____

_____

_____

IDENTIFY

Underline the lines on this page that give the first hint that something is wrong with Mr. Hooper.

VOCABULARY

semblance (sem'blens) *n.:* outward appearance.

The sexton[1] stood in the porch of Milford meetinghouse, pulling lustily at the bell rope. The old people of the village came stooping along the street. Children, with bright faces, tripped merrily beside their parents, or mimicked a graver gait, in the conscious dignity of their Sunday clothes. Spruce[2] bachelors looked sidelong at the pretty maidens, and fancied that the Sabbath sunshine made them prettier than on weekdays. When the throng had mostly streamed into the porch, the sexton began to toll the bell, keeping his eye on the Reverend Mr.

10 Hooper's door. The first glimpse of the clergyman's figure was the signal for the bell to cease its summons.

"But what has good Parson Hooper got upon his face?" cried the sexton in astonishment.

All within hearing immediately turned about, and beheld the **semblance** of Mr. Hooper, pacing slowly his meditative[3] way toward the meetinghouse. With one accord they started, expressing more wonder than if some strange minister were coming to dust the cushions of Mr. Hooper's pulpit.

---

1. **sexton** *n.:* church officer or employee whose duties may include maintenance, ringing the bells, and digging graves.
2. **spruce** *adj.:* neat in appearance.
3. **meditative** *adj.:* deeply thoughtful.

"Are you sure it is our parson?" inquired Goodman[4] Gray of the sexton.

"Of a certainty it is good Mr. Hooper," replied the sexton. "He was to have exchanged pulpits with Parson Shute of Westbury; but Parson Shute sent to excuse himself yesterday, being to preach a funeral sermon."

The cause of so much amazement may appear sufficiently slight. Mr. Hooper, a gentlemanly person of about thirty, though still a bachelor, was dressed with due clerical neatness, as if a careful wife had starched his band, and brushed the weekly dust from his Sunday's garb. There was but one thing remarkable in his appearance. Swathed about his forehead, and hanging down over his face, so low as to be shaken by his breath, Mr. Hooper had on a black veil. On a nearer view, it seemed to consist of two folds of crape,[5] which entirely concealed his features, except the mouth and chin, but probably did not intercept his sight, farther than to give a darkened aspect to all living and inanimate[6] things. With this gloomy shade before him, good Mr. Hooper walked onward, at a slow and quiet pace, stooping somewhat and looking on the ground, as is customary with abstracted[7] men, yet nodding kindly to those of his parishioners who still waited on the meetinghouse steps. But so wonder-struck were they, that his greeting hardly met with a return.

"I can't really feel as if good Mr. Hooper's face was behind that piece of crape," said the sexton.

"I don't like it," muttered an old woman, as she hobbled into the meetinghouse. "He has changed himself into something awful, only by hiding his face."

"Our parson has gone mad!" cried Goodman Gray, following him across the threshold.

---

4. **Goodman:** form of polite address similar to *mister*.
5. **crape** *n.:* kind of black cloth worn as a sign of mourning; from the French word *crêpe*.
6. **inanimate** *adj.:* lifeless.
7. **abstracted** *adj.:* lost in thought.

IDENTIFY

Re-read lines 25–32. Circle the words that describe how Mr. Hooper's appearance has changed.

FLUENCY

Read the boxed passage aloud two times. Punctuation clues indicate when to pause briefly (commas), and when to pause longer (periods). Which sentence would you emphasize in your reading?

INTERPRET

Pause at line 48. What do the congregation's comments reveal about the veil's effect?

IDENTIFY

Underline the words and phrases that describe how people react to Mr. Hooper's appearance (lines 49–57).

IDENTIFY

Underline or highlight the words that describe how Mr. Hooper acts when he enters the church (lines 57–62).

VOCABULARY

obscurity (əb·skyoor′ə·tē) n.: darkness.

Obscurity is more often used to mean "state of being not well-known or famous."

CLARIFY

Read lines 77–87 carefully. What is the minister's usual style of preaching? Is he using the same style now?

_____

_____

_____

_____

_____

_____

_____

_____

_____

A rumor of some unaccountable phenomenon had pre-
50   ceded Mr. Hooper into the meetinghouse, and set all the congregation astir. Few could refrain from twisting their heads toward
the door; many stood upright, and turned directly about; while
several little boys clambered upon the seats, and came down
again with a terrible racket. There was a general bustle, a rustling
of the women's gowns and shuffling of the men's feet, greatly at
variance[8] with that hushed repose which should attend the
entrance of the minister. But Mr. Hooper appeared not to notice
the perturbation[9] of his people. He entered with an almost
noiseless step, bent his head mildly to the pews on each side, and
60   bowed as he passed his oldest parishioner, a white-haired
great-grandsire, who occupied an armchair in the center of the
aisle. It was strange to observe, how slowly this venerable man
became conscious of something singular in the appearance of
his pastor. He seemed not fully to partake of the prevailing wonder, till Mr. Hooper had ascended the stairs, and showed himself
in the pulpit, face to face with his congregation, except for the
black veil. That mysterious emblem was never once withdrawn.
It shook with his measured breath as he gave out the psalm; it
threw its **obscurity** between him and the holy page, as he read
70   the Scriptures; and while he prayed, the veil lay heavily on his up-
lifted countenance. Did he seek to hide it from the dread Being
whom he was addressing?

Such was the effect of this simple piece of crape, that
more than one woman of delicate nerves was forced to leave the
meetinghouse. Yet perhaps the pale-faced congregation was
almost as fearful a sight to the minister, as his black veil to them.

Mr. Hooper had the reputation of a good preacher, but not
an energetic one: He strove to win his people heavenward, by
mild persuasive influences, rather than to drive them thither, by
80   the thunders of the Word. The sermon which he now delivered,

---

8. **at variance:** not in agreement.
9. **perturbation** *n.:* state of alarm.

was marked by the same characteristics of style and manner, as the general series of his pulpit oratory. But there was something, either in the sentiment of the discourse itself, or in the imagination of the auditors, which made it greatly the most powerful effort that they had ever heard from their pastor's lips. It was tinged, rather more darkly than usual, with the gentle gloom of Mr. Hooper's temperament. The subject had reference to secret sin, and those sad mysteries which we hide from our nearest and dearest, and would fain conceal from our own consciousness,

90 even forgetting that the Omniscient[10] can detect them. A subtle power was breathed into his words. Each member of the congregation, the most innocent girl, and the man of hardened breast, felt as if the preacher had crept upon them, behind his awful veil, and discovered their hoarded **iniquity** of deed or thought. Many spread their clasped hands on their bosoms. There was nothing terrible in what Mr. Hooper said; at least, no violence; and yet, with every tremor of his melancholy voice, the hearers quaked. An unsought pathos[11] came hand in hand with awe. So sensible were the audience of some unwonted attribute in their minister,

100 that they longed for a breath of wind to blow aside the veil, almost believing that a stranger's visage[12] would be discovered, though the form, gesture, and voice were those of Mr. Hooper.

At the close of the services, the people hurried out with indecorous[13] confusion, eager to communicate their pent-up amazement, and conscious of lighter spirits, the moment they lost sight of the black veil. Some gathered in little circles, huddled closely together, with their mouths all whispering in the center; some went homeward alone, wrapped in silent meditation; some talked loudly, and profaned[14] the Sabbath day with

110 **ostentatious** laughter. A few shook their **sagacious** heads,

---

10. **the Omniscient:** the all-knowing God.
11. **pathos** n.: feelings of pity, sympathy, and sorrow.
12. **visage** n.: face.
13. **indecorous** adj.: improper; lacking good taste.
14. **profaned** v.: showed disrespect for.

IDENTIFY

Underline the subject of Mr. Hooper's sermon (lines 82–90).

WORD STUDY

Fain (fān) in line 89 is an old-fashioned word that means "with eagerness" or "gladly."

IDENTIFY CAUSE & EFFECT

Why is the congregation so moved and upset? Re-read lines 91–94, and underline the reasons.

VOCABULARY

iniquity (i·nik′wi·tē) n.: wickedness.

ostentatious (äs′tən·tā′shəs) adj.: deliberately attracting notice.

sagacious (sə·gā′shəs) adj.: wise; keenly perceptive.

IDENTIFY

Re-read lines 115–126, and circle the four things that Mr. Hooper does after the sermon. How do the parishioners react to his actions?

_____

_____

_____

_____

_____

INFER

Pause at line 131. Do you think Mr. Hooper knows he has upset the members of his church? Explain.

_____

_____

_____

_____

_____

_____

_____

_____

IDENTIFY

Pause at line 141. What effect does the veil have on the minister's appearance, according to the village physician? Underline his description of the veil's impact.

intimating[15] that they could penetrate the mystery; while one or two affirmed that there was no mystery at all, but only that Mr. Hooper's eyes were so weakened by the midnight lamp, as to require a shade. After a brief interval, forth came good Mr. Hooper also, in the rear of his flock. Turning his veiled face from one group to another, he paid due reverence to the hoary[16] heads, saluted the middle-aged with kind dignity, as their friend and spiritual guide, greeted the young with mingled authority and love, and laid his hands on the little children's heads to bless

120 them. Such was always his custom on the Sabbath day. Strange and bewildered looks repaid him for his courtesy. None, as on former occasions, aspired to the honor of walking by their pastor's side. Old Squire Saunders, doubtless by an accidental lapse of memory, neglected to invite Mr. Hooper to his table, where the good clergyman had been wont[17] to bless the food, almost every Sunday since his settlement. He returned, therefore, to the parsonage, and, at the moment of closing the door, was observed to look back upon the people, all of whom had their eyes fixed upon the minister. A sad smile gleamed faintly from beneath the

130 black veil, and flickered about his mouth, glimmering as he disappeared.

"How strange," said a lady, "that a simple black veil, such as any woman might wear on her bonnet, should become such a terrible thing on Mr. Hooper's face!"

"Something must surely be amiss with Mr. Hooper's intellects," observed her husband, the physician of the village. "But the strangest part of the affair is the effect of this vagary,[18] even on a sober-minded man like myself. The black veil, though it covers only our pastor's face, throws its influence over his whole

140 person, and makes him ghostlike from head to foot. Do you not feel it so?"

---

15. **intimating** v. used as adj.: indirectly suggesting.
16. **hoary** adj.: white or gray, as with age.
17. **wont** adj.: accustomed.
18. **vagary** n.: odd, unexpected action.

"Truly do I," replied the lady; "and I would not be alone with him for the world. I wonder he is not afraid to be alone with himself!"

"Men sometimes are so," said her husband.

The afternoon service was attended with similar circumstances. At its conclusion, the bell tolled for the funeral of a young lady. The relatives and friends were assembled in the house, and the more distant acquaintances stood about the door, speaking of the good qualities of the deceased, when their talk was interrupted by the appearance of Mr. Hooper, still covered with his black veil. It was now an appropriate emblem. The clergyman stepped into the room where the corpse was laid, and bent over the coffin, to take a last farewell of his deceased parishioner. As he stooped, the veil hung straight down from his forehead, so that, if her eyelids had not been closed forever, the dead maiden might have seen his face. Could Mr. Hooper be fearful of her glance, that he so hastily caught back the black veil? A person, who watched the interview between the dead and living, scrupled[19] not to affirm, that, at the instant when the clergyman's features were disclosed, the corpse had slightly shuddered, rustling the shroud[20] and muslin cap, though the countenance retained the composure of death. A superstitious old woman was the only witness of this prodigy.[21] From the coffin, Mr. Hooper passed into the chamber of the mourners, and thence to the head of the staircase, to make the funeral prayer. It was a tender and heart-dissolving prayer, full of sorrow, yet so imbued with celestial[22] hopes, that the music of a heavenly harp, swept by the fingers of the dead, seemed faintly to be heard among the saddest accents of the minister. The people trembled, though they but darkly understood him, when he prayed that they, and himself, and all of mortal race, might be ready, as he

---

19. **scrupled** v.: hesitated.
20. **shroud** n.: cloth used to wrap a body for burial.
21. **prodigy** n.: something extraordinary or inexplicable.
22. **celestial** adj.: heavenly.

CLARIFY

Re-read lines 155–164. What did Mr. Hooper do when his veil swung forward while praying with the corpse? What did an observer say happened then?

INTERPRET

According to lines 166–170, what was Mr. Hooper's prayer like?

_____

_____

_____

_____

_____

_____

_____

_____

_____

_____

_____

_____

_____

VOCABULARY

portend (pôr·tend′) *v.:* signify.

IDENTIFY

Pause at line 200. How does the veil affect people at the wedding? Underline the answer.

trusted this young maiden had been, for the dreadful hour that should snatch the veil from their faces. The bearers went heavily forth, and the mourners followed, saddening all the street, with the dead before them, and Mr. Hooper in his black veil behind.

"Why do you look back?" said one in the procession to his partner.

"I had a fancy," replied she, "that the minister and the maiden's spirit were walking hand in hand."

"And so had I, at the same moment," said the other.

That night, the handsomest couple in Milford village were to be joined in wedlock. Though reckoned a melancholy man, Mr. Hooper had a placid cheerfulness for such occasions, which often excited a sympathetic smile, where livelier merriment would have been thrown away. There was no quality of his dis-position which made him more beloved than this. The company at the wedding awaited his arrival with impatience, trusting that the strange awe, which had gathered over him throughout the day, would now be dispelled. But such was not the result. When Mr. Hooper came, the first thing that their eyes rested on was the same horrible black veil, which had added deeper gloom to the funeral, and could **portend** nothing but evil to the wedding. Such was its immediate effect on the guests, that a cloud seemed to have rolled duskily from beneath the black crape, and dimmed the light of the candles. The bridal pair stood up before the minister. But the bride's cold fingers quivered in the tremu-lous[23] hand of the bridegroom, and her deathlike paleness caused a whisper, that the maiden who had been buried a few hours before, was come from her grave to be married. If ever another wedding were so dismal, it was that famous one, where they tolled the wedding knell.[24] After performing the ceremony, Mr. Hooper raised a glass of wine to his lips, wishing happiness to the new-married couple, in a strain of mild pleasantry that ought to have brightened the features of the guests, like a cheer-

23. **tremulous** *adj.:* trembling.
24. **If . . . wedding knell:** reference to Hawthorne's story "The Wedding Knell." A knell is the ringing of a bell.

ful gleam from the hearth. At that instant, catching a glimpse of his figure in the looking glass, the black veil involved his own spirit in the horror with which it overwhelmed all others. His frame shuddered—his lips grew white—he spilt the untasted wine upon the carpet—and rushed forth into the darkness. For the Earth, too, had on her Black Veil.

The next day, the whole village of Milford talked of little else than Parson Hooper's black veil. That, and the mystery concealed behind it, supplied a topic for discussion between acquaintances meeting in the street, and good women gossiping at their open windows. It was the first item of news that the tavern keeper told to his guests. The children babbled of it on their way to school. One imitative little imp covered his face with an old black handkerchief, thereby so affrighting his playmates, that the panic seized himself, and he well nigh lost his wits by his own waggery.[25]

It was remarkable, that, of all the busybodies and impertinent people in the parish, not one ventured to put the plain question to Mr. Hooper, wherefore he did this thing. Hitherto, whenever there appeared the slightest call for such interference, he had never lacked advisers, nor shown himself averse to be guided by their judgment. If he erred at all, it was by so painful a degree of self-distrust, that even the mildest censure[26] would lead him to consider an indifferent action as a crime. Yet, though so well acquainted with this amiable[27] weakness, no individual among his parishioners chose to make the black veil a subject of friendly remonstrance.[28] There was a feeling of dread, neither plainly confessed nor carefully concealed, which caused each to shift the responsibility upon another, till at length it was found expedient to send a deputation[29] of the church, in order to deal with Mr. Hooper about the mystery, before it should grow into a scandal. Never did an embassy so ill discharge its duties. The

---

25. **waggery** *n.:* joke.
26. **censure** *n.:* expression of strong disapproval or criticism.
27. **amiable** *adj.:* friendly; likable.
28. **remonstrance** *n.:* protest; complaint.
29. **deputation** *n.:* group of representatives.

IDENTIFY
CAUSE & EFFECT

Why does Mr. Hooper flee from the reception (lines 206–210)? Underline the cause.

CLARIFY

What is being **personified** in lines 210–211? What is referred to as "Earth's black veil"?

_____

_____

_____

_____

WORD STUDY

The word *wherefore* (line 224) is no longer in common use. It means "why."

INFER

Think back on Mr. Hooper's behavior so far in this story. Why do you think he begins wearing the veil?

_____

_____

IDENTIFY

What does the congregation do to address the problem of the veil (lines 232–237)?

_____

_____

_____

_____

IDENTIFY

Re-read lines 240–246, and circle what the veil has come to **symbolize** to the people of the church. *(Grade 9–10 Review)*

CLARIFY

Pause at line 253. Was the delegation successful in their mission? Why or why not?

_____

_____

_____

_____

_____

_____

_____

_____

IDENTIFY

Pause at line 263. Who is the next person to speak to Mr. Hooper?

_____

_____

_____

_____

_____

_____

_____

_____

minister received them with friendly courtesy, but became silent, after they were seated, leaving to his visitors the whole burden of introducing their important business. The topic, it might be supposed, was obvious enough. There was the black veil, swathed round Mr. Hooper's forehead, and concealing every feature above his placid mouth, on which, at times, they could perceive the glimmering of a melancholy smile. But that piece of crape, to their imagination, seemed to hang down before his heart, the symbol of a fearful secret between him and them. Were the veil but cast aside, they might speak freely of it, but not till then. Thus they sat a considerable time, speechless, confused, and shrinking uneasily from Mr. Hooper's eye, which they felt to be fixed upon them with an invisible glance. Finally, the deputies returned abashed to their constituents, pronouncing the matter too weighty to be handled, except by a council of the churches, if, indeed, it might not require a general synod.[30]

But there was one person in the village, unappalled by the awe with which the black veil had impressed all beside herself. When the deputies returned without an explanation, or even venturing to demand one, she, with the calm energy of her character, determined to chase away the strange cloud that appeared to be settling round Mr. Hooper, every moment more darkly than before. As his plighted[31] wife, it should be her privilege to know what the black veil concealed. At the minister's first visit, therefore, she entered upon the subject, with a direct simplicity, which made the task easier both for him and her. After he had seated himself, she fixed her eyes steadfastly upon the veil, but could discern nothing of the dreadful gloom that had so over-awed the multitude: It was but a double fold of crape, hanging down from his forehead to his mouth, and slightly stirring with his breath.

"No," said she aloud, and smiling, "there is nothing terrible in this piece of crape, except that it hides a face which I am always glad to look upon. Come, good sir, let the sun shine from

---

30. **synod** (sin′əd) *n.:* governing body of a group of churches.
31. **plighted** *v.* used as *adj.:* promised.

behind the cloud. First lay aside your black veil: Then tell me why you put it on."

Mr. Hooper's smile glimmered faintly.

"There is an hour to come," said he, "when all of us shall cast aside our veils. Take it not amiss, beloved friend, if I wear this piece of crape till then."

"Your words are a mystery too," returned the young lady. "Take away the veil from them, at least."

280 "Elizabeth, I will," said he, "so far as my vow may suffer me. Know, then, this veil is a type and a symbol, and I am bound to wear it ever, both in light and darkness, in solitude and before the gaze of multitudes, and as with strangers, so with my familiar friends. No mortal eye will see it withdrawn. This dismal shade must separate me from the world: Even you, Elizabeth, can never come behind it!"

"What grievous affliction hath befallen you," she earnestly inquired, "that you should thus darken your eyes forever?"

"If it be a sign of mourning," replied Mr. Hooper, "I, per-
290 haps, like most other mortals, have sorrows dark enough to be typified by a black veil."

"But what if the world will not believe that it is the type of an innocent sorrow?" urged Elizabeth. "Beloved and respected as you are, there may be whispers, that you hide your face under the consciousness of secret sin. For the sake of your holy office, do away this scandal!"

The color rose into her cheeks, as she intimated the nature of the rumors that were already abroad in the village. But Mr. Hooper's mildness did not forsake him. He even smiled again—
300 that same sad smile, which always appeared like a faint glimmering of light, proceeding from the obscurity beneath the veil.

"If I hide my face for sorrow, there is cause enough," he merely replied; "and if I cover it for secret sin, what mortal might not do the same?"

And with this gentle, but unconquerable obstinacy,[32] did he resist all her entreaties. At length Elizabeth sat silent. For a few

---

32. **obstinacy** *n.:* stubbornness; willfulness.

INTERPRET

Underline Mr. Hooper's response to Elizabeth's request to take off the veil (lines 275–276). His response has **symbolic** meaning. What do you think it means? *(Grade 9–10 Review)*

_____

_____

_____

INTERPRET

Lines 280–286 are a key passage in the story. Re-read this passage, and explain what you learn from it.

_____

_____

_____

_____

_____

IDENTIFY

Pause at line 296. What argument does Elizabeth use to try to persuade Mr. Hooper to remove his veil?

_____

_____

_____

_____

_____

IDENTIFY

What change has come over
Elizabeth in lines 311–315?

_____

_____

_____

_____

_____

_____

CLARIFY

What does Mr. Hooper
attempt to get Elizabeth to
do (lines 319–325)? Underline
his arguments.

IDENTIFY

Pause at line 331. How is the
matter between Elizabeth
and Mr. Hooper resolved?

_____

_____

_____

_____

_____

_____

_____

_____

_____

_____

_____

moments she appeared lost in thought, considering, probably,
what new methods might be tried, to withdraw her lover
from so dark a fantasy, which, if it had no other meaning,
was perhaps a symptom of mental disease. Though of a firmer
character than his own, the tears rolled down her cheeks. But, in
an instant, as it were, a new feeling took the place of sorrow: Her
eyes were fixed insensibly on the black veil, when, like a sudden
twilight in the air, its terrors fell around her. She arose, and
stood trembling before him.

"And do you feel it then at last?" said he mournfully.

She made no reply, but covered her eyes with her hand, and
turned to leave the room. He rushed forward and caught her arm.

"Have patience with me, Elizabeth!" cried he passionately.
"Do not desert me, though this veil must be between us here on
earth. Be mine, and hereafter there shall be no veil over my face,
no darkness between our souls! It is but a mortal veil—it is not
for eternity! Oh! you know not how lonely I am, and how frightened to be alone behind my black veil. Do not leave me in this
miserable obscurity forever!"

"Lift the veil but once, and look me in the face," said she.

"Never! It cannot be!" replied Mr. Hooper.

"Then, farewell!" said Elizabeth.

She withdrew her arm from his grasp, and slowly departed,
pausing at the door, to give one long, shuddering gaze, that
seemed almost to penetrate the mystery of the black veil. But,
even amid his grief, Mr. Hooper smiled to think that only a
material emblem had separated him from happiness, though the
horrors which it shadowed forth, must be drawn darkly between
the fondest of lovers.

From that time no attempts were made to remove Mr.
Hooper's black veil, or, by a direct appeal, to discover the secret
which it was supposed to hide. By persons who claimed a supe-
riority to popular prejudice, it was reckoned merely an eccentric
whim, such as often mingles with the sober actions of men otherwise rational, and tinges them all with its own semblance of

> Her eyes were fixed insensibly on the black veil, when, like a sudden twilight in the air, its terrors fell around her.

insanity. But with the multitude, good Mr. Hooper was irreparably a bugbear.[33] He could not walk the streets with any peace of mind, so conscious was he that the gentle and timid would turn aside to avoid him, and that others would make it a point of hardihood to throw themselves in his way. The impertinence of the latter class compelled him to give up his customary walk, at sunset, to the burial ground; for when he leaned **pensively** over the gate, there would always be faces behind the grave-

350 stones, peeping at his black veil. A fable went the rounds, that the stare of the dead people drove him thence. It grieved him, to the very depth of his kind heart, to observe how the children fled from his approach, breaking up their merriest sports, while his melancholy figure was yet afar off. Their instinctive dread caused him to feel, more strongly than aught else, that a preternatural[34] horror was interwoven with the threads of the black crape. In truth, his own **antipathy** to the veil was known to be so great, that he never willingly passed before a mirror, nor stooped to drink at a still fountain, lest, in its peaceful bosom, he should

360 be affrighted by himself. This was what gave **plausibility** to the whispers, that Mr. Hooper's conscience tortured him for some great crime, too horrible to be entirely concealed, or otherwise than so obscurely intimated. Thus, from beneath the black veil, there rolled a cloud into the sunshine, an ambiguity of sin or sorrow, which enveloped the poor minister, so that love or sympathy could never reach him. It was said, that ghost and fiend

---

33. **bugbear** *n.:* source of irrational fears.
34. **preternatural** *adj.:* abnormal; supernatural.

INTERPRET

Pause at line 346. How do the villagers treat Mr. Hooper?

VOCABULARY

pensively (pen′siv·lē) *adv.:* in deep thought.
antipathy (an·tip′ə·thē) *n.:* strong dislike.
plausibility (plô·zə·bil′ə·tē) *n.:* believability.

IDENTIFY

Pause at the end of this page. Underline details that might give you a clue about the veil's meaning.

INTERPRET

Pause at line 373. What effect does the veil have on Mr. Hooper's outlook?

_____

_____

_____

_____

_____

INTERPRET

Re-read lines 374–381. Underline the words that describe how the black veil affected Hooper's relationship with the villagers. What do you think the black veil is a **symbol** of at this point in the story? *(Grade 9–10 Review)*

_____

_____

_____

_____

CLARIFY

Pause at line 389. In what way did the veil make Mr. Hooper a popular minister?

_____

_____

_____

_____

consorted with him there. With self-shudderings and outward terrors, he walked continually in its shadow, groping darkly within his own soul, or gazing through a medium that saddened
370 the whole world. Even the lawless wind, it was believed, respected his dreadful secret, and never blew aside the veil. But still good Mr. Hooper sadly smiled, at the pale visages of the worldly throng as he passed by.

Among all its bad influences, the black veil had the one desirable effect, of making its wearer a very efficient clergyman. By the aid of his mysterious emblem—for there was no other apparent cause—he became a man of awful power, over souls that were in agony for sin. His converts always regarded him with a dread peculiar to themselves, affirming, though but fig-
380 uratively, that, before he brought them to celestial light, they had been with him behind the black veil. Its gloom, indeed, enabled him to sympathize with all dark affections. Dying sinners cried aloud for Mr. Hooper, and would not yield their breath till he appeared; though ever, as he stooped to whisper consolation, they shuddered at the veiled face so near their own. Such were the terrors of the black veil, even when Death had bared his visage! Strangers came long distances to attend service at his church, with the mere idle purpose of gazing at his figure, because it was forbidden them to behold his face. But many
390 were made to quake ere they departed! Once, during Governor Belcher's[35] administration, Mr. Hooper was appointed to preach the election sermon. Covered with his black veil, he stood before the chief magistrate, the council, and the representatives, and wrought so deep an impression, that the legislative measures of that year, were characterized by all the gloom and piety of our earliest ancestral sway.

In this manner Mr. Hooper spent a long life, irreproachable[36] in outward act, yet shrouded in dismal suspicions; kind

---

35. **Governor Belcher's:** Jonathan Belcher (1681?–1757) was governor of the Massachusetts Bay Colony from 1730 to 1741.
36. **irreproachable** *adj.*: blameless.

and loving, though unloved, and dimly feared; a man apart from men, shunned in their health and joy, but ever summoned to their aid in mortal anguish. As years wore on, shedding their snows above his sable veil, he acquired a name throughout the New England churches, and they called him Father Hooper. Nearly all his parishioners, who were of mature age when he was settled, had been borne away by many a funeral: He had one congregation in the church, and a more crowded one in the churchyard; and having wrought so late into the evening, and done his work so well, it was now good Father Hooper's turn to rest.

Several persons were visible by the shaded candlelight, in the death chamber of the old clergyman. Natural connections he had none. But there was the decorously grave, though unmoved physician, seeking only to mitigate[37] the last pangs of the patient whom he could not save. There were the deacons, and other eminently pious members of his church. There, also, was the Reverend Mr. Clark, of Westbury, a young and zealous divine, who had ridden in haste to pray by the bedside of the expiring minister. There was the nurse, no hired handmaiden of death, but one whose calm affection had endured thus long, in secrecy, in solitude, amid the chill of age, and would not perish, even at the dying hour. Who, but Elizabeth! And there lay the hoary head of good Father Hooper upon the death-pillow, with the black veil still swathed about his brow and reaching down over his face, so that each more difficult gasp of his faint breath caused it to stir. All through life that piece of crape had hung between him and the world: It had separated him from cheerful brotherhood and woman's love, and kept him in that saddest of all prisons, his own heart; and still it lay upon his face, as if to deepen the gloom of his darksome chamber, and shade him from the sunshine of eternity.

For some time previous, his mind had been confused, wavering doubtfully between the past and the present, and

---

37. mitigate v.: make less painful.

INTERPRET

What does the phrase "it was now good Father Hooper's turn to rest" mean in lines 408–409?

CLARIFY

What do you learn about Elizabeth in lines 418–421?

IDENTIFY

Underline details that suggest the meaning of the black veil (lines 421–430).

INFER

Pause at line 442. Why do you think Elizabeth would have replaced the veil if it had fallen away?

_____

_____

_____

_____

_____

_____

_____

PREDICT

Pause at line 453. Do you think Hooper will reveal why he has worn the black veil for so many years? Explain.

_____

_____

_____

_____

_____

_____

_____

_____

IDENTIFY

Re-read lines 456–464. Underline the reasons the minister of Westbury gives for wanting to lift the black veil.

hovering forward, as it were, at intervals, into the indistinctness of the world to come. There had been feverish turns, which tossed him from side to side, and wore away what little strength he had. But in his most convulsive struggles, and in the wildest vagaries of his intellect, when no other thought retained its sober influence, he still showed an awful solicitude lest the black veil should slip aside. Even if his bewildered soul could have for-
440   gotten, there was a faithful woman at his pillow, who, with avert-ed eyes, would have covered that aged face, which she had last beheld in the comeliness of manhood. At length the death-stricken old man lay quietly in the torpor[38] of mental and bodily exhaustion, with an imperceptible pulse, and breath that grew fainter and fainter, except when a long, deep, and irregular inspi-ration[39] seemed to prelude the flight of his spirit.

The minister of Westbury approached the bedside.

"Venerable Father Hooper," said he, "the moment of your release is at hand. Are you ready for the lifting of the veil, that
450   shuts in time from eternity?"

Father Hooper at first replied merely by a feeble motion of his head; then, apprehensive, perhaps, that his meaning might be doubtful, he exerted himself to speak.

"Yea," said he, in faint accents, "my soul hath a patient weariness until that veil be lifted."

"And is it fitting," resumed the Reverend Mr. Clark, "that a man so given to prayer, of such a blameless example, holy in deed and thought, so far as mortal judgment may pronounce; is it fitting that a father in the church should leave a shadow on his
460   memory, that may seem to blacken a life so pure? I pray you, my venerable brother, let not this thing be! Suffer us to be glad-dened by your triumphant aspect, as you go to your reward. Before the veil of eternity be lifted, let me cast aside this black veil from your face!"

And thus speaking, the Reverend Mr. Clark bent forward to reveal the mystery of so many years. But, exerting a sudden

---

38. **torpor** _n._: dull or sluggish state.
39. **inspiration** _n._: inhaling.

energy, that made all the beholders stand aghast, Father Hooper snatched both his hands from beneath the bedclothes, and pressed them strongly on the black veil, **resolute** to struggle, if the minister of Westbury would contend with a dying man.

"Never!" cried the veiled clergyman. "On earth, never!"

"Dark old man!" exclaimed the affrighted minister, "with what horrible crime upon your soul are you now passing to the judgment?"

Father Hooper's breath heaved; it rattled in his throat; but, with a mighty effort, grasping forward with his hands, he caught hold of life, and held it back till he should speak. He even raised himself in bed; and there he sat, shivering with the arms of death around him, while the black veil hung down, awful, at that last moment, in the gathered terrors of a lifetime. And yet the faint, sad smile, so often there, now seemed to glimmer from its obscurity, and linger on Father Hooper's lips.

"Why do you tremble at me alone?" cried he, turning his veiled face round the circle of pale spectators. "Tremble also at each other! Have men avoided me, and women shown no pity, and children screamed and fled, only for my black veil? What, but the mystery which it obscurely typifies, has made this piece of crape so awful? When the friend shows his inmost heart to his friend; the lover to his best beloved; when man does not vainly shrink from the eye of his Creator, loathsomely treasuring up the secret of his sin; then deem me a monster, for the symbol beneath which I have lived, and die! I look around me, and, lo! on every visage a Black Veil!"

While his auditors shrank from one another, in mutual affright, Father Hooper fell back upon his pillow, a veiled corpse, with a faint smile lingering on the lips. Still veiled, they laid him in his coffin, and a veiled corpse they bore him to the grave. The grass of many years has sprung up and withered on that grave, the burial stone is moss-grown, and good Mr. Hooper's face is dust; but awful is still the thought, that it moldered beneath the Black Veil!

VOCABULARY

resolute (rez′ə·l‾oot′) *adj.:* determined.

CLARIFY

Lines 483–493 contain the climax of the story. What does Mr. Hooper say made the veil so awful?

_____

_____

_____

_____

_____

_____

_____

INFER

This story is a **parable:** It teaches a moral lesson. What do you think is the moral lesson of "The Minister's Black Veil"?

_____

_____

_____

_____

_____

_____

_____

_____

The Minister's Black Veil

Reading Skills: Drawing Inferences   "The Minister's Black Veil" contains details that help you make inferences about Mr. Hooper, about the deceased woman, about what the veil symbolizes, and about the moral lesson the story teaches.

The following chart contains passages from "The Minister's Black Veil." Write the inferences you make about these passages in the space provided to the right.

Story Details	Inferences About . . .
"'I had a fancy,' replied she, 'that the minister and the maiden's spirit were walking hand in hand.'" (lines 179–180)	**Mr. Hooper:**
"All through life that piece of crape had hung between him and the world: It had separated him from cheerful brotherhood and woman's love, and kept him in that saddest of all prisons, his own heart. . . . " (lines 425–428)	**The veil:**
"'When the friend shows his inmost heart to his friend; the lover to his best beloved; when man does not vainly shrink from the eye of his Creator, loathsomely treasuring up the secret of his sin; then deem me a monster. . . .'" (lines 488–491)	**The moral lesson:**
"'. . . Lo! on every visage a Black Veil!'" (lines 492–493)	**People everywhere:**

The Minister's Black Veil

VOCABULARY IN CONTEXT

DIRECTIONS: Write vocabulary words from the Word Box to complete the paragraph below. Not all of the words will be used.

Word Box

semblance

obscurity

iniquity

ostentatious

sagacious

portend

pensively

antipathy

plausibility

resolute

Nathaniel Hawthorne was a great nineteenth-century American novelist and short-story writer. After graduating from college, he lived in quiet (1) _____ as a little-known writer for more than ten years. Early in his career, Hawthorne often wrote about (2) _____ and the effect of wickedness on individuals and their community. Characters in Hawthorne's stories have the (3) _____ of normalcy; however, their outward appearances are often deceiving. Like most storytellers, Hawthorne creates suspense with details that (4) _____ future events. In his stories and novels, Hawthorne reveals his (5) _____ for hypocrisy and moral blindness.

CONTEXT CLUES

You can figure out the meaning of an unknown word by using **context clues,** which are the surrounding words, phrases, and sentences.

DIRECTIONS: In each sentence below, circle the words or phrases that provide clues to the meaning of the boldface vocabulary word. Then, explain the meaning of the boldface word based on its context.

1. Mr. Hooper, though a mild man, was **resolute** in his determination not to remove the veil.

   Explanation: _____

2. The lonely minister often walked **pensively** as the villagers greeted each other. He seriously considered how their lives differed from his own.

   Explanation: _____

3. The minister didn't want the black veil to be **ostentatious**; however, it still attracted a lot of notice in the village.

   Explanation: _____

Reading Standard 1.1 (Grade 9–10 Review) Identify and use the literal and figurative meanings of words and understand word derivations.

 Check your Standards Mastery at the back of this book.

The Raven by Edgar Allan Poe

BEFORE YOU READ

REVIEW SKILLS

Reinforce your mastery of this literary concept as you read "The Raven":

SYMBOLISM
The use of a person, a place, a thing, or an event to stand both for itself and for something beyond itself.

Reading Standard 3.3
Analyze the ways in which irony, tone, mood, the author's style, and the "sound" of language achieve specific rhetorical or aesthetic purposes or both.

Reading Standard 3.4
Analyze the ways in which poets use imagery, personification, figures of speech, and sounds to evoke readers' emotions.

Reading Standard 3.7 (Grade 9–10 Review)
Recognize and understand the significance of various literary devices, including figurative language, imagery, ...ism.

LITERARY FOCUS: SOUND EFFECTS

Edgar Allan Poe was a master at creating sound effects in his stories and poems. Here is a list of some of Poe's favorite sound devices:

Sound Device	Example from "The Raven"
Refrain: Repeated lines.	"Nevermore."
End rhyme: Rhymes at the ends of lines.	"'Tis some visitor," I muttered, "tapping at my chamber **door**—/ Only this and nothing **more.**"
Internal rhyme: Rhyme that occurs within lines.	While I nodded, nearly **napping,** suddenly there came a **tapping**
Alliteration: Repetition of a consonant sound.	While I **n**odded, **n**early **n**apping, suddenly there came a tapping
Onomatopoeia: Use of words with sounds that echo their sense.	While I nodded, nearly napping, suddenly there came a **tapping**
Meter: Regular pattern of stressed and unstressed syllables in a poem.	Once upon a midnight dreary, while I pondered, weak and weary,

READING SKILLS: ORAL READING

To enjoy Poe, and to be sure you have caught the meaning of each line of this famous poem, read the poem aloud. Feel the beat of the lines and listen for the rhyming sounds, the repeated consonant sounds, and the use of onomatopoeia. After you have read the poem aloud at least once, you will find that your comprehension of the text has improved.

Use the Skill After one oral reading of the poem, stop to mark up its sound devices. You could circle or underline or box examples of alliteration, rhyme, and onomatopoeia. Then, read the poem aloud again, this time to a classmate. Give special emphasis to those sound devices you marked.

The Raven

Edgar Allan Poe

Once upon a midnight dreary, while I pondered, weak and
    weary,
Over many a quaint and curious volume of forgotten lore—
While I nodded, nearly napping, suddenly there came a tapping,
As of someone gently rapping, rapping at my chamber door—
5   " 'Tis some visitor," I muttered, "tapping at my chamber door—
    Only this and nothing more."

Ah, distinctly I remember it was in the bleak December;
And each separate dying ember wrought its ghost upon the
    floor.
Eagerly I wished the morrow;—vainly I had sought to borrow
10 From my books surcease[1] of sorrow—sorrow for the lost
    Lenore—
For the rare and radiant maiden whom the angels name Lenore—
    Nameless *here* for evermore.

And the silken, sad, uncertain rustling of each purple curtain
Thrilled me—filled me with fantastic terrors never felt before;
15 So that now, to still the beating of my heart, I stood repeating
" 'Tis some visitor entreating[2] entrance at my chamber door—
Some late visitor entreating entrance at my chamber door;—
    This it is and nothing more."

Presently my soul grew stronger; hesitating then no longer,
20 "Sir," said I, "or Madam, truly your forgiveness I implore;[3]
But the fact is I was napping, and so gently you came rapping,

---

1. **surcease** *n.:* end.
2. **entreating** *v.:* begging; asking.
3. **implore** *v.:* plead; ask.

ANALYZE

Circle the rhyming words in lines 1–6. What kind of **mood,** or atmosphere, do the rhymes create?

_____

_____

_____

_____

_____

CLARIFY

Re-read lines 9–10. What is the speaker trying to do?

_____

_____

_____

_____

_____

FLUENCY

Read the boxed passage silently at first, and mark up the sound devices it contains (alliteration, rhyme, rhythm, and so on). Then, read the passage aloud, and focus on conveying simple meaning. Read the passage aloud a second time, and bring the sound effects to life.

IDENTIFY

What happens in lines 25–30? Mark up the sound devices you find while you re-read.

_____

_____

_____

_____

_____

_____

INTERPRET

Re-read lines 31–36. What does the narrator say might be causing the tapping? Do you think he really believes his own explanation?

_____

_____

_____

_____

_____

_____

IDENTIFY

Who enters the speaker's chamber (lines 37–42)?

_____

_____

_____

And so faintly you came tapping, tapping at my chamber door,

That I scarce was sure I heard you"—here I opened wide the
    door;—

        Darkness there and nothing more.

25 Deep into that darkness peering, long I stood there wondering,
    fearing,

Doubting, dreaming dreams no mortal ever dared to dream
    before;

But the silence was unbroken, and the stillness gave no token,

And the only word there spoken was the whispered word,
    "Lenore?"

This I whispered, and an echo murmured back the word,
    "Lenore!"

30   Merely this and nothing more.

Back into the chamber turning, all my soul within me burning,

Soon again I heard a tapping somewhat louder than before.

"Surely," said I, "surely that is something at my window lattice;[4]

Let me see, then, what thereat is, and this mystery explore—

35 Let my heart be still a moment and this mystery explore;—

        'Tis the wind and nothing more!"

Open here I flung the shutter, when, with many a flirt and flutter,

In there stepped a stately Raven of the saintly days of yore;[5]

Not the least obeisance[6] made he; not a minute stopped or
    stayed he;

40 But, with mien[7] of lord or lady, perched above my chamber
    door—

---

4. **lattice** _n.:_ shutter or screen formed by strips or bars overlaid in a criss-cross pattern.
5. **Raven . . . of yore:** _Of yore_ is an obsolete way of saying "of time long past." Poe's allusion is to 1 Kings 17:1–6, which tells of the prophet Elijah being fed by ravens in the wilderness.
6. **obeisance** (ō·bā′səns) _n.:_ gesture of respect.
7. **mien** (mēn) _n.:_ manner.

Perched upon a bust of Pallas[8] just above my chamber door—
        Perched, and sat, and nothing more.

Then this ebony bird beguiling[9] my sad fancy into smiling,
By the grave and stern decorum of the countenance it wore,
45 "Though thy crest be shorn and shaven, thou," I said, "art sure
        no craven,
Ghastly grim and ancient Raven wandering from the Nightly
        shore—
Tell me what thy lordly name is on the Night's Plutonian shore!"[10]
        Quoth the Raven "Nevermore."

Much I marveled this ungainly[11] fowl to hear discourse so plainly,
50 Though its answer little meaning—little relevancy bore;
For we cannot help agreeing that no living human being
Ever yet was blessed with seeing bird above his chamber door—
Bird or beast upon the sculptured bust above his chamber door,
        With such name as "Nevermore."

55 But the Raven, sitting lonely on the placid bust, spoke only
That one word, as if his soul in that one word he did outpour.
Nothing farther then he uttered—not a feather then he fluttered—
Till I scarcely more than muttered "Other friends have flown
        before—
On the morrow *he* will leave me, as my Hopes have flown before."
60   Then the bird said "Nevermore."

Startled at the stillness broken by reply so aptly spoken,
"Doubtless," said I, "what it utters is its only stock and store
Caught from some unhappy master whom unmerciful Disaster

---

8. **Pallas:** Pallas Athena, the Greek goddess of wisdom.
9. **beguiling** *v.* used as *adj.:* deceiving.
10. **Plutonian shore:** Pluto is the Greek god of the underworld—the land of darkness—called Hades (hā′dēz′). Hades is separated from the world of the living by several rivers; hence, the mention of a shore.
11. **ungainly** *adj.:* unattractive.

CLARIFY

Re-read lines 43–48. Underline the question the speaker asks the raven. Circle the raven's reply.

INTERPRET

Re-read lines 55–60. What does the speaker compare the raven's probable departure to?

_____
_____
_____
_____
_____
_____

CLARIFY

How does the speaker explain the bird's ability to say the word *nevermore* (lines 61–63)?

_____
_____
_____
_____
_____
_____
_____
_____
_____
_____

Followed fast and followed faster till his songs one burden bore—
65   Till the dirges of his Hope that melancholy burden bore
                Of 'Never—nevermore.' "

But the Raven still beguiling my sad fancy into smiling,
Straight I wheeled a cushioned seat in front of bird, and bust
                and door;
Then, upon the velvet sinking, I betook myself to linking
70   Fancy unto fancy, thinking what this ominous bird of yore—
What this grim, ungainly, ghastly, gaunt, and ominous bird of
                yore
                Meant in croaking "Nevermore."

This I sat engaged in guessing, but no syllable expressing
To the fowl whose fiery eyes now burned into my bosom's core;
75   This and more I sat divining,[12] with my head at ease reclining
On the cushion's velvet lining that the lamplight gloated o'er,
But whose velvet-violet lining with the lamplight gloating o'er,
                She shall press, ah, nevermore!

12. **divining** *v.* used as *adj.:* guessing; supposing.

READ & REREAD

Read lines 67–72 once for basic meaning. Then, read them again, and underline examples of alliteration, circle rhymes, and box onomatopoeic words.

Then, methought, the air grew denser, perfumed from an
    unseen censer

80 Swung by seraphim[13] whose footfalls tinkled on the tufted floor.
"Wretch," I cried, "thy God hath lent thee—by these angels he
    hath sent thee
Respite—respite and nepenthe[14] from thy memories of Lenore;
Quaff,[15] oh quaff this kind nepenthe and forget this lost
    Lenore!"
          Quoth the Raven "Nevermore."

85 "Prophet!" said I, "thing of evil!—prophet still, if bird or devil!—
Whether Tempter sent, or whether tempest tossed thee here
    ashore,
Desolate yet all undaunted,[16] on this desert land enchanted—
On this home by Horror haunted—tell me truly, I implore—
Is there—*is* there balm in Gilead?[17]—tell me—tell me, I implore!"
90   Quoth the Raven "Nevermore."

"Prophet!" said I, "thing of evil!—prophet still, if bird or devil!
By that Heaven that bends above us—by that God we both
    adore—
Tell this soul with sorrow laden if, within the distant Aidenn,[18]
It shall clasp a sainted maiden whom the angels name Lenore—
95 Clasp a rare and radiant maiden whom the angels name
    Lenore."
          Quoth the Raven "Nevermore."

---

13. **seraphim** *n. pl.:* highest of the nine ranks of angels.
14. **nepenthe** (nē·pen′thē) *n.:* sleeping potion that people once believed would relieve pain and sorrow.
15. **quaff** *v.:* drink heartily.
16. **undaunted** *adj.:* unafraid.
17. **Is . . . Gilead:** literally, "Is there any relief from my sorrow?" Poe paraphrases a line from Jeremiah 8:22: "Is there no balm in Gilead?" Gilead was a region in ancient Palestine known for its healing herbs, such as balm, a healing ointment.
18. **Aidenn:** Arabic for "Eden; Heaven."

CLARIFY

Pause at line 84. Who does the speaker say sent the raven? Why, according to the speaker, was he sent?

_____

_____

_____

_____

FLUENCY

Read the boxed passage aloud twice, taking careful note of how it is punctuated and what sounds are repeated. How would you describe the speaker's state of mind here?

_____

_____

INTERPRET

Re-read lines 91–96. Circle the question that the narrator asks the raven in this stanza. Then, underline the raven's answer. In your own words, restate the question and answer.

_____

_____

_____

_____

_____

_____

_____

_____

Re-read lines 103–108. Underline the words that describe the raven. What do you think the bird **symbolizes**? *(Grade 9–10 Review)*

"Be that word our sign of parting, bird or fiend!" I shrieked, upstarting—

"Get thee back into the tempest and the Night's Plutonian shore!

Leave no black plume as a token of that lie thy soul hath spoken!

100   Leave my loneliness unbroken!—quit the bust above my door!

Take thy beak from out my heart, and take thy form from off my door!"

           Quoth the Raven "Nevermore."

And the Raven, never flitting, still is sitting, *still* is sitting

On the pallid[19] bust of Pallas just above my chamber door;

105   And his eyes have all the seeming of a demon's that is dreaming,

And the lamplight o'er him streaming throws his shadow on the floor;

And my soul from out that shadow that lies floating on the floor

           Shall be lifted—nevermore!

---

19. pallid *adj.*: pale.

The Raven

Literary Focus: Sound Effects   Look back over the sound effects you marked up in the poem. Find an example of each of the following types of sound effects, and enter it in the chart below.

Sound Effect	Example from "The Raven"
Repetition	
Rhyme (internal or end)	
Alliteration	
Onomatopoeia	

Evaluate   Review the details you recorded in the chart above. What do the sound effects contribute to the poem?

_____

_____

_____

_____

_____

 Check your Standards Mastery at the back of this book.

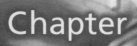

American Masters: Whitman and Dickinson

American Masters:
Whitman and Dickinson

Reading Standard 3.5a–c
Analyze recognized works of American literature representing a variety of genres and traditions.

John Malcolm Brinnin

The following essay provides highlights of the contributions made by Whitman and Dickinson to American poetry. For a more detailed version of this essay, see *Holt Literature and Language Arts,* pages 302–305.

The two greatest American poets of the nineteenth century were so different from each other, both as artists and as personalities, that only a nation as varied in character as the United States could contain them.

Walt Whitman (1819–1892) worked with bold strokes on a broad canvas; Emily Dickinson (1830–1886) worked with the delicacy of a miniaturist. Whitman was sociable and loved company, a traveler; Dickinson was private and shy, content to remain in one secluded spot throughout her lifetime.

10 While both poets were close observers of people and of life's daily activities, the emphasis they gave to what impressed them was so distinct as to make them opposites. Whitman was the public spokesman of the masses and the prophet of progress: "I hear America singing," he said, and he joined his voice to that chorus. Dickinson was the homebody, peering through the curtains of her house in a country town, who found in nature metaphors for the spirit and recorded them with no hope of an audience. Whitman expected that his celebration of universal brotherhood and the bright destiny of democracy

20 would be carried like a message into the future. Dickinson expected nothing but a box in a dusty attic for the poetry that was her "letter to the World."

WORD STUDY

The word *miniaturist* in line 7 refers to a person who paints small, delicate portraits. What kind of poet might be called a miniaturist?

_____

_____

_____

_____

_____

_____

_____

_____

COMPARE & CONTRAST

Re-read lines 12–24. How do Whitman's and Dickinson's expectations about their audiences differ? Underline the answers.

Two Seams in the Fabric

Whitman's career might be regarded as another American success story—the story of a pleasant young man who drifted into
his thirties, working at one job after another, never finding himself until, at his own expense, he boldly published *Leaves of Grass*
30   in 1855. The book made him famous around the world.
Dickinson's career as a poet began after her death. It is one of
those ironies of history in which a writer dies unknown, only to
have fame thrust upon her by later generations of readers.

    Whitman and Dickinson represent two distinct seams in
the fabric of American poetry, one slightly uneven and the other
carefully measured and stitched tight. Whitman was as extrava-
gant with words as he was careless with repetition and self-
contradiction. He filled his pages with long lists and strained to
catalog everything in sight. His technique is based on **cadence**—
40   the long, easy sweep of sound that echoes the Bible and the
speeches of orators and preachers. This cadence is the basis for
his **free verse**—poetry without rhyme or meter.

IDENTIFY

Pause at line 33. What is the
title of Whitman's famous
book of poetry? Underline
the answer.

IDENTIFY

Re-read lines 34–38.
Underline the metaphor that
states the difference
between Whitman and
Dickinson. According to the
text, which poet's use of
words is "slightly uneven"?

_____

_____

IDENTIFY

What is *cadence*? What is
free verse? Underline the
definitions.

_____

_____

_____

_____

_____

_____

_____

_____

_____

_____

_____

_____

_____

Dickinson, on the other hand, wrote with the precision of a diamond cutter. She was always searching for the one right phrase that would fix a thought in the mind. Her technique is economical, and her neat stanzas are controlled by the demands of rhyme and by the meters she found in her hymn book.

Models for Future Poets

As the history of our poetry shows, both Whitman's and
50   Dickinson's styles have continued to be used by American writers. Both poets have served as models for modern poets who have been drawn to the visions Dickinson and Whitman fulfilled and the techniques they mastered. Poetry as public speech written in the cadences of free verse remains a part of our literature; poetry as private observation, carefully crafted in rhyme and meter, still attracts young writers who tend to regard poems as experiences rather than statements.

Whitman and Dickinson together mark a turning point in American poetry.

IDENTIFY

Re-read lines 43–47. What influenced Emily Dickinson's use of meter? Underline the answer.

CONNECT

Why are Whitman and Dickinson such important poets?

I Hear America Singing by Walt Whitman

LITERARY FOCUS: CATALOG

A **catalog** is a list of things, people, or events that are related in some way. Whitman frequently used catalogs in his poetry, extolling and celebrating various people and aspects of American life.

Create Your Own Catalog   Walt Whitman celebrates the qualities that make America unique or special. Imagine that you are developing an ad campaign to encourage people to visit the place you live in. Make a catalog of the things that make *your* town or city unique.

My town or city is unique because . . .
1.
2.
3.
4.
5.

READING SKILLS: IDENTIFYING PARALLEL STRUCTURE

Parallel structure refers to the repetition of words, phrases, and sentences that have the same grammatical structures. When a writer uses parallel structure, he or she might use a series of adjectives, prepositional phrases, verb phrases, or sentence patterns. If you write "I sang, cooked, and washed up," you are using parallel structure: You have used a series of three verbs in the past tense. If you say "I sang a song, I cooked a dinner, and I raked the yard," you are also using parallel structure. You are repeating three sentence patterns that use subject-verb-object.

Whitman uses parallel structures as he catalogs the songs he hears America singing.

Use the Skill   As you read the poem, mark up the parallel sentence patterns that are repeated over and over again. Be sure to read the poem aloud to feel the rhythmic effects of all this repetition.

I Hear America Singing

Walt Whitman

I hear America singing, the varied carols I hear,

Those of mechanics, each one singing his as it should be blithe
and strong,

The carpenter singing his as he measures his plank or beam,

The mason singing his as he makes ready for work, or leaves off
work,

The boatman singing what belongs to him in his boat, the

5   deckhand singing on the steamboat deck,

The shoemaker singing as he sits on his bench, the hatter singing
as he stands,

The wood-cutter's song, the plowboy's on his way in the morning, or at noon intermission or at sundown,

The delicious singing of the mother, or of the young wife at
work, or of the girl sewing or washing,

Each singing what belongs to him or her and to none else,

10   The day what belongs to the day—at night the party of young
fellows, robust, friendly,

Singing with open mouths their strong melodious songs.

I Hear America Singing

Reading Skills: Identifying Parallel Structure   "I Hear America Singing" is full of parallel structures. In the chart below, list examples of parallel words, phrases, and sentence structures in the spaces provided.

Parallel Structure	Examples from the Poem
Repetition of words	
Repetition of phrases	
Repetition of sentence patterns	

 Check your Standards Mastery at the back of this book.

from Song of Myself, Number 33 by Walt Whitman

LITERARY FOCUS: FREE VERSE

Free verse is poetry that does not follow a regular meter (a pattern of stressed and unstressed syllables) or rhyme scheme. Instead of having a set number of syllables, for example, a line in a free verse poem can be of any length. Although free verse abandons some elements of traditional poetry, it uses many others. As you read the excerpt from "Song of Myself, Number 33," which is written in free verse, notice how the following devices add to the power and the message of the poem

alliteration	The repetition of consonant sounds: "I understand the large **h**earts of **h**eroes,"
assonance	The repetition of vowel sounds: "How the silent old-faced **i**nfants and the l**i**fted sick,"
onomatopoeia	The use of words whose sounds echo their meanings: "Hell and despair are upon me, **crack** and again **crack** the marksmen,"
parallel structure	The repetition of phrases, clauses, or sentences that have the same grammatical structure: "**Again the** long roll of the drummers, **Again the** attacking cannon, mortars,"

READING SKILLS: PARAPHRASING

When you **paraphrase**, you restate a writer's ideas in your own words. A paraphrase should include all the details of the original. It is unlike a **summary,** which includes only the most important details. Paraphrasing is a useful skill for explaining difficult terms or ideas. It can also help you check your comprehension of what you've read. Here is an example:

Original Line: "I understand the large hearts of heroes, / The courage of present times and all times, . . . "

Sample Paraphrase: "I know that heroes have enormous compassion. Their courage is everlasting."

Use the Skill   As you read this excerpt from the poem, paraphrase passages you have trouble understanding.

REVIEW SKILLS

Look for examples of **figurative language** as you read the following poem.

FIGURATIVE LANGUAGE
Words or phrases that describe one thing in terms of another, very different thing, and are not meant to be taken literally. Figures of speech include similes, metaphors, and personification.

Reading Standard 3.3
Analyze the ways in which the author's style and the "sound" of language achieve specific rhetorical or aesthetic purposes.

Reading Standard 3.4
Analyze ways in which poets use imagery, personification, figures of speech, and sounds to evoke readers' emotions.

Reading Standard 3.7 (Grade 9–10 Review):
Recognize and understand the significance of figurative language and imagery.

from Song of Myself

Walt Whitman

PARAPHRASE

Locate and circle the example of **personification** in line 3. Then, paraphrase the line. *(Grade 9–10 Review)*

_____

_____

_____

_____

_____

_____

_____

_____

_____

_____

_____

IDENTIFY

Imagery is the use of language that appeals to the senses. Circle the imagery Whitman uses to describe the people who were rescued (lines 8–9). To what sense do these images mostly appeal?

_____

_____

_____

_____

_____

from 33

I understand the large hearts of heroes,

The courage of present times and all times,

How the skipper saw the crowded and rudderless wreck of the
    steam-ship, and Death chasing it up and down the storm,

How he knuckled tight and gave not back an inch, and was
    faithful of days and faithful of nights,

And chalk'd in large letters on a board, *Be of good cheer, we will*
5   *not desert you;*

How he follow'd with them and tack'd with them three days and
    would not give it up,

How he saved the drifting company at last,

How the lank loose-gown'd women look'd when boated from
    the side of their prepared graves,

How the silent old-faced infants and the lifted sick, and the
    sharp-lipp'd unshaved men;

10 All this I swallow, it tastes good, I like it well, it becomes mine,

I am the man, I suffer'd, I was there.[1]

---

1. **I understand . . . I was there:** This stanza was inspired by an incident that occurred in 1853. According to reports in the New York *Weekly Tribune* of January 21, 1854, the ship *San Francisco* sailed from New York City on December 22, 1853, destined for South America. A violent storm hit the ship several hundred miles out of port, washing many passengers overboard. The captain of another ship helped rescue the survivors. A copy of the newspaper story was found among Whitman's papers after his death.

The disdain and calmness of martyrs,

The mother of old, condemn'd for a witch, burnt with dry
wood, her children gazing on,

The hounded slave that flags in the race, leans by the fence,
blowing, cover'd with sweat,

The twinges that sting like needles his legs and neck, the
15   murderous buckshot and the bullets,

All these I feel or am.

I am the hounded slave, I wince at the bite of the dogs,

Hell and despair are upon me, crack and again crack the
marksmen,

I clutch the rails of the fence, my gore dribs,² thinn'd with the
ooze of my skin,

20   I fall on the weeds and stones,

The riders spur their unwilling horses, haul close,

Taunt my dizzy ears and beat me violently over the head with
whip-stocks.

Agonies are one of my changes of garments,

I do not ask the wounded person how he feels, I myself become
the wounded person,

25   My hurts turn livid upon me as I lean on a cane and observe.

I am the mash'd fireman with breast-bone broken,

Tumbling walls buried me in their debris,

Heat and smoke I inspired,³ I heard the yelling shouts of my
comrades,

I heard the distant click of their picks and shovels,

30   They have clear'd the beams away, they tenderly lift me forth.

---

2. **dribs** *n. pl.:* dribbles.
3. **inspired** *v.:* breathed in.

IDENTIFY

Underline the two martyrs the speaker mentions in lines 12–16.

INTERPRET

A **metaphor** is a comparison of unlike things that does not include connecting words such as *like* or *as.* Circle the metaphor in line 23, and explain its meaning. *(Grade 9–10 Review)*

_____

_____

_____

_____

_____

_____

_____

_____

_____

_____

_____

IDENTIFY

Re-read lines 26–30, and find examples of sound devices. Circle examples of **alliteration.** Underline examples of **assonance.** Put a box around repeated words.

_____

_____

_____

_____

_____

_____

_____

_____

_____

_____

FLUENCY

Read aloud the boxed passage that tells about the gruesome experiences of an artillery soldier. Note that *plaudits* means "applause," *rent* means "torn," and *entrenchments* means "a fortification of trenches." Look up in a dictionary any other words you don't know. Mark up examples of parallel structures. Then, see how smoothly and dramatically you can read these stanzas, being careful to let the parallel structures create a rhythm.

I lie in the night air in my red shirt, the pervading hush is for
    my sake,

Painless after all I lie exhausted but not so unhappy,

White and beautiful are the faces around me, the heads are
    bared of their fire-caps,

The kneeling crowd fades with the light of the torches.

35   Distant and dead resuscitate,

They show as the dial or move as the hands of me, I am the
    clock myself.

I am an old artillerist, I tell of my fort's bombardment,

I am there again.

Again the long roll of the drummers,

40   Again the attacking cannon, mortars,

Again to my listening ears the cannon responsive.

I take part, I see and hear the whole,

The cries, curses, roar, the plaudits for well-aim'd shots,

The ambulanza[4] slowly passing trailing its red drip,

45   Workmen searching after damages, making indispensable
    repairs,

The fall of grenades through the rent roof, the fan-shaped
    explosion,

The whizz of limbs, heads, stone, wood, iron, high in the air.

Again gurgles the mouth of my dying general, he furiously
    waves with his hand,

He gasps through the clot *Mind not me—mind—the
    entrenchments.*

---

4. **ambulanza** (ăm·bōō·länt′sə): Italian for "ambulance."

from Song of Myself, Number 33

Reading Skills: Paraphrasing   In the left-hand column of the chart below are passages from "Song of Myself, Number 33." Paraphrase each in the space at the right. Remember to include all details of the original; paraphrases are not summaries. Once you've finished paraphrasing, answer the final question that appears below the chart.

Passage from Poem	Paraphrase
I am the hounded slave, I wince at the bite of the dogs, Hell and despair are upon me, crack and again crack the marksmen, I clutch the rails of the fence, my gore dribs, thinn'd with the ooze of my skin, I fall on the weeds and stones, The riders spur their unwilling horses, haul close, Taunt my dizzy ears and beat me violently over the head with whip-stocks. (lines 17–22)	
I lie in the night air in my red shirt, the pervading hush is for my sake, Painless after all I lie exhausted but not so unhappy, White and beautiful are the faces around me, the heads are bared of their fire-caps, The kneeling crowd fades with the light of the torches. (lines 31–34)	

Evaluate   Compare your paraphrases with the original verses from the poem. What is "lost" in translation?

_____

_____

Check your Standards Mastery at the back of this book.

from Song of Myself, Number 52 by Walt Whitman

LITERARY FOCUS: THEME

Walt Whitman's revelations about human experience are his **themes.** Whitman, like most good writers, never states his themes directly. To discover the theme in one of Whitman's poems, follow these steps:

- Read the poem carefully. Be sure you understand all its figures of speech.

- Identify the subject of the poem—what is it "about"?

- Think about the language in the poem: Is there a particular line that seems very important, or a word that seems key to the poem?

- Think about the title of the poem. Is it significant?

- Ask yourself: "What does this poem say to me about our human experience?"

- Try out several statements of theme. There is no one correct way to express a theme. In fact, different readers will almost always come up with different statements of theme.

Keep in mind that a theme is different from a work's subject, or topic. A theme comments on the topic in some way. See below:

Sample Topics	Sample Themes
baseball	The game of baseball is like the game of life.
mountain climbing	We find what we are capable of when faced with deadly obstacles.
art	Imagination is the quality that makes us human.

READING SKILLS: COMPARING THEMES ACROSS TEXTS

"Song of Myself, Number 52" is the final section of Walt Whitman's long poem. This conclusion is a **coda,** a summing up and restatement of the different themes running throughout the poem. Once you've read this selection, think about Whitman's "Song of Myself, Number 33." Find passages of "Song of Myself, Number 52" that echo ideas you read about in "Song of Myself, Number 33." Then compare the themes of the two poems.

from Song of Myself

Walt Whitman

52

The spotted hawk swoops by and accuses me, he complains of
    my gab and my loitering.

I too am not a bit tamed, I too am untranslatable,
I sound my barbaric yawp over the roofs of the world.

The last scud[1] of day holds back for me,
5 It flings my likeness after the rest and true as any on the
    shadow'd wilds,
It coaxes me to the vapor and the dusk.

I depart as air, I shake my white locks at the runaway sun,
I effuse[2] my flesh in eddies, and drift it in lacy jags.

I bequeath myself to the dirt to grow from the grass I love,
10 If you want me again look for me under your boot-soles.

You will hardly know who I am or what I mean,
But I shall be good health to you nevertheless,
And filter and fiber your blood.

Failing to fetch me at first keep encouraged,
15 Missing me one place search another,
I stop somewhere waiting for you.

---

1. **scud** *n.:* windblown mist and
   low clouds.
2. **effuse** *v.:* spread out.

CLARIFY

Re-read lines 1–3. What is the speaker comparing him-self to? Underline the words in line 2 that alert you to the comparison.

_____

_____

INTERPRET

Where does the speaker tell us to look for him (lines 9–10)? Why is that? What larger meaning might the **images** in this line have?

_____

_____

_____

_____

_____

_____

INTERPRET

In what way can Whitman be "good health" to the reader (line 12)?

_____

_____

_____

_____

_____

Song of Myself, Number 52

Reading Skills: Comparing Themes Across Texts The chart below lists some details from "Song of Myself, Number 33" and "Song of Myself, Number 52." For each selection, fill in a **theme** the details suggest to you. When you finish, think about the themes you have listed. Are they the same or similar? Write your response on the lines below the chart.

Details from "Song of Myself, Number 33"	Possible Theme
"All this I swallow, it tastes good, I like it well, it becomes mine," (line 10)	
"All these I feel or am." (line 16)	
"I take part, I see and hear the whole," (line 42)	
Details from "Song of Myself, Number 52"	**Possible Theme**
"I sound my barbaric yawp over the roofs of the world." (line 3)	
"I bequeath myself to the dirt to grow from the grass I love," (line 9)	
"I stop somewhere waiting for you." (line 16)	

Comparing Themes: In what way are the themes in the two poems similar or the same?

_____

_____

_____

✓ Check your Standards Mastery at the back of this book.

Full Powers by Pablo Neruda

BEFORE YOU READ

LITERARY FOCUS: METAPHOR

Which description is more exciting to read: *Many ants ate the picnic food* or *An army of ants attacked the picnic basket?* You probably preferred the second sentence, in which ants are compared to an attacking army. This comparison is an example of a metaphor. A **metaphor** is a figure of speech that makes a comparison between two unlike things without using a word such as *like, than, as,* or *resembles.*

As you read Pablo Neruda's "Full Powers," think about the metaphors he creates. Then, think about why he chose to make those comparisons and how they add meaning to the poem.

READING SKILLS: COMPARING AND CONTRASTING POEMS

Walt Whitman, an American, and Pablo Neruda, a Chilean, came from different parts of the world and lived in different centuries, yet their writing shares certain similarities in style and theme. In fact, Neruda has said he was inspired by Whitman and owed him "this marvelous debt that has helped me to live."

When you compare and contrast poems, you look for ways in which they are similar and ways in which they differ. As you compare and contrast poems, think about the elements of poetry and how the poems you are working on make use of those elements. Some of the elements of poetry you should consider in making comparisons and contrasts are these:

Subject:	What is each poem about?
Sounds:	What sound devices does each poet use? Are the poems written with strict regard for meter and rhyme, or are they written in free verse?
Imagery:	What pictures does each poem create?
Figures of speech:	What metaphors and similes are found in each poem?
Tone:	What is the tone of each poem, or its attitude toward life or toward its subject?
Theme:	What does the poem reveal about human life or human experience?

Reading Standard 3.4 Analyze ways in which poets use imagery to evoke readers' emotions.

Reading Standard 3.7 Analyze recognized works of world literature.

Reading Standard 3.7 (Grade 9–10 Review) Recognize and understand the significance of various literary devices, including figurative language, imagery, allegory, and symbolism, and explain their appeal.

Full Powers

Pablo Neruda
translated by Ben Belitt *and* Alastair Reid

CLARIFY

Re-read lines 1–5. What might the speaker mean when he says he uses the night's interruption to "recover space" and "gather shadows"?

_____

_____

_____

_____

INTERPRET

What does the speaker mean by the **metaphors** "keys" and "locks" in lines 6–11?

_____

_____

_____

_____

_____

_____

INTERPRET

What does the speaker mean by his comment in line 14?

_____

_____

_____

I write in the clear sun, in the teeming street,
at full sea-tide, in a place where I can sing;
only the wayward night inhibits me,
but, interrupted by it, I recover space,
5   I gather shadows to last me a long time.

The black crop of the night is growing
while my eyes meanwhile take measure of the meadows.
So, from one sun to the next, I forge the keys.
In the darkness, I look for the locks
10 and keep on opening broken doors to the sea,
for it to fill the wardrobes with its foam.

And I do not weary of going and returning.
Death, in its stone aspect, does not halt me.
I am weary neither of being nor of non-being.

15 Sometimes I puzzle over origins—
was it from my father, my mother, or the mountains
that I inherited debts to minerality,

the fine threads spreading from a sea on fire?
And I know that I keep on going for the going's sake,
20 and I sing because I sing and because I sing.

There is no way of explaining what does happen
when I close my eyes and waver
as between two lost channels under water.
One lifts me in its branches toward my dying,
25 and the other sings in order that I may sing.

And so I am made up of a non-being,
and, as the sea goes battering at a reef
in wave on wave of salty white-tops
and drags back stones in its retreating wash,
30   so what there is in death surrounding me
opens in me a window out to living,
and, in the spasm of being, I go on sleeping.
In the full light of day, I walk in the shade.

IDENTIFY

According to the speaker, what makes him "keep on going" (line 19)? Why does he "sing" (line 20)? Underline the answers he gives.

INTERPRET

Re-read lines 26–33. What does the speaker mean when he says that death "opens in me a window out to living"? (line 31)

_____

_____

_____

_____

_____

_____

_____

_____

_____

_____

FLUENCY

Read aloud the boxed passage twice. Remember, in reading most poems you must not stop at the ends of lines unless a punctuation mark indicates that you should pause (comma or dash) or make a full stop because it is the end of a sentence (period). In your second reading, try to use your voice to express the tone of these lines.

Full Powers

Reading Skills: Comparing and Contrasting Poems   Pablo Neruda acknowledged his debt to Whitman for his poetic inspiration. Compare "Full Powers" to the three Whitman poems you have just read. Fill out the chart below with details you find in the poems.

Elements of Poetry	Whitman's poems	Neruda's poem
Subject		
Sounds		
Imagery		
Figures of speech		
Theme		

 Check your Standards Mastery at the back of this book.

The Soul selects her own Society;
If you were coming in the Fall by Emily Dickinson

BEFORE YOU READ

LITERARY FOCUS: SLANT RHYME

Not that long ago exact rhyme was part of every poet's craft. An **exact rhyme** occurs when the accented syllables and all following syllables of two or more words share the same sound, such as *love* and *dove* or *number* and *slumber.* Many poets in more recent times, however, have chosen not to use rhyme at all. Some do not like the constraint of a rhyme scheme, and some feel that all the good rhymes have been used already.

Other poets choose to use slant rhyme, also called approximate rhyme. **Slant rhyme** is a close, but not exact, rhyming sound. Examples of slant rhyme are *follow* and *fellow,* and *mystery* and *mastery.* Look for exact rhymes and slant rhymes in the following two poems by Emily Dickinson.

Finding Slant Rhymes   Some poets like to have a list of rhymes on hand when they sit down to write a poem. Use the chart below to start your own list. The first row has been done to get you started.

Word	Exact Rhyme	Slant Rhyme
love	dove, glove, above	leave, live, loaf, grove
moon		
fight		
shimmer		

READING SKILLS: ANALYZING FIGURATIVE LANGUAGE

A major element of Emily Dickinson's poetry is her use of **figures of speech.** In her poems, you'll find **similes,** comparisons of two unlike things using words such as *like, as, than,* and *resembles;* **metaphors,** comparisons that do not use direct words of comparison; and **personification,** a type of metaphor that gives inanimate things human characteristics. You'll also find **extended metaphors,** metaphors developed over several lines or even over the whole poem. As you read Dickinson's poems, think about what the figures of speech mean and what they help you visualize.

REVIEW SKILLS

As you read "The Soul selects her own Society" and "If you were coming in the Fall," look for the following literary device.

FIGURATIVE LANGUAGE
Words or phrases that describe one thing in terms of another, very different thing. Figurative language is not meant to be understood on a literal level.

Reading Standard 3.4
Analyze the ways in which poets use imagery, personification, figures of speech, and sounds to evoke readers' emotions.

Reading Standard 3.7 (Grade 9–10 Review):
Recognize and understand the significance of various literary devices, including figurative language, imagery, allegory, and symbolism, and explain their appeal.

The Soul selects her own Society

Emily Dickinson

IDENTIFY

What does Dickinson **personify** in lines 1–4? Draw a box around the example you find.

ANALYZE

In this poem, Dickinson uses an **extended metaphor,** in which she compares the soul to a queen. How would you explain the chariots at the gate and the kneeling emperor in lines 5–8? *(Grade 9–10 Review)*

_____

_____

_____

_____

_____

IDENTIFY

Every other line in this poem rhymes. Underline the **slant rhymes,** and circle the **exact rhyme.**

FLUENCY

Read the poem aloud until you can read it smoothly. The dashes are an indication to pause, but don't pause too long. Be sure *not* to pause at the end of the only line without a dash at the end.

The Soul selects her own Society—
Then—shuts the Door—
To her divine Majority—
Present no more—

5　Unmoved—she notes the Chariots—pausing—
At her low Gate—
Unmoved—an Emperor be kneeling
Upon her Mat—

I've known her—from an ample nation—
10　Choose One—
Then—close the Valves of her attention—
Like Stone—

Emily Dickinson's bedroom window.

If you were coming in the Fall

Emily Dickinson

If you were coming in the Fall,
I'd brush the Summer by
With half a smile, and half a spurn,
As Housewives do, a Fly.

5   If I could see you in a year,
I'd wind the months in balls—
And put them each in separate Drawers,
For fear the numbers fuse—

If only Centuries, delayed,
10   I'd count them on my Hand,
Subtracting, till my fingers dropped
Into Van Dieman's Land.°

If certain, when this life was out—
That your's and mine, should be
15   I'd toss it yonder, like a Rind,
And take Eternity—

But, now, uncertain of the length
Of this, that is between,
It goads me, like the Goblin Bee—
20   That will not state—it's sting.

°**Van Dieman's** (dē′mənz) **Land:** former name
of Tasmania, an island that is a state of
Australia.

INTERPRET

What does the speaker say she'll do with the months (lines 5–8)? Why would she do that? (*Grade 9–10 Review*)

_____

_____

_____

IDENTIFY

In this poem, the second and fourth lines of each stanza rhyme. Circle **exact rhymes,** and underline **slant rhymes.**

INTERPRET

In folklore, a goblin is a tormenting creature. What point is the speaker making by comparing waiting for a bee sting with waiting for her love (lines 17–20)?

_____

_____

_____

_____

EVALUATE

What corrections to lines 14 and 20 would you make if you were editing this poem?

_____

_____

_____

The Soul selects her own Society; If you were coming in the Fall

Reading Skills: Analyzing Figurative Language Sometimes the meaning of figurative language is very clear. When something *stings like a bee,* you know that it hurts. But when it *goads like a Goblin Bee,* you have to infer or interpret the meaning based on the surrounding text and your own prior knowledge.

The chart below lists some figures of speech from Emily Dickinson's poems. In the other columns, identify the two things being compared, and then write what you think each figure of speech means.

Figures of Speech from "The Soul . . ."	Comparison	Meaning
1. "The Soul selects her own Society—" (line 1)		
2. "I've known her—from an ample nation— / Choose One—" (lines 9–10)		
Figures of Speech from "If you were . . ."		
3. "I'd brush the Summer by / . . . / As Housewives do, a Fly." (lines 2 and 4)		
4. "I'd toss [this life] yonder, like a Rind, / And take Eternity—" (lines 15–16)		

Check your Standards Mastery at the back of this book.

Because I could not stop for Death;
I heard a Fly buzz—when I died by Emily Dickinson

LITERARY FOCUS: IRONY

Stories or poems can surprise you. You may expect something to happen based on what you have read so far, and instead the opposite happens. This literary "surprise" is an example of irony. **Irony** is a contrast between expectations and reality. There are three main kinds of irony:

- **Situational irony** is the kind described above—a contrast between what happens and what we expect to happen.

- **Verbal irony** is a contrast between what is said and what is meant.

- **Dramatic irony** occurs when the reader knows something a character does not know.

The following poems by Emily Dickinson rely on situational and verbal irony.

READING SKILLS: SUMMARIZING A TEXT

Have you ever read the capsule reviews of movies in the TV listings? They usually summarize a movie's plot in just a few sentences. A **summary** of a text is a brief retelling of its main events and most important ideas. The best summaries are complete but short. They include important information only. Summarizing a text is a useful reading skill because it can help you gain a better understanding of what you read.

Use the Skill   Both of these poems by Emily Dickinson tell a very brief story. To follow the events, stop at the end of each stanza and summarize what just happened.

REVIEW SKILLS

As you read "Because I could not stop for Death" and "I heard a Fly buzz—when I died," look for the use of **symbols**.

SYMBOL
A person, place, thing, or event that has meaning in itself and stands for something beyond itself as well. The dove, for example, is a symbol of peace.

Reading Standard 3.3
Analyze the ways in which irony, tone, mood, the author's style, and the "sound" of language achieves specific rhetorical or aesthetic purposes.

Reading Standard 3.7 **(Grade 9–10 Review)**
Recognize and understand the significance of various literary devices, including figurative language, imagery, allegory, and symbolism, and explain their appeal.

Because I could not stop for Death

Emily Dickinson

Because I could not stop for Death—
He kindly stopped for me—
The Carriage held but just Ourselves—
And Immortality.

5 We slowly drove—He knew no haste
And I had put away
My labor and my leisure too,
For His Civility—

We passed the School, where Children strove
10 At Recess—in the Ring—
We passed the Fields of Gazing Grain—
We passed the Setting Sun—

Or rather—He passed Us—
The Dews drew quivering and chill—
15 For only Gossamer,[1] my Gown—
My Tippet—only Tulle[2]—

---

1. **gossamer** *n.:* thin, soft material.
2. **tippet . . . tulle:** shawl made of fine netting.

IDENTIFY

Underline the word in line 2 that describes death in an **ironic** way.

INTERPRET

What is happening in lines 5–8?

_____

_____

_____

_____

_____

_____

INTERPRET

In lines 9–12, what do the playing children, the fields of grain, and the sunset **symbolize,** or stand for, other than themselves? *(Grade 9–10 Review)*

_____

_____

_____

_____

_____

We paused before a House that seemed

A Swelling of the Ground—

The Roof was scarcely visible—

20   The Cornice[3]—in the Ground—

Since then—'tis Centuries—and yet

Feels shorter than the Day

I first surmised the Horses' Heads

Were toward Eternity—

---

3.   **cornice** *n.:* molding at the top of a building.

INTERPRET

What do you think the "House" is in line 17?

_____

_____

_____

_____

_____

_____

New England Cemetery—Augusta, Maine (1997) by Fred Danziger (20" × 23").
Collection of the artist.

SUMMARIZE

When does this poem end? Where is the speaker now?

_____

_____

_____

_____

_____

_____

_____

_____

_____

_____

_____

_____

_____

I heard a Fly buzz— when I died

Emily Dickinson

CLARIFY

What happens as the speaker dies (lines 1–4)?

_____

_____

ANALYZE

Whom do the speaker and the others in the room expect to see (lines 5–12)? Whom or what do they see instead? In what way is the situation **ironic**?

_____

_____

_____

_____

_____

INTERPRET

What does the speaker mean when she says the "Windows failed" in line 15?

_____

_____

_____

FLUENCY

Read the poem aloud twice. On your second reading, decide how you will treat the dashes.

I heard a Fly buzz—when I died—
The Stillness in the Room
Was like the Stillness in the Air—
Between the Heaves of Storm—

5   The Eyes around—had wrung them dry—
And Breaths were gathering firm
For that last Onset—when the King
Be witnessed—in the Room—

I willed my Keepsakes—Signed away
10   What portion of me be
Assignable—and then it was
There interposed a Fly—

With Blue—uncertain stumbling Buzz—
Between the light—and me—
15   And then the Windows failed—and then
I could not see to see—

"465: I heard a Fly buzz—when I died" from *The Poems of Emily Dickinson,* edited by Thomas H. Johnson. Copyright © 1951, 1955, 1979, 1983 by the President and Fellows of Harvard College. Published by The Belknap Press of Harvard University Press, Cambridge, Mass. Reprinted by permission of **Harvard University Press and the Trustees of Amherst College.**

Because I could not stop for Death; I heard a Fly buzz—when I died

Reading Skills: Summarizing a Text In the chart below, write brief **summaries** of the two poems. Include only the important events or ideas. Summarize stanza by stanza.

Summary of "Because I could not stop for Death":

Summary of "I heard a Fly buzz—when I died":

Check your Standards Mastery at the back of this book.

The Rise of Realism
The Civil War to 1914

Home, Sweet Home (detail) (1863) by Winslow Homer (1836–1910).
Oil on canvas ($21\frac{1}{2}'' \times 16\frac{1}{2}''$).

The Rise of Realism
The Civil War to 1914
Gary Q. Arpin

Reading Standard 3.5a–c
Analyze recognized works of American literature representing a variety of genres and traditions.

The following essay provides highlights of the historical period. For a more detailed version of this essay, see *Holt Literature and Language Arts,* pages 382–395.

On the evening of April 12, 1861, Walt Whitman attended the opera at the Academy of Music in Manhattan. After the opera he was walking down Broadway toward Brooklyn when, as he later wrote, "I heard in the distance the loud cries of the newsboys, who came presently tearing and yelling up the street, rushing from side to side even more furiously than usual. I bought an extra and crossed to the Metropolitan Hotel . . . and, with a crowd of others, who gathered impromptu, read the news, which was evidently authentic."

10　　The news that Whitman and the others read was of the Confederate attack on Fort Sumter, the opening shots of the Civil War. Thus began one of the greatest cataclysms in U.S. history.

Slavery Divides the Country

What had brought the country to the point of the Civil War? It had but a "single cause," asserted the historian James Ford Rhodes in 1913, and that cause was slavery. Today historians acknowledge additional causes of the war, but slavery lay at the heart of this conflict.

　　From the personal accounts of people held in slavery—
20　such as Frederick Douglass and Harriet A. Jacobs—we learn firsthand about the horrors and injustices of slavery. Increasing numbers of Northerners viewed slaveholding as a monstrous violation of the basic American principle of equality, but Southerners wanted to preserve the institution of slavery. The conflict reached a fever pitch and erupted at Fort Sumter.

WORD STUDY

The word *extra* (line 7), in this context, means "a special edition of a newspaper." Extras used to be put out between regular newspaper editions in order to cover important breaking news.

WORD STUDY

Cataclysms (kat'ə·kliz'əmz), in line 12, refers to great upheavals, such as earthquakes or war, that result in violent destruction. *Cataclysm* comes from the Greek *kata*–, meaning "down," and *klyzein,* meaning "to wash." As you might infer from its origin, *cataclysm* literally means "flood."

IDENTIFY CAUSE & EFFECT

What was the main cause of the Civil War (lines 14–18)? Circle the answer.

COMPARE & CONTRAST

What opposing views on slavery did Northerners and Southerners hold (lines 19–25)? Underline the details that give you this information.

ANALYZE

Re-read lines 30–38. How did Emerson respond to the war?

_____

_____

_____

_____

_____

_____

_____

_____

_____

_____

_____

_____

_____

_____

_____

_____

_____

_____

_____

A Response to the War: Idealism

In Concord, Massachusetts, army volunteers met in 1861 at the bridge that Ralph Waldo Emerson had immortalized in "Concord Hymn," his famous poem about the beginning of the

30   American Revolution. Emerson had for decades warned that this day would come if slavery were not abolished. Now that the day had arrived, he was filled with patriotic fervor. He had great respect for the Southern will to fight, however, and he suspected that the war would not be over in a few months, as some people had predicted. When the Concord volunteers returned a few months later from the First Battle of Bull Run (July 1861), defeated and disillusioned, Emerson maintained his conviction that the war must be pursued.

A Reality of the War: Appalling Suffering

40   Late in 1862, Walt Whitman traveled to Virginia to find his brother George, who had been wounded in battle. After George was nursed back to health, Whitman served as a hospital volunteer. The condition of the wounded was appalling. Many of the injured had to remain on the battlefield for two or three days until the camp hospitals had room for them. Antiseptics were primitive, as were operating-room techniques. A major wound meant

50   amputation or even death.

    Whitman estimated that in three years as a camp hospital volunteer, he visited tens of thousands of wounded men.

Photograph by Mathew Brady.

IDENTIFY

Why was the condition of the wounded soldiers so bad (lines 43–50)? Underline the details that describe their hardships.

Wounded Soldier Being Given a Drink from a Canteen (1864) by Winslow Homer. Charcoal and white chalk on green paper (36.5 cm × 50 cm).

Cooper-Hewitt, National Design Museum, Smithsonian Institution; Gift of Charles Savage Homer, Jr./Courtesy Art Resource, New York.

A Result of the War: Disillusionment

Herman Melville's poems about the war, collected in *Battle-Pieces and Aspects of the War* (1866), were often dark and foreboding. Of the elation following the firing on Fort Sumter, Melville wrote:

60   O, the rising of the People
        Came with the springing of the grass,
They rebounded from dejection
        After Easter came to pass.
And the young were all elation
        Hearing Sumter's cannon roar. . . .
But the elders with foreboding
        Mourned the days forever o'er,
And recalled the forest proverb,
        The Iroquois' old saw:
70 *Grief to every graybeard*
        When young Indians lead the war.

The poems in *Battle-Pieces*, based on newspaper accounts of the battles as well as visits to battlefields, record the heroism and futility of the fighting on both sides and demonstrate respect for Southern soldiers as well as Northern troops.

The War in Literature

Although many works of historical interest—soldiers' letters and diaries, as well as journalistic writings—came out of the war, works of literary significance were rare, prompting the question,

80 Why didn't an event of such magnitude result in more literary output?

One reason is that few major American writers saw the Civil War firsthand. Emerson was in Concord during most of the war, "knitting socks and mittens for soldiers," as he wrote to his son, and "writing patriotic lectures." Thoreau, who had been a fervent abolitionist, died in 1862, and Hawthorne died two years later. Emily Dickinson remained in Amherst, Massachusetts, and the country's grief over the war seems not to have

90 informed her poetry. Perhaps most important, the traditional literary forms of the time were inadequate to express the horrifying details of the Civil War. The literary form most appropriate for handling such strong material—the **realistic novel**—had not yet been fully developed in the United States.

CLARIFY

Why did so few writers respond to the war in their literary works (lines 82–102)? Underline the details that tell you.

Woman freed from slavery, learning to read.
Leib Image Archives, York, Pennsylvania.

100 Thus, the great novel of the war, *The Red Badge of Courage,* had to wait to be written by a man who was not born until six years after the war had ended: Stephen Crane.

The Rise of Realism

After the Civil War a new generation of writers came of age. They were known as **realists.** Their subjects were drawn from the slums of the rapidly growing cities, from the factories that were replacing farmlands, and from the lives of far-from-idealized characters—poor factory workers, corrupt politicians, and even prostitutes.

Realism Takes Root in Europe

110 Realism was well entrenched in Europe by the time it began to flower in the United States. It developed in the work of such writers as Daniel Defoe, George Eliot, Anthony Trollope, Honoré de Balzac, Stendhal, Gustave Flaubert, and Leo Tolstoy. These writers tried to represent faithfully the environment and the manners of everyday life.

Realism sought to explain why ordinary people behave the way they do. Realistic novelists often relied on the emerging sciences of human and animal behavior—biology, psychology, and 120 sociology—as well as on their own insights and observations.

American Regionalism: Brush Strokes of Local Color

In America, realism had its roots in **regionalism,** literature that emphasizes a specific geographic setting and that makes use of the speech and manners of the people who live in that region. While regionalists tried to be realistic in depicting speech patterns and manners, they were often unrealistic in their depiction of character and social environment. Realism went far beyond regionalism in its concern for accuracy in portraying social con130 ditions and human motivations.

IDENTIFY

Re-read lines 104–109. What kinds of people did realists write about?

_____

_____

_____

_____

_____

_____

_____

_____

_____

_____

_____

_____

_____

_____

_____

ANALYZE

Re-read lines 111–120. What are some of the basic characteristics of **realism**? Underline those details.

IDENTIFY

What is **regionalism** (lines 123–130)? Underline the answer.

Mark Twain is the best-known example of a regional writer whose realism far surpassed local bounds. Although he first established his reputation as a regional humorist, Twain evolved into a writer whose comic view of society became increasingly satiric. His most widely read novel, *Adventures of Huckleberry Finn* (1884), describes the moral growth of a comic character in an environment that is at the same time physically beautiful and morally offensive. *Huckleberry Finn* combines a biting picture of some of the injustices of pre-Civil War life with a lyrical portrait

140 of the American landscape.

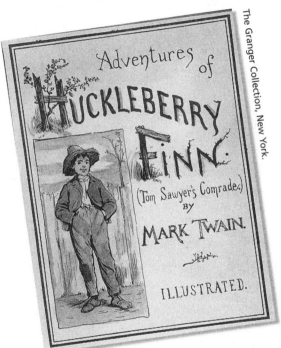

The Granger Collection, New York.

Original edition of Mark Twain's *Adventures of Huckleberry Finn* (1885).

Realism and Naturalism: A Lens on Everyday Life

■ "Smiling Realism"

The most active proponent of realism in American fiction was William Dean Howells, editor of the influential magazine *The Atlantic Monthly*. Howells insisted that realism should deal with

Children in Mullen's Alley, off Cherry Street, New York City (c. 1888). Photograph by Jacob Riis.
The Granger Collection, New York.

DRAW CONCLUSIONS

Re-read lines 144–151. Why do you think Howells's approach to realism was referred to as "smiling realism"?

the lives of ordinary people, be faithful to the development of character even at the expense of action, and discuss social questions perplexing Americans. Howells's "smiling realism" por-
150 trayed an America where people may act foolishly but where their good qualities eventually win out.

Other realistic novelists viewed life as a much rougher clash of contrary forces. The Californian Frank Norris, for example,

IDENTIFY

Pause at line 162. What two notable novels examined social institutions with a view to reforming them? Circle their titles.

IDENTIFY

Re-read lines 164–168. Whom are the **naturalists** compared to?

_____

_____

ANALYZE

Re-read lines 168–174. What did the naturalists believe? Underline the details that support your answer.

_____

_____

_____

_____

_____

_____

_____

_____

_____

_____

_____

_____

_____

found Howells's fiction too straitlaced and narrow. Norris was an earthier writer, interested in the impact of large social forces on individuals. His best-known novel, *The Octopus* (1901), is about the struggles between wheat farmers and the railroad monopoly in California. Norris was not the first to use the novel to examine social institutions with the aim of reforming them:

160 Harriet Beecher Stowe's novel *Uncle Tom's Cabin* (1852) had been published before the Civil War and, according to Lincoln (and many historians), played a part in bringing about the war.

■ Grim Naturalism

Norris is generally considered a **naturalist.** Following the lead of the French novelist Émile Zola, naturalists relied heavily on the emerging scientific disciplines of psychology and sociology. In their fiction, the naturalists attempted to dissect human behavior with as much objectivity as a scientist would use. For naturalists, human behavior was determined by forces beyond the

170 individual's power, especially by biology and environment. The naturalists tended to look at human life as a grim losing battle. In the eyes of some naturalist writers, human beings are totally subject to the natural laws of the universe; like animals, they live crudely, by instinct, unable to control their own destinies.

Psychological Realism: Inside the Human Mind

■ Exploring Motivation

On the other hand, the New York–born Henry James concentrated on fine distinctions in character motivation. James was a

180 realist, but no realist could be further from the blunt, naturalistic view that people were driven by animal-like instincts. In his finely tuned studies of human motivation, James was mainly interested in complex social and psychological situations. Many of his novels, including *Daisy Miller* (1878) and *The Portrait of a Lady* (1881), take place in Europe. James frequently contrasts

innocent, eager Americans with sophisticated, more manipulative Europeans. In a typical James novel a straightforward American confronts the complexities of European society and either defeats or is defeated by them.

190 ■ **Examining Characters in Crisis**

Stephen Crane was as insightful a psychologist as James. Crane's principal interest was the human character at moments of stress. For James the proper setting for an examination of human behavior under pressure was the drawing room; for Crane it was the battlefield, the streets of a slum, or a lifeboat lost at sea. Although Crane is sometimes referred to as a naturalist, he is probably best thought of as an **ironist**. Of all the nineteenth-century realists, only Crane could describe a stabbing death (in his story "The Blue Hotel") in this coolly cynical manner: "[The 200 blade] shot forward, and a human body, this citadel of virtue, wisdom, power, was pierced as easily as if it had been a melon." It would take this sensibility to get the "real war" into the books at last.

Endings and Beginnings

The period from around the turn of the century up to 1914 saw the continuation of many nineteenth-century trends and, at the same time, the early flowerings of modernism. Still, the currents of realism and naturalism evoked by the Civil War continued to dominate American literature.

210 In the period between the end of the Civil War and the outbreak of World War I in 1914, the American nation was transformed from an isolated, rural nation to an industrialized world power. Even these changes would soon be dwarfed, however. World War I would rock the world and shake people's faith in humanity. Idealism would turn to cynicism, and thinkers and writers called modernists would seek new literary forms for exploring the social and spiritual upheavals wrought once again by war.

COMPARE & CONTRAST

Re-read lines 178–189. How did Henry James's literary approach differ from that of the naturalists?

_____

_____

_____

_____

_____

_____

_____

WORD STUDY

An *ironist* (line 197) is someone who uses irony to make a larger comment on life. In general, irony is the difference between what we expect to happen and what actually happens. Underline Crane's ironic description of a stabbing.

IDENTIFY

Pause at line 209. What dominated American literature up to 1914? Circle the details that give you this information.

IDENTIFY

This chapter deals with the Civil War. What war breaks out early in the next century?

_____

_____

from Narrative of the Life of Frederick Douglass by Frederick Douglass

LITERARY FOCUS: METAPHOR

Writers use metaphors to help us see things in new, imaginative ways. A **metaphor** is a figure of speech that makes a comparison between two things that are basically unalike. Metaphors, unlike similes, do not use the words *like, as,* or *resembles.*

A poet, for example, describes the moon by saying, "The moon was a ghostly galleon." This metaphor compares the moon moving across the night sky to a sailing ship. Another writer might express the metaphor differently and say, "The moon sails across the sky."

As you near the end of this selection, look for a powerful metaphor. In it, Douglass compares a personal victory to coming back from the dead: "It was a glorious resurrection, from the tomb of slavery, to the heaven of freedom." By connecting a physical victory with a victory of the soul, this metaphor helps readers understand the depth of Douglass's feelings.

READING SKILLS: ANALYZING A WRITER'S PURPOSE

Frederick Douglass clearly states his purpose in the first paragraph of this excerpt. To make his point clear and dramatic, he uses narration and description. He uses narration to tell us about a series of related events. He uses descriptive language to help us imagine his pain.

Use the Skill   As you read, look for ways in which Douglass uses narration and description to describe the horrors of slavery. You will notice that Douglass also uses some powerful metaphors to describe his experience.

Frederick Douglass.
Chester County Historical Society, West Chester, Pennsylvania.

Reading Standard 2.4
Make warranted and reasonable assertions about the author's arguments by using elements of the text to defend and clarify interpretations.

Reading Standard 3.4
Analyze ways in which poets use figures of speech to evoke readers' emotions.

Reading Standard 3.8
Analyze the clarity and consistency of political assumptions in a selection of literary works or essays on a topic.

from Narrative of the Life of Frederick Douglass

Frederick Douglass

> Frederick Douglass was born into slavery. Soon after his birth, Douglass was separated from his mother. At the age of eight, he was sent to Baltimore to work as a house servant. Later he was sent to the country to work in the fields. This selection describes an event that happened when Douglass was sixteen years old. At that time, Douglass was "owned" by a man named Thomas. Another man, Mr. Covey, had paid Thomas to use Douglass for one year.

The Battle with Mr. Covey

I have already **intimated** that my condition was much worse, during the first six months of my stay at Mr. Covey's, than in the last six. The circumstances leading to the change in Mr. Covey's course toward me form an epoch[1] in my humble history. You have seen how a man was made a slave; you shall see how a slave was made a man. On one of the hottest days of the month of August, 1833, Bill Smith, William Hughes, a slave named Eli, and myself, were engaged in fanning wheat.[2] Hughes was clearing

10 the fanned wheat from before the fan, Eli was turning, Smith was feeding, and I was carrying wheat to the fan. The work was simple, requiring strength rather than intellect; yet, to one entirely unused to such work, it came very hard.

About three o'clock of that day, I broke down; my strength failed me; I was seized with a violent aching of the head, attended with extreme dizziness; I trembled in every limb. Finding what was coming, I nerved myself up, feeling it would never do

---

1. **epoch** (ep'ək) *n.:* noteworthy period of time.
2. **fanning wheat:** separating out usable grain.

From *The Narrative of the Life of Frederick Douglass: An American Slave Written by Himself,* edited by Benjamin Quarles. Copyright © 1960, 1988 by the President and Fellows of Harvard College. Published by The Belknap Press of Harvard University Press, Cambridge, Mass., pages 97–105. Reprinted by permission of **Harvard University Press.**

VOCABULARY

intimated (in'tə·māt'·id) *v.:* stated indirectly; hinted.

AUTHOR'S PURPOSE

In lines 2–7, Douglass describes his purpose for writing. Describe this purpose in your own words.

_____

_____

_____

CLARIFY

What happens to Douglass while he is fanning wheat (lines 14–20)?

_____

_____

INTERPRET

Underline the main events Douglass narrates in lines 32–46. Would you describe Douglass's **tone** as angry or emotional?

_____

_____

_____

_____

_____

_____

_____

_____

_____

VOCABULARY

comply (kəm·plī′) *v.:* obey; agree to a request.

IDENTIFY

Pause at line 48. What does Douglass decide to do for the first time in his life? Circle the answer.

to stop work. I stood as long as I could stagger to the hopper with grain. When I could stand no longer, I fell, and felt as if

20 held down by an immense weight. The fan of course stopped; everyone had his own work to do; and no one could do the work of the other, and have his own go on at the same time.

Mr. Covey was at the house, about one hundred yards from the treading yard where we were fanning. On hearing the fan stop, he left immediately, and came to the spot where we were. He hastily inquired what the matter was. Bill answered that I was sick, and there was no one to bring wheat to the fan. I had by this time crawled away under the side of the post-and-rail fence by which the yard was enclosed, hoping to find relief by

30 getting out of the sun. He then asked where I was. He was told by one of the hands.

He came to the spot, and, after looking at me awhile, asked me what was the matter. I told him as well as I could, for I scarce had strength to speak. He then gave me a savage kick in the side, and told me to get up. I tried to do so, but fell back in the attempt. He gave me another kick, and again told me to rise. I again tried, and succeeded in gaining my feet; but, stooping to get the tub with which I was feeding the fan, I again staggered and fell. While down in this situation, Mr. Covey took up the

40 hickory slat with which Hughes had been striking off the half-bushel measure, and with it gave me a heavy blow upon the head, making a large wound, and the blood ran freely; and with this again told me to get up. I made no effort to **comply**, having now made up my mind to let him do his worst. In a short time after receiving this blow, my head grew better. Mr. Covey had now left me to my fate.

At this moment I resolved, for the first time, to go to my master, enter a complaint, and ask his protection. In order to [do] this, I must that afternoon walk seven miles; and this,

50 under the circumstances, was truly a severe undertaking. I was exceedingly feeble; made so as much by the kicks and blows which I received, as by the severe fit of sickness to which I had

been subjected. I, however, watched my chance, while Covey was looking in an opposite direction, and started for St. Michael's. I succeeded in getting a considerable distance on my way to the woods, when Covey discovered me, and called after me to come back, threatening what he would do if I did not come. I disregarded both his calls and his threats, and made my way to the woods as fast as my feeble state would allow; and thinking I might be overhauled by him if I kept the road, I walked through the woods, keeping far enough from the road to avoid detection, and near enough to prevent losing my way.

I had not gone far before my little strength again failed me. I could go no farther. I fell down, and lay for a considerable time. The blood was yet oozing from the wound on my head. For a time I thought I should bleed to death; and think now that I should have done so, but that the blood so matted my hair as to stop the wound. After lying there about three quarters of an hour, I nerved myself up again, and started on my way, through bogs and briers, barefooted and bareheaded, tearing my feet sometimes at nearly every step; and after a journey of about seven miles, occupying some five hours to perform it, I arrived at master's store. I then presented an appearance enough to affect any but a heart of iron. From the crown of my head to my feet, I was covered with blood. My hair was all clotted with dust and blood; my shirt was stiff with blood. My legs and feet were torn in sundry places with briers and thorns, and were also covered with blood. I suppose I looked like a man who had escaped a den of wild beasts, and barely escaped them.

In this state I appeared before my master, humbly entreating him to **interpose** his authority for my protection. I told him all the circumstances as well as I could, and it seemed, as I spoke, at times to affect him. He would then walk the floor, and seek to justify Covey by saying he expected I deserved it. He asked me what I wanted. I told him, to let me get a new home; that as sure as I lived with Mr. Covey again, I should live with but to die with him; that Covey would surely kill me; he was in a fair way

The Life of Frederick Douglass (1938–1939), No. 10, by Jacob Lawrence. "The master of Douglass, seeing he was of a rebellious nature, sent him to a Mr. Covey, a man who had built up a reputation as a "slave breaker." A second attempt by Covey to flog Douglass was unsuccessful. This was one of the most important incidents in the life of Frederick Douglass: He was never again attacked by Covey. His philosophy: A slave easily flogged is flogged oftener; a slave who resists flogging is flogged less." (17⅞" × 12").

Notes

IDENTIFY

Re-read lines 88–95. Circle the reasons Thomas gives for refusing to help Douglass.

for it. Master Thomas ridiculed the idea that there was any danger of Mr. Covey's killing me, and said that he knew Mr. Covey;

90 that he was a good man, and that he could not think of taking me from him; that, should he do so, he would lose the whole year's wages; that I belonged to Mr. Covey for one year, and that

I must go back to him, come what might; and that I must not trouble him with any more stories, or that he would himself *get hold of me.* After threatening me thus, he gave me a very large dose of salts, telling me that I might remain in St. Michael's that night (it being quite late), but that I must be off back to Mr. Covey's early in the morning; and that if I did not, he would *get hold of me,* which meant that he would whip me.

100   I remained all night, and, according to his orders, I started off to Covey's in the morning (Saturday morning), wearied in body and broken in spirit. I got no supper that night, or breakfast that morning. I reached Covey's about nine o'clock; and just as I was getting over the fence that divided Mrs. Kemp's fields from ours, out ran Covey with his cowskin, to give me another whipping. Before he could reach me, I succeeded in getting to the cornfield; and as the corn was very high, it **afforded** me the means of hiding. He seemed very angry, and searched for me a long time. My behavior was altogether unaccountable. He finally
110   gave up the chase, thinking, I suppose, that I must come home for something to eat; he would give himself no further trouble in looking for me. I spent that day mostly in the woods, having the alternative before me—to go home and be whipped to death, or stay in the woods and be starved to death.

That night, I fell in with Sandy Jenkins, a slave with whom I was somewhat acquainted. Sandy had a free wife who lived about four miles from Mr. Covey's; and it being Saturday, he was on his way to see her. I told him my circumstances, and he very kindly invited me to go home with him. I went home with him,
120   and talked this whole matter over, and got his advice as to what course it was best for me to pursue. I found Sandy an old advisor.[3] He told me, with great **solemnity,** I must go back to Covey; but that before I went, I must go with him into another part of the woods, where there was a certain *root,* which, if I would take some of it with me, carrying it *always on my right side,* would

---

3. **an old advisor:** someone who can offer good advice.

Notes _____

IDENTIFY

Underline two choices, or alternatives, Douglass has now (lines 112–114).

CLARIFY

Pause at line 119. What new person enters the narrative at this point?

VOCABULARY

afforded (ə·fôrd′id) *v.:* gave; provided.
solemnity (sə·lem′nə·tē) *n.:* seriousness.

render (ren′dər) v.: make.

singular (siŋ′gyə·lər) adj.: remarkable.

attributed (ə·trib′yoot·id) v.: thought of as resulting from.

CLARIFY

What surprises Douglass about Covey's conduct (lines 137–145)?

_____

_____

_____

_____

_____

_____

_____

CLARIFY

Re-read lines 147–158. Underline what Covey does to Douglass. Then, underline Douglass's response.

ANALYZE

Circle the **figure of speech** Douglass uses to describe Covey's reaction to his resistance (line 160). Is this comparison a **metaphor** or a **simile**? Explain.

_____

_____

_____

_____

render it impossible for Mr. Covey, or any other white man, to whip me. He said he had carried it for years; and since he had done so, he had never received a blow, and never expected to while he carried it. I at first rejected the idea, that the simple car-
130 rying of a root in my pocket would have any such effect as he had said, and was not disposed to take it; but Sandy impressed the necessity with much earnestness, telling me it could do no harm, if it did no good. To please him, I at length took the root, and, according to his direction, carried it upon my right side. This was Sunday morning.

I immediately started for home; and upon entering the yard gate, out came Mr. Covey on his way to meeting. He spoke to me very kindly, made me drive the pigs from a lot nearby, and passed on toward the church. Now, this **singular** conduct of Mr.
140 Covey really made me begin to think that there was something in the *root* which Sandy had given me; and had it been on any other day than Sunday, I could have **attributed** the conduct to no other cause than the influence of that root; and as it was, I was half inclined to think the *root* to be something more than I at first had taken it to be. All went well till Monday morning. On this morning, the virtue of the *root* was fully tested.

Long before daylight, I was called to go and rub, curry, and feed the horses. I obeyed, and was glad to obey. But while thus engaged, while in the act of throwing down some blades from
150 the loft, Mr. Covey entered the stable with a long rope; and just as I was half out of the loft, he caught hold of my legs, and was about tying me. As soon as I found what he was up to, I gave a sudden spring, and as I did so, he holding to my legs, I was brought sprawling on the stable floor. Mr. Covey seemed now to think he had me, and could do what he pleased; but at this moment—from whence came the spirit I don't know—I resolved to fight; and, suiting my action to the resolution, I seized Covey hard by the throat; and as I did so, I rose. He held on to me, and I to him. My resistance was so entirely unex-
160 pected, that Covey seemed taken all aback. He trembled like a leaf.

This gave me assurance, and I held him uneasy, causing the blood to run where I touched him with the ends of my fingers. Mr. Covey soon called out to Hughes for help. Hughes came, and, while Covey held me, attempted to tie my right hand. While he was in the act of doing so, I watched my chance, and gave him a heavy kick close under the ribs. This kick fairly sickened Hughes, so that he left me in the hands of Mr. Covey.

This kick had the effect of not only weakening Hughes, but Covey also. When he saw Hughes bending over with pain, his
170 courage quailed.[4] He asked me if I meant to persist in my resistance. I told him I did, come what might; that he had used me like a brute for six months, and that I was determined to be used so no longer. With that, he strove to drag me to a stick that was lying just out of the stable door. He meant to knock me down. But just as he was leaning over to get the stick, I seized him with both hands by his collar, and brought him by a sudden snatch to the ground. By this time, Bill came. Covey called upon him for assistance. Bill wanted to know what he could do. Covey said, "Take hold of him, take hold of him!" Bill said his master hired
180 him out to work, and not to help to whip me; so he left Covey and myself to fight our own battle out. We were at it for nearly two hours. Covey at length let me go, puffing and blowing at a great rate, saying that if I had not resisted, he would not have whipped me half so much. The truth was, that he had not whipped me at all. I considered him as getting entirely the worst end of the bargain; for he had drawn no blood from me, but I had from him. The whole six months afterward, that I spent with Mr. Covey, he never laid the weight of his finger upon me in anger. He would occasionally say, he didn't want to get hold
190 of me again. "No," thought I, "you need not; for you will come off worse than you did before."

---

4. **quailed** *v.*: faltered.

from Narrative of the Life of Frederick Douglass   **169**

Notes _____

_____

_____

_____

_____

_____

_____

_____

_____

_____

_____

_____

_____

_____

_____

IDENTIFY

Pause at line 173. Underline the reason Douglass gives for his determination to resist Mr. Covey.

IDENTIFY

Pause at line 182. For how long did Covey and Douglass fight? Underline the words that tell you.

IDENTIFY CAUSE & EFFECT

Pause at line 191. Underline the result, or effect, of the fight in the stable.

expiring (ek·spīr′iŋ) *v.* used as *adj.:* dying.

Circle the **metaphor** Douglass uses to describe freedom (line 193). What truth does the comparison reveal?

_____

_____

_____

_____

_____

How does the **tone** of the final paragraph differ from the tone of the rest of the story?

_____

_____

_____

Locate and circle another **metaphor,** in lines 200–201. What three comparisons does Douglass make in it?

_____

_____

_____

_____

_____

This battle with Mr. Covey was the turning point in my career as a slave. It rekindled the few **expiring** embers of freedom, and revived within me a sense of my own manhood. It recalled the departed self-confidence, and inspired me again with a determination to be free. The gratification afforded by the triumph was a full compensation for whatever else might follow, even death itself. He only can understand the deep satisfaction which I experienced, who has himself repelled by force the bloody arm of slavery. I felt as I never felt before. It was a glorious resurrection,[5] from the tomb of slavery, to the heaven of freedom. My long-crushed spirit rose, cowardice departed, bold defiance took its place; and I now resolved that, however long I might remain a slave in form, the day had passed forever when I could be a slave in fact.

200

_____

5. **resurrection** *n.:* coming back to life.

These people were formerly held in slavery.

from Narrative of the Life of Frederick Douglass

Reading Skills: Analyzing a Writer's Purpose   Complete this chart to show how Douglass supports his purpose, which is stated in the first paragraph of the text. First, state Douglass's purpose, using his own words. Then, find examples of description and narration that support his purpose. Also, find at least one strong metaphor that supports his purpose.

Author's Purpose	
Use of Narration	
Use of Description	
Use of Strong Metaphors	

from Narrative of the Life of Frederick Douglass

VOCABULARY DEVELOPMENT

VOCABULARY IN CONTEXT

DIRECTIONS: Write words from the Word Box in the blanks to complete the paragraph below. Not all words will be used.

Word Box

intimated

comply

interpose

afforded

solemnity

render

singular

attributed

expiring

Learning to read was a (1) _____ achievement for a slave. Douglass was (2) _____ the opportunity when he was sent to live in Baltimore, Maryland. He (3) _____ his first reading skills to Sophia Auld, the wife of his master, who taught him. When her husband discovered that Douglass could read, he was furious. At the time it was illegal to teach a slave to read. Hugh Auld was determined to (4) _____ with the law. The lessons stopped immediately, but Douglass's passion for learning was in no danger of (5) _____.

CONTEXT CLUES

Underline the context clue that helps you guess at the meaning of each boldface word below. Then, write the word's meaning in the space provided.

Reading Standard 1.3 (Grade 8 Review)
Use word meanings within the appropriate context and show ability to verify those meanings by definition, restatement, example, comparison, or contrast.

Context	Meaning
As I watched the trees **expiring,** I realized I could not let them die.	
The **solemnity** of the occasion was evident: Everyone was quiet and serious.	
She **intimated** that Sam lied, a hint that would cause her trouble later.	
The boy tried to **comply** with the order, but his mother refused to let him obey it.	

 Check your Standards Mastery at the back of this book.

A Mystery of Heroism by Stephen Crane

LITERARY FOCUS: SITUATIONAL IRONY

Situational irony is the difference between what you expect will happen and what actually happens. Suppose, for example, a person plans carefully for a worldwide disaster by stocking an underground room with provisions. As it turns out, a disaster does occur, and the man is pleased with himself and his foresight. As he goes to prepare his first meal in the shelter, he realizes that he forgot to stock a can opener. The hundreds of cans of food he stockpiled are useless to him.

READING SKILLS: IDENTIFYING THEME

When you finish a story you often ask: "What was the meaning of that story?" When you ask that question, you are asking about theme. **Theme** is the insight or truth about human experience revealed in a story. We learn about this truth as we share the events of the story and the discoveries the story characters make. When you are looking for theme, ask: "What have these actions revealed to me about our lives? What have the events of the story revealed to the main character? What has he or she learned?"

To help you think about theme, fill out this chart after your first reading of the story:

Main events in story	
What character(s) discover	
Significance of title	
Key details	

Reading Standard 3.3 Analyze the ways in which irony, tone, mood, the author's style, and the "sound" of language achieve specific rhetorical or aesthetic purposes or both.

Reading Standard 3.8 Analyze the clarity and consistency of political assumptions in a selection of literary works or essays on a topic. (Political approach)

Reading Standard 3.8 (Grade 9–10 Review) Interpret and evaluate the impact of ambiguities, subtleties, contradictions, ironies, and incongruities in a text.

A Mystery of Heroism

Stephen Crane

Notes

WORD STUDY

The word *duck* in line 10 refers to heavy cotton cloth. This use of *duck* comes from the Dutch word for cloth (*doek*).

The dark uniforms of the men were so coated with dust from the incessant wrestling of the two armies that the regiment almost seemed a part of the clay bank which shielded them from the shells. On the top of the hill a battery[1] was arguing in tremendous roars with some other guns, and to the eye of the infantry, the artillerymen, the guns, the caissons,[2] the horses, were distinctly outlined upon the blue sky. When a piece was fired, a red streak as round as a log flashed low in the heavens, like a monstrous bolt of lightning. The men of the battery wore
10 white duck trousers, which somehow emphasized their legs, and when they ran and crowded in little groups at the bidding of the

---

1. **battery** *n.:* set of heavy guns.
2. **caissons** (kā′sənz) *n. pl.:* ammunition wagons.

shouting officers, it was more impressive than usual to the infantry.

Fred Collins of A Company was saying: "Thunder, I wisht I had a drink. Ain't there any water round here?" Then somebody yelled: "There goes th' bugler!"

As the eyes of half of the regiment swept in one machine-like movement, there was an instant's picture of a horse in a great convulsive leap of a death wound and a rider leaning back
20 with a crooked arm and spread fingers before his face. On the ground was the crimson terror of an exploding shell, with fibers of flame that seemed like lances. A glittering bugle swung clear of the rider's back as fell headlong the horse and the man. In the air was an odor as from a **conflagration.**

Sometimes they of the infantry looked down at a fair little meadow which spread at their feet. Its long, green grass was rippling gently in a breeze. Beyond it was the gray form of a house half torn to pieces by shells and by the busy axes of soldiers who had pursued firewood. The line of an old fence was now dimly
30 marked by long weeds and by an occasional post. A shell had blown the well house to fragments. Little lines of gray smoke ribboning upward from some embers indicated the place where had stood the barn.

From beyond a curtain of green woods there came the sound of some stupendous scuffle as if two animals of the size of islands were fighting. At a distance there were occasional appearances of swift-moving men, horses, batteries, flags, and, with the crashing of infantry, volleys were heard, often, wild and frenzied cheers. In the midst of it all, Smith and Ferguson, two
40 privates of A Company, were engaged in a heated discussion, which involved the greatest questions of the national existence.

The battery on the hill presently engaged in a frightful duel. The white legs of the gunners scampered this way and that way and the officers redoubled their shouts. The guns, with their

CLARIFY

Re-read lines 17–24. What has happened to the bugler?

_____

_____

_____

_____

_____

VOCABULARY

conflagration
(kän′flə·grā′shən) *n.:* huge fire.

COMPARE & CONTRAST

Re-read lines 25–41. How does the narrator describe the natural setting? How does he describe the battle raging within the setting?

_____

_____

_____

_____

_____

WORD STUDY

Lines 34–36 contain a **metaphor** and a **simile.** Underline the metaphor (a comparison that does not use the words *like* or *as*), and circle the simile (a comparison that uses the words *like* or *as*).

stolidity (stə·lid′ə·tē) *n.:*
absence of emotional
reactions.

CLARIFY

Re-read lines 58–65.
What has happened to
the lieutenant?

_____

_____

_____

_____

_____

_____

IDENTIFY

Pause at line 76. Why would
it be difficult for Collins to
get a drink of water from
the old well?

_____

_____

_____

_____

_____

_____

**COMPARE &
CONTRAST**

Underline the words in lines
69–76 that describe the
meadow before the battle.
Then, circle the words that
describe the meadow during
the battle.

demeanors of **stolidity** and courage, were typical of something infinitely self-possessed in this clamor of death that swirled around the hill.

One of a "swing" team was suddenly smitten quivering to the ground and his maddened brethren dragged his torn body in 50 their struggle to escape from this turmoil and danger. A young soldier astride one of the leaders swore and fumed in his saddle and furiously jerked at the bridle. An officer screamed out an order so violently that his voice broke and ended the sentence in a falsetto[3] shriek.

The leading company of the infantry regiment was somewhat exposed and the colonel ordered it moved more fully under the shelter of the hill. There was the clank of steel against steel.

A lieutenant of the battery rode down and passed them, holding his right arm carefully in his left hand. And it was as if 60 this arm was not at all a part of him, but belonged to another man. His sober and reflective charger[4] went slowly. The officer's face was grimy and perspiring and his uniform was tousled as if he had been in direct grapple with an enemy. He smiled grimly when the men stared at him. He turned his horse toward the meadow.

Collins of A Company said: "I wisht I had a drink. I bet there's water in that there ol' well yonder!"

"Yes; but how you goin' to git it?"

For the little meadow which intervened was now suffering a 70 terrible onslaught of shells. Its green and beautiful calm had vanished utterly. Brown earth was being flung in monstrous handfuls. And there was a massacre of the young blades of grass. They were being torn, burned, obliterated. Some curious fortune of the battle had made this gentle little meadow the object of the red hate of the shells and each one as it exploded seemed like an imprecation[5] in the face of a maiden.

---

3. **falsetto** *n.* used as *adj.:* artificially high voice.
4. **charger** *n.:* horse trained for battle.
5. **imprecation** *n.:* curse.

The wounded officer who was riding across this expanse said to himself: "Why, they couldn't shoot any harder if the whole army was massed here!"

A shell struck the gray ruins of the house and as, after the roar, the shattered wall fell in fragments, there was a noise which resembled the flapping of shutters during a wild gale of winter. Indeed the infantry paused in the shelter of the bank, appeared as men standing upon a shore contemplating a madness of the sea. The angel of calamity[6] had under its glance the battery upon the hill. Fewer white-legged men labored about the guns. A shell had smitten one of the pieces, and after the flare, the smoke, the dust, the wrath of this blow was gone, it was possible to see white legs stretched horizontally upon the ground. And at that interval to the rear, where it is the business of battery horses to stand with their noses to the fight awaiting the command to drag their guns out of the destruction or into it or wheresoever these incomprehensible humans demanded with whip and spur— in this line of passive and dumb spectators, whose fluttering hearts yet would not let them forget the iron laws of man's control of them—in this rank of brute soldiers there had been relentless and hideous carnage. From the ruck[7] of bleeding and prostrate[8] horses, the men of the infantry could see one animal raising its stricken body with its forelegs and turning its nose with mystic and profound eloquence toward the sky.

Some comrades joked Collins about his thirst. "Well, if yeh want a drink so bad, why don't yeh go git it?"

"Well, I will in a minnet if yeh don't shut up."

A lieutenant of artillery floundered his horse straight down the hill with as great concern as if it were level ground. As he galloped past the colonel of the infantry, he threw up his hand in swift salute. "We've got to get out of that," he roared angrily. He was a black-bearded officer, and his eyes, which resembled

---

6. **calamity** *n.:* disaster; misfortune.
7. **ruck** *n.:* mass; crowd.
8. **prostrate** *adj.:* lying flat on the ground.

PARAPHRASE

The narrator uses vivid, eloquent language to describe the events of the battle. What has happened in lines 80–85? Restate the events in your own words.

_____

_____

_____

_____

_____

_____

_____

_____

AUTHOR'S PURPOSE

Re-read lines 89–100. Which is more understandable: the humans' behavior or the animals' behavior? What might the purpose of this passage be?

_____

_____

_____

_____

_____

_____

_____

_____

CLARIFY

Pause at line 115. Where is the black-bearded officer going, and why?

_____

_____

_____

_____

_____

_____

_____

_____

_____

_____

_____

_____

_____

_____

_____

_____

_____

CLARIFY

Re-read lines 121–128. Underline the information that tells what happened to the lieutenant who was injured earlier in the story.

beads, sparkled like those of an insane man. His jumping horse
110 sped along the column of infantry.

The fat major standing carelessly with his sword held horizontally behind him and with his legs far apart, looked after the receding horseman and laughed. "He wants to get back with orders pretty quick or there'll be no batt'ry left," he observed.

The wise young captain of the second company hazarded[9] to the lieutenant colonel that the enemy's infantry would probably soon attack the hill, and the lieutenant colonel snubbed him.

A private in one of the rear companies looked out over the
120 meadow and then turned to a companion and said: "Look there, Jim." It was the wounded officer from the battery, who some time before had started to ride across the meadow, supporting his right arm carefully with his left hand. This man had encountered a shell apparently at a time when no one perceived him and he could now be seen lying face downward with a stirruped foot stretched across the body of his dead horse. A leg of the charger extended slantingly upward precisely as stiff as a stake. Around this motionless pair the shells still howled.

There was a quarrel in A Company. Collins was shaking his
130 fist in the faces of some laughing comrades. "Dern yeh! I ain't afraid t' go. If yeh say much, I will go!"

"Of course, yeh will! Yeh'll run through that there medder, won't yeh?"

Collins said, in a terrible voice: "You see, now!" At this **ominous** threat his comrades broke into renewed jeers.

Collins gave them a dark scowl and went to find his captain. The latter was conversing with the colonel of the regiment.

"Captain," said Collins, saluting and standing at attention. In those days all trousers bagged at the knees. "Captain, I want
140 t' git permission to go git some water from that there well over yonder!"

---

9. **hazarded** v.: risked saying.

The colonel and the captain swung about simultaneously and stared across the meadow. The captain laughed. "You must be pretty thirsty, Collins?"

"Yes, sir; I am."

"Well—ah," said the captain. After a moment he asked: "Can't you wait?"

"No, sir."

The colonel was watching Collins's face. "Look here, my lad," he said, in a pious[10] sort of a voice. "Look here, my lad." Collins was not a lad. "Don't you think that's taking pretty big risks for a little drink of water?"

"I dunno," said Collins, uncomfortably. Some of the resentment toward his companions, which perhaps had forced him into this affair, was beginning to fade. "I dunno wether 'tis."

The colonel and the captain contemplated him for a time.

"Well," said the captain finally.

"Well," said the colonel, "if you want to go, why go."

Collins saluted. "Much obliged t' yeh."

As he moved away, the colonel called after him. "Take some of the other boys' canteens with you an' hurry back now."

"Yes, sir. I will."

The colonel and the captain looked at each other then, for it had suddenly occurred that they could not for the life of them tell whether Collins wanted to go or whether he did not.

They turned to regard Collins, and as they perceived him surrounded by **gesticulating** comrades, the colonel said: "Well, by thunder! I guess he's going."

Collins appeared as a man dreaming. In the midst of the questions, the advice, the warnings, all the excited talk of his company mates, he maintained a curious silence.

They were very busy in preparing him for his ordeal. When they inspected him carefully, it was somewhat like the examination that grooms give a horse before a race; and they were

---

10. **pious** *adj.:* seemingly virtuous.

IDENTIFY CAUSE & EFFECT

Why does Collins ask to get some water from the well across the meadow (lines 142–155)?

VOCABULARY

gesticulating
(jes·tik′yoo·lāt′iŋ) *v.* used as *adj.:* gesturing, especially with the hands and arms.

The Hornet's Nest (1895) by Thomas Corwin Lindsay.
Oil on canvas.
Courtesy Cincinnati Historical Society.

CLARIFY

What is the "long animal-like thing" (line 184)?

amazed, staggered by the whole affair. Their astonishment found vent in strange repetitions.

"Are yeh sure a-goin'?" they demanded again and again.

"Certainly I am," cried Collins, at last furiously.

He strode sullenly[11] away from them. He was swinging five

180 or six canteens by their cords. It seemed that his cap would not remain firmly on his head, and often he reached and pulled it down over his brow.

There was a general movement in the compact column. The long animal-like thing moved slightly. Its four hundred eyes were turned upon the figure of Collins.

"Well, sir, if that ain't th' derndest thing. I never thought Fred Collins had the blood in him for that kind of business."

"What's he goin' to do, anyhow?"

---

11. **sullenly** *adv.:* in a resentful manner; sulkily.

"He's goin' to that well there after water."

"We ain't dyin' of thirst, are we? That's foolishness."

"Well, somebody put him up to it an' he's doin' it."

"Say, he must be a desperate cuss."

When Collins faced the meadow and walked away from the regiment, he was vaguely conscious that a chasm, the deep valley of all prides, was suddenly between him and his comrades. It was **provisional,** but the provision was that he return as a victor. He had blindly been led by quaint emotions and laid himself under an obligation to walk squarely up to the face of death.

But he was not sure that he wished to make a **retraction** even if he could do so without shame. As a matter of truth he was sure of very little. He was mainly surprised.

It seemed to him supernaturally strange that he had allowed his mind to maneuver his body into such a situation. He understood that it might be called dramatically great.

However, he had no full appreciation of anything excepting that he was actually conscious of being dazed. He could feel his dulled mind groping after the form and color of this incident.

Too, he wondered why he did not feel some keen agony of fear cutting his sense like a knife. He wondered at this because human expression had said loudly for centuries that men should feel afraid of certain things and that all men who did not feel this fear were phenomena, heroes.

He was then a hero. He suffered that disappointment which we would all have if we discovered that we were ourselves capable of those deeds which we most admire in history and legend. This, then, was a hero. After all, heroes were not much.

INTERPRET

What do the words of the soldiers reveal about Collins's actions (lines 186–195)?

_____
_____
_____
_____
_____
_____
_____
_____
_____
_____
_____
_____
_____
_____
_____
_____

VOCABULARY

provisional (prō·vizh′ə·nəl) *adj.*: temporary; serving for the time being.

retraction (ri·trak′shən) *n.*: withdrawal.

IDENTIFY

Re-read lines 212–219. How does Collins feel as he sets out to get the water? Underline your answer.

No, it could not be true. He was not a hero. Heroes had no shames in their lives and, as for him, he remembered borrowing fifteen dollars from a friend and promising to pay it back the next day, and then avoiding that friend for ten months. When at home his mother had aroused him for the early labor of his life on the farm, it had often been his fashion to be irritable, child-

230 ish, diabolical, and his mother had died since he had come to the war.

He saw that in this matter of the well, the canteens, the shells, he was an intruder in the land of fine deeds.

He was now about thirty paces from his comrades. The regiment had just turned its many faces toward him.

From the forest of terrific noises there suddenly emerged a little uneven line of men. They fired fiercely and rapidly at distant foliage on which appeared little puffs of white smoke. The spatter of skirmish firing was added to the thunder of the guns

240 on the hill. The little line of men ran forward. A color sergeant fell flat with his flag as if he had slipped on ice. There was hoarse cheering from this distant field.

Collins suddenly felt that two demon fingers were pressed into his ears. He could see nothing but flying arrows, flaming red. He lurched from the shock of this explosion, but he made a mad rush for the house, which he viewed as a man submerged to the neck in a boiling surf might view the shore. In the air, little pieces of shell howled and the earthquake explosions drove him insane with the menace of their roar. As he ran, the can-

250 teens knocked together with a rhythmical tinkling.

As he neared the house, each detail of the scene became vivid to him. He was aware of some bricks of the vanished chimney lying on the sod. There was a door which hung by one hinge.

Rifle bullets called forth by the insistent skirmishers came from the far-off bank of foliage. They mingled with the shells and the pieces of shells until the air was torn in all directions by hootings, yells, howls. The sky was full of fiends who directed all their wild rage at his head.

260   When he came to the well, he flung himself face downward
and peered into its darkness. There were furtive silver glintings
some feet from the surface. He grabbed one of the canteens and,
unfastening its cap, swung it down by the cord. The water
flowed slowly in with an **indolent** gurgle.

       And now as he lay with his face turned away, he was sud-
denly smitten with the terror. It came upon his heart like the
grasp of claws. All the power faded from his muscles. For an
instant he was no more than a dead man.

       The canteen filled with a maddening slowness in the manner
270 of all bottles. Presently he recovered his strength and addressed a
screaming oath to it. He leaned over until it seemed as if he
intended to try to push water into it with his hands. His eyes as
he gazed down into the well shone like two pieces of metal and
in their expression was a great appeal and a great curse. The stupid water derided[12] him.

       There was the blaring thunder of a shell. Crimson light
shone through the swift-boiling smoke and made a pink reflec-
tion on part of the wall of the well. Collins jerked out his arm
and canteen with the same motion that a man would use in with-
280 drawing his head from a furnace.

       He scrambled erect and glared and hesitated. On the ground
near him lay the old well bucket, with a length of rusty chain. He
lowered it swiftly into the well. The bucket struck the water and
then turning lazily over, sank. When, with hand reaching trem-
blingly over hand, he hauled it out, it knocked often against the
walls of the well and spilled some of its contents.

       In running with a filled bucket, a man can adopt but one
kind of gait. So through this terrible field over which screamed
practical angels of death Collins ran in the manner of a farmer
290 chased out of a dairy by a bull.

       His face went staring white with anticipation—anticipation
of a blow that would whirl him around and down. He would fall
as he had seen other men fall, the life knocked out of them so

---

12. **derided** *v.:* mocked.

A Mystery of Heroism   **183**

VOCABULARY

indolent (in′də·lənt) *adj.:*
lazy.

CLARIFY

Re-read lines 265–268. What
new feeling overtakes Collins
as he tries to fill his first
canteen?

_____

_____

_____

_____

**IDENTIFY
CAUSE & EFFECT**

Pause at line 286. Why does
Collins fill a bucket with
water instead of the can-
teens?

_____

_____

_____

_____

_____

_____

CLARIFY

What are the "practical
angels of death" (line 289)?

_____

_____

_____

_____
_____
_____
_____
_____
_____
_____
_____

VOCABULARY

blanched (blancht) *v.* used as *adj.:* drained of color.

CLARIFY

Re-read lines 308–321. Whom does Collins encounter while he is running across the meadow? What does this person want?

_____
_____
_____
_____
_____
_____
_____
_____
_____
_____

suddenly that their knees were no more quick to touch the ground than their heads. He saw the long blue line of the regi-

300 ment, but his comrades were standing looking at him from the edge of an impossible star. He was aware of some deep wheel ruts and hoof prints in the sod beneath his feet.

The artillery offi-cer who had fallen in

310 this meadow had been making groans in the teeth of the tempest of sound. These futile cries, wrenched from him by his agony, were heard only by shells, bullets. When wild-eyed Collins came running, this officer raised himself. His face con-torted and **blanched** from pain, he was about to utter some

320 great beseeching cry. But suddenly his face straightened and he called: "Say, young man, give me a drink of water, will you?"

Collins had no room amid his emotions for surprise. He was mad from the threats of destruction.

"I can't," he screamed, and in this reply was a full descrip-tion of his quaking apprehension. His cap was gone and his hair was riotous. His clothes made it appear that he had been dragged over the ground by the heels. He ran on.

Charge of VMI Cadets at New Market (1914) by Benjamin West Clinedinst. Oil on canvas (18″ × 23″).
Virginia Military Institute, Lexington, Virginia.

The officer's head sank down and one elbow crooked. His foot in its brass-bound stirrup still stretched over the body of his horse and the other leg was under the steed.

But Collins turned. He came dashing back. His face had now turned gray and in his eyes was all terror. "Here it is! Here it is!"

The officer was as a man gone in drink. His arm bended like a twig. His head drooped as if his neck was of willow. He was sinking to the ground, to lie face downward.

Collins grabbed him by the shoulder. "Here it is. Here's your drink. Turn over! Turn over, man, for God's sake!"

With Collins hauling at his shoulder, the officer twisted his body and fell with his face turned toward that region where lived the unspeakable noises of the swirling missiles. There was the faintest shadow of a smile on his lips as he looked at Collins. He gave a sigh, a little primitive breath like that from a child.

Collins tried to hold the bucket steadily, but his shaking hands caused the water to splash all over the face of the dying man. Then he jerked it away and ran on.

The regiment gave him a welcoming roar. The grimed faces were wrinkled in laughter.

His captain waved the bucket away. "Give it to the men!"

The two genial,[13] skylarking[14] young lieutenants were the first to gain possession of it. They played over it in their fashion.

When one tried to drink, the other teasingly knocked his elbow. "Don't, Billie! You'll make me spill it," said the one. The other laughed.

Suddenly there was an oath, the thud of wood on the ground, and a swift murmur of astonishment from the ranks. The two lieutenants glared at each other. The bucket lay on the ground empty.

---

13. **genial** *adj.*: friendly; cheerful.
14. **skylarking** *v.* used as *adj.*: frolicking; playful.

INFER

Why does Collins turn and go back to the officer (lines 331–332)?

_____

_____

_____

_____

_____

_____

ANALYZE

Pause at line 345. Circle the word that tells what will happen to the officer after Collins leaves. How does the officer's fate make Collins's act of heroism **ironic**?

_____

_____

_____

INTERPRET

Re-read lines 354–357. The ending of the story is **ambiguous**; it is open to more than one interpretation. In your own words, explain what you think has happened.

_____

_____

_____

_____

_____

A Mystery of Heroism

Reading Skills: Identifying Theme   Fill in the chart below with details from the story that illustrate the elements in the left-hand column. Then, review your chart entries and state the story's theme at the bottom of the chart.

Main events in story	
What character(s) discover	
Significance of title	
Key details	
Statement of Theme	

A Mystery of Heroism

VOCABULARY
DEVELOPMENT

VOCABULARY IN CONTEXT

DIRECTIONS: Write words from the Word Box in the blanks to complete the paragraph below. Not all words will be used.

Word Box

conflagration
stolidity
ominous
gesticulating
provisional
retraction
indolent
blanched

Nate Forrester of B Company felt almost sleepy. The steady noise had been ringing in his ears for so many hours that the blasts no longer sounded (1) _____ or even frightened him. His company was staying behind a (2) _____ wall they had just built. Lying on his back, he watched the flames from the (3) _____. From a distance the relaxed soldier could be mistaken for an (4) _____ young boy. But the noise suddenly stopped. Forrester snapped out of his daze. His face (5) _____ with fear, he wondered what new horrors the silence would bring.

ETYMOLOGY

A word's **etymology** is its history. Dictionaries usually provide an etymology after a word's pronunciation or following its definitions.

DIRECTIONS: A list of word etymologies is given at the right, in column B. Match each etymology with the appropriate "military" word in column A, on the left. On the lines at the bottom, list any words you can think of that might share these roots. The root words are in italics in column B.

A	B
____ **1.** infantry	**a.** from the Old French *atillier,* meaning "to equip"
____ **2.** regiment	**b.** from the Latin *caballus,* meaning "horse"
____ **3.** cavalry	**c.** from the Latin *infans,* meaning "child"
____ **4.** artillery	**d.** from the Latin *regere,* meaning "to rule"

_____

_____

_____

_____

Reading Standard 1.1
Trace the etymology of significant terms used in political science and history.

 Check your Standards Mastery at the back of this book.

A Pair of Silk Stockings by Kate Chopin

LITERARY FOCUS: MOTIVATION

The reason for a character's actions is called **motivation.** Writers sometimes state motivations directly. More often, however, writers give readers clues about why characters act the way they do. The readers then have to use the clues—and their own life experiences—to infer what feelings, desires, and needs motivated the characters.

In "A Pair of Silk Stockings," Mrs. Sommers makes a series of surprising choices. The narrator does not explain exactly why Mrs. Sommers makes each choice. Instead, we are given clues that help us understand Mrs. Sommers's motivation.

READING SKILLS: ANALYZING HISTORICAL CONTEXT

To understand a story, you need to know something about the time in which it was written and the time in which it takes place. Kate Chopin wrote this story in the 1890s, which is when the story also takes place. At that time, women in the United States could not vote. They had fewer opportunities for education and work. Some people were beginning to fight for women's rights, but progress was slow. The dollar was worth a lot more back then: Fifteen dollars could buy more than a couple of fast-food meals.

On the fashion front, most women in the 1890s wore thick cotton stockings. Silk stockings were a pure luxury that were beyond the average woman's means.

Use the Skill   As you read Chopin's story, note the differences between life then and life as it is today.

- Think about the position of women in the 1890s.
- Think about how the story would change if it took place today.

A Pair of Silk Stockings

Kate Chopin

Little Mrs. Sommers one day found herself the unexpected possessor of fifteen dollars. It seemed to her a very large amount of money, and the way in which it stuffed and bulged her worn old *porte-monnaie*[1] gave her a feeling of importance such as she had not enjoyed for years.

The question of investment was one that occupied her greatly. For a day or two she walked about apparently in a dreamy state, but really absorbed in speculation[2] and calculation. She did not wish to act hastily, to do anything she might afterward regret. But it was during the still hours of the night when she lay awake revolving plans in her mind that she seemed to see her way clearly toward a proper and **judicious** use of the money.

A dollar or two should be added to the price usually paid for Janie's shoes, which would ensure their lasting an **appreciable** time longer than they usually did. She would buy so-and-so many yards of percale[3] for new shirtwaists for the boys and Janie and Mag. She had intended to make the old ones do by skillful patching. Mag should have another gown. She had seen some beautiful patterns, **veritable** bargains in the shop windows. And still there would be left enough for new stockings—two pairs apiece—and what darning that would save for a while! She would get caps for the boys and sailor hats for the girls. The vision of her little brood looking fresh and dainty and new for once in their lives excited her and made her restless and wakeful with anticipation.

---

1. *porte-monnaie* (pôrt · mô · ne′): French for "purse."
2. **speculation** *n.:* deep thought; meditation.
3. **percale** *n.:* finely woven cotton cloth.

INFER

Re-read lines 1–5. Why do you think the narrator refers to the main character as "Little Mrs. Sommers"?

_____

_____

_____

_____

VOCABULARY

judicious (jōō · dish′əs) *adj.:* cautious; wise.
appreciable (ə · prē′shə · bəl) *adj.:* measurable.
veritable (ver′i · tə · bəl) *adj.:* genuine; true.

MOTIVATION

Re-read lines 14–26. Circle the things that Mrs. Sommers plans to buy with her fifteen dollars. What do her plans reveal about her motivations?

_____

_____

_____

_____

_____

_____

Pause at line 33. Compare Mrs. Sommers's present with her past. How has her life changed from what it once was?

Self Portrait (1880) by Mary Cassatt. Watercolor on paper (13″ × 9⅝″).
National Portrait Gallery, Smithsonian Institution, Washington, DC.

The neighbors sometimes talked of certain "better days" that little Mrs. Sommers had known before she had ever thought of being Mrs. Sommers. She herself indulged in no such morbid retrospection.[4] She had no time—no second of time to devote to the past. The needs of the present absorbed her every faculty. A vision of the future like some dim, gaunt monster sometimes appalled[5] her, but luckily tomorrow never comes.

Mrs. Sommers was one who knew the value of bargains; who could stand for hours making her way inch by inch toward the desired object that was selling below cost. She could elbow her way if need be; she had learned to clutch a piece of goods and hold it and stick to it with persistence and determination till her turn came to be served, no matter when it came.

But that day she was a little faint and tired. She had swallowed a light luncheon—no! when she came to think of it, between getting the children fed and the place righted, and preparing herself for the shopping bout, she had actually forgotten to eat any luncheon at all!

She sat herself upon a revolving stool before a counter that was comparatively deserted, trying to gather strength and courage to charge through an eager multitude that was besieging breastworks[6] of shirting and figured lawn. An all-gone limp feeling had come over her and she rested her hand aimlessly upon the counter. She wore no gloves. By degrees she grew aware that her hand had encountered something very soothing, very pleasant to touch. She looked down to see that her hand lay upon a pile of silk stockings. A placard nearby announced that they had been reduced in price from two dollars and fifty cents to one dollar and ninety-eight cents; and a young girl who stood behind the counter asked her if she wished to examine their line of silk hosiery. She smiled, just as if she had been asked to

4. **morbid retrospection:** brooding on things in the past.
5. **appalled** v.: shocked; dismayed.
6. **breastworks** n. pl.: low walls put up as barricades during battle. The bolts of shirting material and fine patterned cotton, or "figured lawn," are compared to barricades being stormed by shoppers.

ANALYZING HISTORICAL CONTEXT

Mrs. Sommers is a good bargain hunter (lines 34–39). Think about the **historical context** of this story. Do you think it was important for a woman in the 1890s to be a careful shopper?

_____

_____

_____

_____

_____

_____

_____

_____

IDENTIFY CAUSE & EFFECT

Pause at line 44. Why is Mrs. Sommers feeling so weak and tired?

_____

_____

_____

_____

WORD STUDY

Lawn (line 48) is a type of linen or cotton. _Figured_ in this context means "decorated with a design or pattern."

PREDICT

Pause at line 63. What do you think Mrs. Sommers is going to do?

_____

_____

INTERPRET

Why is Mrs. Sommers's purchase of silk stockings surprising (lines 72–75)?

_____

_____

_____

_____

_____

VOCABULARY

acute (ə·kyo͞ot′) *adj.*: keen; sharp.

laborious (lə·bôr′ē·əs) *adj.*: difficult; involving hard work.

reveling (rev′əl·iŋ) *v.*: taking pleasure.

CLARIFY

Re-read lines 79–86. Does Mrs. Sommers try to under-stand why she acted so impulsively? Explain.

_____

_____

_____

_____

_____

inspect a tiara of diamonds with the ultimate view of purchasing
it. But she went on feeling the soft, sheeny luxurious things—

60 with both hands now, holding them up to see them glisten, and
to feel them glide serpentlike through her fingers.

Two hectic blotches came suddenly into her pale cheeks.
She looked up at the girl.

"Do you think there are any eights-and-a-half among
these?"

There were any number of eights-and-a-half. In fact, there
were more of that size than any other. Here was a light blue pair;
there were some lavender, some all black, and various shades of
tan and gray. Mrs. Sommers selected a black pair and looked at

70 them very long and closely. She pretended to be examining their
texture, which the clerk assured her was excellent.

"A dollar and ninety-eight cents," she mused aloud. "Well,
I'll take this pair." She handed the girl a five-dollar bill and waited
for her change and for her parcel. What a very small parcel it was!
It seemed lost in the depths of her shabby old shopping bag.

Mrs. Sommers after that did not move in the direction of
the bargain counter. She took the elevator, which carried her to
an upper floor into the region of the ladies' waiting rooms.
Here, in a retired corner, she exchanged her cotton stockings for

80 the new silk ones which she had just bought. She was not going
through any **acute** mental process or reasoning with herself, nor
was she striving to explain to her satisfaction the motive of her
action. She was not thinking at all. She seemed for the time to be
taking a rest from that **laborious** and fatiguing function and to
have abandoned herself to some mechanical impulse[7] that
directed her actions and freed her of responsibility.

How good was the touch of the raw silk to her flesh! She
felt like lying back in the cushioned chair and **reveling** for a
while in the luxury of it. She did for a little while. Then she

90 replaced her shoes, rolled the cotton stockings together, and

---

7. **impuls**e *n.*: sudden, driving force.

thrust them into her bag. After doing this she crossed straight over to the shoe department and took her seat to be fitted.

She was **fastidious.** The clerk could not make her out; he could not reconcile[8] her shoes with her stockings, and she was not too easily pleased. She held back her skirts and turned her feet one way and her head another way as she glanced down at the polished, pointed-tipped boots. Her foot and ankle looked very pretty. She could not realize that they belonged to her and were a part of herself. She wanted an excellent and stylish fit, she told the young fellow who served her, and she did not mind the difference of a dollar or two more in the price so long as she got what she desired.

It was a long time since Mrs. Sommers had been fitted with gloves. On rare occasions when she had bought a pair they were always "bargains," so cheap that it would have been **preposterous** and unreasonable to have expected them to be fitted to the hand.

Now she rested her elbow on the cushion of the glove counter, and a pretty, pleasant young creature, delicate and deft of touch, drew a long-wristed "kid" over Mrs. Sommers's hand. She smoothed it down over the wrist and buttoned it neatly, and both lost themselves for a second or two in admiring contemplation of the little symmetrical gloved hand. But there were other places where money might be spent.

There were books and magazines piled up in the window of a stall a few paces down the street. Mrs. Sommers bought two high-priced magazines such as she had been accustomed to read in the days when she had been accustomed to other pleasant things. She carried them without wrapping. As well as she could she lifted her skirts at the crossings. Her stockings and boots and well-fitting gloves had worked marvels in her bearing—had given her a feeling of assurance, a sense of belonging to the well-dressed multitude.

---

8. **reconcile** *v.:* make compatible; bring into agreement.

VOCABULARY

fastidious (fa·stid′ē·əs) *adj.:* difficult to please; critical.

preposterous (prē·päs′tər·əs) *adj.:* ridiculous.

MOTIVATION

Re-read lines 93–102, and underline the passage that reveals that Mrs. Sommers has changed her shopping plan. What might have motivated this change?

_____

_____

_____

_____

FLUENCY

Read the boxed passage aloud two times. On your second read, try to capture the women's admiration of the gloves.

INFER

How do you think Mrs. Sommers's purchases make her feel (lines 119–123)?

_____

_____

_____

_____

_____

INFER

Re-read lines 124–128. Why do you think Mrs. Sommers doesn't want to have a snack at home?

_____

_____

_____

_____

_____

_____

_____

_____

_____

_____

ANALYZING HISTORICAL CONTEXT

Locate and underline the detail in lines 141–144 that reveals this story takes place long ago.

MOTIVATION

Read on to line 154. What motivates Mrs. Sommers to leave an extra coin on the waiter's tray?

_____

_____

_____

_____

_____

_____

She was very hungry. Another time she would have stilled the cravings for food until reaching her own home, where she would have brewed herself a cup of tea and taken a snack of anything that was available. But the impulse that was guiding her would not suffer her to entertain any such thought.

There was a restaurant at the corner. She had never entered
130 its doors; from the outside she had sometimes caught glimpses of spotless damask and shining crystal, and soft-stepping waiters serving people of fashion.

When she entered, her appearance created no surprise, no consternation, as she had half feared it might. She seated herself at a small table alone, and an attentive waiter at once approached to take her order. She did not want a profusion;[9] she craved a nice and tasty bite—a half dozen bluepoints,[10] a plump chop with cress, a something sweet—a crème-frappé,[11] for instance; a glass of Rhine wine, and after all a small cup of black
140 coffee.

While waiting to be served she removed her gloves very leisurely and laid them beside her. Then she picked up a magazine and glanced through it, cutting the pages with a blunt edge of her knife.[12] It was all very agreeable. The damask was even more spotless than it had seemed through the window, and the crystal more sparkling. There were quiet ladies and gentlemen, who did not notice her, lunching at the small tables like her own. A soft, pleasing strain of music could be heard, and a gentle breeze was blowing through the window. She tasted a bite,
150 and she read a word or two, and she sipped the amber wine and wiggled her toes in the silk stockings. The price of it made no difference. She counted the money out to the waiter and left an

---

9. **profusion** *n.:* abundance; great wastefulness.
10. **bluepoints** *n. pl.:* small oysters.
11. **crème-frappé** (krem · fra · pā′) *n.:* dessert similar to ice cream.
12. **cutting . . . knife:** At one time, magazines and books were often sold with folded, untrimmed pages. These outer edges had to be cut apart before one could read them.

extra coin on his tray, whereupon he bowed before her as before a princess of royal blood.

There was still money in her purse, and her next temptation presented itself in the shape of a matinée poster.

It was a little later when she entered the theater, the play had begun, and the house seemed to her to be packed. But there were vacant seats here and there, and into one of them she was ushered, between brilliantly dressed women who had gone there to kill time and eat candy and display their **gaudy** attire. There were many others who were there solely for the play and acting. It is safe to say there was no one present who bore quite the attitude which Mrs. Sommers did to her surroundings. She gathered in the whole—stage and players and people in one wide impression, and absorbed it and enjoyed it. She laughed at the comedy and wept—she and the gaudy woman next to her wept over the tragedy. And they talked a little together over it. And the gaudy woman wiped her eyes and sniffled on a tiny square of filmy, perfumed lace and passed little Mrs. Sommers her box of candy.

The play was over, the music ceased, the crowd filed out. It was like a dream ended. People scattered in all directions. Mrs. Sommers went to the corner and waited for the cable car.

A man with keen eyes, who sat opposite her, seemed to like the study of her small, pale face. It puzzled him to decipher what he saw there. In truth, he saw nothing—unless he were wizard enough to detect a **poignant** wish, a powerful longing that the cable car would never stop anywhere, but go on and on with her forever.

VOCABULARY

gaudy (gô′dē) adj.: showy but lacking in good taste.
poignant (poin′yənt) adj.: emotionally moving.

INTERPRET

What is the ending of the play compared to, in line 173? Underline the comparison. What else might be ending?

_____

_____

_____

INTERPRET

Re-read lines 175–180. Why do you think Mrs. Sommers wishes the cable car would never stop? What revelation about life might this wish convey? *(Grade 9–10 Review)*

_____

_____

_____

_____

_____

_____

_____

_____

_____

A Pair of Silk Stockings

Reading Skills: Analyzing Historical Context   Complete this chart to help you understand this story's historical context. Read each statement about the historical context in the left-hand column. Find a passage from the story that relates to that statement. Write the passage in the space provided.

Historical Context	Story Passage
Because most women in the 1890s had very limited opportunities for working, having pocket money was rare.	
A woman was expected to take care of her entire family.	
A woman's style of dress said a lot about her class.	
Many store clerks gave rich customers special treatment.	
A woman's social position was determined by her husband's position.	

A Pair of Silk Stockings

VOCABULARY DEVELOPMENT

VOCABULARY IN CONTEXT

DIRECTIONS: Write words from the Word Box in the blanks to complete the paragraph below. Not all words will be used.

Word Box

- judicious
- appreciable
- veritable
- acute
- laborious
- reveling
- fastidious
- preposterous
- gaudy
- poignant

Mrs. Walters was clearly a (1)_____ dresser. Every ribbon on her dress was perfectly tied. She even enjoyed the (2)_____ task of polishing her tiny black shirt buttons. Even though she wore six layers and four colors, the effect was not at all (3)_____. She was a (4)_____ rainbow of fabric. As she walked down the theater aisle, she looked like she was (5)_____ in her own private painting.

ANALOGIES

An **analogy** is made of two pairs of words. The words in one pair relate to each other in the same way as the words in the second pair relate to each other. Many word pairs in analogies are synonyms or antonyms.

Synonyms The words in each pair have the same meaning.
        WISE : SMART :: fair : just
Antonyms The words in each pair have opposite meanings.
        LOVE : HATE :: believe : doubt

DIRECTIONS: Write words from the Word Box to complete each analogy. Not all words will be used.

1. MARVELOUS : WONDERFUL :: fussy : _____

2. AVERAGE : NORMAL :: sharp : _____

3. BRAVE : COWARDLY :: sensible : _____

4. RAPID : SLOW :: untrue : _____

Reading Standard 1.3 Discern the meaning of analogies encountered, analyzing specific comparisons as well as relationships and inferences.

 Check your Standards Mastery at the back of this book.

5

The Moderns
(1914–1939)

Welcome to Our City (1921) by Charles Henry Demuth.
Oil on canvas (25$\frac{1}{8}$″ × 20$\frac{1}{8}$″).
Terra Foundation for the Arts, Daniel J. Terra Collection.

The Moderns (1914–1939)

John Leggett and John Malcolm Brinnin

Reading Standard 3.5c
Analyze recognized works of American literature representing a variety of genres and traditions.

The following essay provides highlights of the historical period. For a more detailed version of this essay, see *Holt Literature and Language Arts,* pages 562–569.

World War I (1914–1918), the so-called Great War, was an event that changed the American voice in fiction. The country appeared to have lost its innocence. Idealism had turned to cynicism for many Americans, who began to question the authority and tradition that was thought to be our bedrock. American writers, like their European counterparts, were also deeply influenced by the **modernist** movement. This movement in literature, painting, music, and the other arts called for bold experimentation and a complete rejection of traditional themes and styles.

IDENTIFY

Re-read lines 1–9. Underline what the modernist movement called for.

ANALYZE

Pause at line 15. Why do you think World War I and the Great Depression led Americans to examine their ideals?

_____
_____
_____
_____
_____
_____
_____
_____
_____
_____
_____
_____
_____

The American Dream: Pursuit of a Promise

10 The devastation of World War I and the economic crash of the Great Depression a decade later caused Americans to reexamine their ideals. Among the ideals that people began to question were three assumptions that, taken together, we have come to call the **American dream.**

■ America as a New Eden

The first element of the American dream is admiration for America as a new Eden: a land of beauty, bounty, and unlimited promise. Both the promise and the disappointment of this idea

20 are reflected in one of the greatest American novels, *The Great Gatsby* (1925) by F. Scott Fitzgerald.

Re-read lines 10–34.
Underline the three elements
of the **American dream.** Do
you think these elements are
still part of the American
dream today?

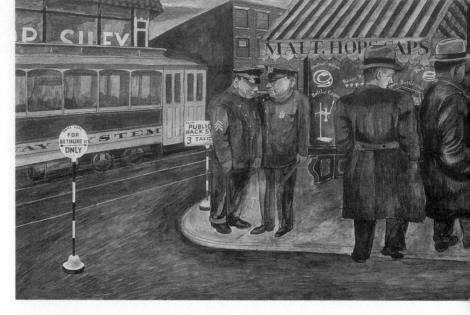

■ A Belief in Progress

The second element is optimism, justified by the ever-expanding
opportunity many people had come to expect. Americans had
come to believe in progress—that life will keep getting better
and that wealth, justice, and joy are just around the corner.

■ Triumph of the Individual

The final element in the American dream is the importance and
ultimate triumph of the individual—the independent, self-
30   reliant person. This ideal was championed by Ralph Waldo
Emerson (page 76), who probably deserves most of the credit
for defining the essence of the American dream, including its
roots in the promise of the "new Eden" and its faith that "things
are getting better all the time."

A Crack in the World: Breakdown of Beliefs and Traditions

In the postwar period, long-held beliefs and traditions began to
be tested. Postwar writers became skeptical of the New England
Puritan tradition and the gentility that had been central to the
40   literary ideal. In fact, the center of American literary life now
finally started to shift away from New England, which had been
the native region of America's most brilliant writers during the

Village Speakeasy, Closed for Violation (c. 1934) by Ben Shahn. Tempera on masonite (16³/₈″ × 47⁷/₈″).

Museum of the City of New York. Permanent Deposit of the Public Art Project through the Whitney Museum. © Estate of Ben Shahn/Licensed by VAGA, New York.

nineteenth century. Many modernist writers, in fact, were born in the South, the Midwest, or the West.

In the postwar period, two new intellectual theories or movements combined to influence previous beliefs and values: **Marxism** and **psychoanalysis**.

Marxism and the Challenge to Free Enterprise

50   In Russia during World War I, a Marxist revolution had toppled and even murdered an anointed ruler, the czar. The socialistic beliefs of Karl Marx (1818–1883) that had powered the Russian Revolution in 1917 conflicted with the American system of capitalism and free enterprise, and Marxists threatened to export their revolution everywhere. Some Americans, however, believed that certain elements of Marxism would provide much-needed rights to workers. After visiting Russia, the American writer Lincoln Steffens reported, "I have seen the future and it works."

Freud and the Unconscious Mind

60   In Vienna, there was another ground-shaking movement. Sigmund Freud (1856–1939), the founder of psychoanalysis, had

IDENTIFY

Re-read lines 45–47. Locate and circle the names of two new theories or movements that sprang up following the Great War.

IDENTIFY

Re-read lines 50–58. What did Americans regard as one positive element of Marxism?

opened the workings of the unconscious mind to examination. He also called for a new understanding of human sexuality and the role it plays in our unconscious thoughts. Throughout America, there was a growing interest in this new field of psychology and a resulting concern about the amount of freedom an individual had if our actions were indeed influenced by an uncontrol-
70 lable subconscious.

Sigmund Freud.

One literary result of this interest in the psyche was the narrative technique called **stream of consciousness.** This writing style abandoned chronology and attempted to imitate the moment-by-moment flow of a character's perceptions and memories. American writers William Faulkner (page 217) and Katherine Anne Porter (page 233) used the stream-of-consciousness technique in their works.

At Home and Abroad: The Jazz Age

In 1919, the U.S. Constitution was amended to prohibit the
80 manufacture and sale of alcohol, which was considered a social evil. Far from inspiring traditional values, however, Prohibition ushered in an age characterized by the bootlegger, the speakeasy, the short-skirted flapper, the new rhythms of jazz, and the gangster. The writer F. Scott Fitzgerald gave this era its name: the Jazz Age.

During the Jazz Age, women too played a prominent role. In 1920, women won the right to vote, and they began to create a presence in artistic, intellectual, and social circles. As energetic as this era was in America, many American artists and writers—
90 F. Scott Fitzgerald among them—abandoned their own shores for life in France. The wave of Americans living abroad was another signal that something had gone wrong with the American dream—with the idea that America was Eden, with our belief in progress, and especially with the conviction that America was a land of heroes.

IDENTIFY CAUSE & EFFECT

What effect did the interest in psychology have on narrative techniques (lines 71–77)?

_____

_____

_____

_____

_____

_____

_____

INTERPRET

Pause at line 85. Do you think Prohibition accomplished what its supporters had hoped? Explain.

_____

_____

_____

_____

_____

_____

_____

_____

IDENTIFY

In lines 86–95, circle the important right women finally won. Underline where some writers chose to live.

Grace Under Pressure:
The New American Hero

The most influential of all the post–World War I writers was
Ernest Hemingway. Hemingway is probably most famous for his
100   literary style, which influenced generations of writers. Like the
Puritans who strove for a plain style centuries earlier,
Hemingway reduced the fanciness of literary language to the
bare bones of the truth it must express.

     Hemingway also introduced a new kind of hero to
American fiction. The Hemingway hero is a man of action, a
warrior, and a tough competitor; he has a code of honor,
courage, and endurance. He shows, in Hemingway's own words,
"grace under pressure." But above all else, the Hemingway hero
is thoroughly disillusioned with the emptiness he finds at the
110   mysterious center of creation. Hemingway found his own
answer to this crisis of faith with a belief in decency, bravery,
and skillfulness, in spite of what he saw as the absolutely unbeat-
able odds waged against us all. A further part of this code is the
importance of recognizing and snatching up the rare, good
moments that life has to offer.

Modern Voices in Poetry:
A Dazzling Period of Experimentation

By the 1920s, the last traces of British influence on American
poetry were washed away, and American poets entered into their
120   most dazzling period of experimentation. Artists and poets
sought new ways of seeing and thinking. Many poets began to
explore the artistic life of Europe, especially Paris, and they
sought to create poems that invited new ways of seeing and
thinking. Ezra Pound (page 205) and T. S. Eliot (page 209) used
the suggestive techniques of **symbolism** to fashion a new, modernist poetry. Pound also was at the head of a related poetic
movement called **imagism.** The imagist and symbolist styles
would prevail in poetry until the mid-twentieth century.

IDENTIFY

Re-read lines 104–115. Name
three characteristics of the
Hemingway hero.

_____

_____

_____

_____

_____

_____

_____

_____

_____

_____

_____

_____

_____

_____

_____

_____

IDENTIFY

Pause at line 126. Circle the
names of the poets who
experimented with the style
called **symbolism.**

COMPARE & CONTRAST

Pause at line 139. How was Robert Frost's poetry different from Eliot's and Pound's poetry?

_____

_____

_____

_____

_____

INTERPRET

Re-read lines 142–151. How did African American poetry during the Harlem Renaissance influence American culture?

_____

_____

_____

_____

INTERPRET

Re-read lines 152–157. What still seems "modern" about Modernism?

_____

_____

_____

_____

_____

_____

_____

Voices of American Character

130 Meanwhile other American poets rejected modernist trends. These poets stayed at home and said what they had to say in plain American speech. Their individual accents reveal the regional diversity of American life and character. Of these poets the greatest was Robert Frost (page 249). Frost's poems were written in ordinary New England speech. He had a gift for taking the most conventional poetic forms and giving them a twist all his own. Frost's ability to bring his own personality to verse resulted in a poetic voice that was unique and impossible to imitate.

The Harlem Renaissance: Voices of the African American Experience

140 In the early 1920s, a group of black poets focused directly on the unique contributions of African American culture to America. Their poetry based its rhythms on spirituals and jazz, its lyrics on songs known as the blues, and its diction on the street talk of the ghettos. African American lyric poets, especially Langston Hughes (page 259), brought literary distinction to the broad movement of artists known as the **Harlem Renaissance**. When African American poetry, along with music, became part of the
150 Jazz Age, it helped usher in a new appreciation of the role of black talent in American culture.

The American Dream Revisited

The writers of the modernist era—some of the best that America has produced—experimented boldly with forms and subject matter. But they were still trying to find the answers to basic human questions: Who are we? Where are we going? What values should guide us on the search for our human identity?

The River-Merchant's Wife: A Letter by Ezra Pound

LITERARY FOCUS: IMAGERY

Which of the following sentences helps you visualize the scene: "We huddled around the campfire, which hissed and crackled in the crisp night air" or "We sat in front of the campfire at night"? The first sentence uses imagery to create a vivid picture of the campfire scene. **Imagery** is language that creates vivid sensory impressions and suggests emotional states. Most images appeal to our sense of sight. However, images may also appeal to our senses of taste, smell, hearing, and touch. Imagery can also suggest emotional states, such as happiness, sadness, or anger.

Ezra Pound based "The River-Merchant's Wife: A Letter" on a poem by Li Po (701–762), In tribute to the great Chinese poet. As you read the poem, notice how simple words are used to evoke vivid images.

READING SKILLS: PARAPHRASING

A **paraphrase** is a restatement of the author's ideas in your own words. Unlike a summary, which is short and includes only the most important details, a paraphrase is often as long as or longer than the original text and restates all the details. Paraphrasing is a useful skill that can help you explain complicated ideas or clarify your understanding of difficult passages. Here is a paraphrase of a poem by Emily Dickinson. Notice that the paraphrase is longer than the poem.

Poem	Paraphrase
Fame is a bee. It has a song— It has a sting— Ah, too, it has a wing.	Fame is like a bee because it can bring joy (the bee's "song"); it can hurt (a bee's sting); and it can disappear, just as a bee can fly away.

The River-Merchant's Wife: A Letter

Ezra Pound

IMAGERY

In lines 1–6, what feelings are evoked by the **images** of the children playing?

_____

_____

_____

INTERPRET

Re-read lines 7–9. How would you describe the speaker's early relationship with her husband?

_____

_____

_____

INTERPRET

Re-read lines 11–14. The speaker's desire to be with her husband, even after death—"my dust to be mingled with yours"—is a **symbol** of her eternal love. What does her lack of interest in climbing the lookout tower represent? *(Grade 9–10 Review)*

_____

_____

_____

While my hair was still cut straight across my forehead
Played I about the front gate, pulling flowers.
You came by on bamboo stilts, playing horse,
You walked about my seat, playing with blue plums.
5 And we went on living in the village of Chokan:
Two small people, without dislike or suspicion.

At fourteen I married My Lord you.
I never laughed, being bashful.
Lowering my head, I looked at the wall.
10 Called to, a thousand times, I never looked back.

At fifteen I stopped scowling,
I desired my dust to be mingled with yours
Forever and forever and forever.
Why should I climb the lookout?

15 At sixteen you departed
You went into far Ku-to-yen, by the river of swirling eddies,
And you have been gone five months.
The monkeys make sorrowful noise overhead.

You dragged your feet when you went out.
20 By the gate now, the moss is grown, the different mosses,
Too deep to clear them away!
The leaves fall early this autumn, in wind.

Figure Crossing a Bridge from *Album of Eight Landscape Paintings* by Shen Chou.

PARAPHRASE

Paraphrase, or describe in your own words, what happens in lines 15–17.

_____

_____

_____

_____

_____

IMAGERY

How does the **imagery** in line 18 reflect the speaker's own feelings?

_____

_____

_____

INTERPRET

In lines 23–25, why does the speaker say the paired butterflies hurt her?

_____

_____

_____

INFER

Why does the speaker want to go and meet her husband?

_____

_____

_____

The paired butterflies are already yellow with August

Over the grass in the West garden;

25   They hurt me. I grow older.

If you are coming down through the narrows of the river Kiang,

Please let me know beforehand.

And I will come out to meet you

         As far as Cho-fu-Sa.

                              —Li T'ai Po

The River-Merchant's Wife: A Letter

Reading Skills: Paraphrasing Paraphrasing can help you understand what a poet is saying. In the chart below are three passages from "The River-Merchant's Wife: A Letter." In the right-hand column, paraphrase each passage in your own words.

Passage from Poem	Paraphrase
At fourteen I married My Lord you. I never laughed, being bashful. Lowering my head, I looked at the wall. Called to, a thousand times, I never looked back. (lines 7–10)	
At fifteen I stopped scowling, I desired my dust to be mingled with yours Forever and forever and forever. Why should I climb the lookout? (lines 11–14)	
The paired butterflies are already yellow with August Over the grass in the West garden; They hurt me. I grow older. (lines 23–25)	

 Check your Standards Mastery at the back of this book.

The Love Song of J. Alfred Prufrock by T. S. Eliot

LITERARY FOCUS: DRAMATIC MONOLOGUE AND STREAM OF CONSCIOUSNESS

A **dramatic monologue** is a poem in which one character speaks directly to one or more listeners. In Eliot's poem the words are spoken by a man named Prufrock. In a dramatic monologue, you learn everything about the setting, the situation, supporting characters, and even the speaker's own personality from the speaker's words. Like people in real life, speakers in dramatic monologues give their own spin to the events and circumstances around them. As you read "The Love Song of J. Alfred Prufrock," you will begin to see the world as Prufrock sees it. Is it the way you see the world?

One reason that Eliot's poem may seem difficult at first is that it uses a **stream-of-consciousness** technique. With stream of consciousness, the writer tries to imitate the natural flow of a character's thoughts, memories, and reflections as the character experiences them. In attempting to capture the random movement of a character's thoughts, the logical connections and transitions of ordinary prose are often left out. Instead, the character jumps from one idea or association to another, as one thought suddenly triggers another, seemingly unrelated, one.

READING SKILLS: IDENTIFYING MAIN IDEAS

The **main idea** of a passage or a work of literature is its most important message, opinion, or lesson. Identifying the main ideas will help you better understand the meaning of a selection. In "The Love Song of J. Alfred Prufrock," look for main ideas about war (the poem was published during World War I), people, and life.

> **REVIEW SKILLS**
>
> As you read "The Love Song of J. Alfred Prufrock," look for the following literary device.
>
> **CHARACTER TRAITS**
> The qualities that a character in a work of literature displays, such as values, habits, likes, and dislikes.

Reading Standard 3.1 Analyze characteristics of subgenres (dramatic monologue).

Reading Standard 3.4 (Grade 9–10 Review) Determine characters' traits by what the characters say about themselves in narration, dialogue, dramatic monologue, and soliloquy.

The LOVE SONG
of J. Alfred Prufrock

T. S. Eliot

BACKGROUND

Thomas Stearns Eliot—known to readers as T. S. Eliot—was born in St. Louis to an intellectual family with deep New England roots. After graduating from Harvard, Eliot studied for a time in Paris and then moved to London to begin his career as a poet. In 1915, just a year after the outbreak of World War I, Eliot published "The Love Song of J. Alfred Prufrock," the poem that made him famous.

"Prufrock" captures the mood of helpless paralysis that many Europeans and Americans felt in the face of the modern forces of technology and industrialism. The individual no longer seemed to count for anything; the war in Europe had quickly turned into a mechanized slaughter in which millions of young men were losing their lives, it seemed, for nothing.

DRAMATIC MONOLOGUE

Circle the pronouns in line 1 that indicate this is a **dramatic monologue,** a poem whose speaker addresses one or more listeners.

INTERPRET

Given the startling **simile**—a comparison using *like, as,* or *than*—in lines 2–3, how do you picture the evening?

_____

_____

_____

_____

_____

_____

S'io credessi che mia risposta fosse

a persona che mai tornasse al mondo,

questa fiamma staria senza più scosse.

Ma per ciò che giammai di questo fondo

non tornò vivo alcun, s'i'odo il vero,

senza tema d'infamia ti rispondo.[1]

Let us go then, you and I,

When the evening is spread out against the sky

Like a patient etherized[2] upon a table;

Let us go, through certain half-deserted streets,

---

1. This quotation is from Dante's epic poem *The Divine Comedy* (1321). The speaker is Guido da Montefeltro, a man sent to Hell for dispensing evil advice. He speaks from a flame that quivers when he talks: "If I thought my answer were to one who ever could return to the world, this flame should shake no more; but since none ever did return alive from this depth, if what I hear be true, without fear of infamy I answer this" (*Inferno,* Canto 27, lines 61–66). Think of Prufrock as speaking from his own personal hell.
2. **etherized:** anesthetized; paralyzed.

5   The muttering retreats

Of restless nights in one-night cheap hotels

And sawdust restaurants with oyster-shells:

Streets that follow like a tedious argument

Of insidious intent

10   To lead you to an overwhelming question . . .

Oh, do not ask, "What is it?"

Let us go and make our visit.

In the room the women come and go

Talking of Michelangelo.[3]

15   The yellow fog that rubs its back upon the window-panes,

The yellow smoke that rubs its muzzle on the window-panes,

Licked its tongue into the corners of the evening,

Lingered upon the pools that stand in drains,

Let fall upon its back the soot that falls from chimneys,

20   Slipped by the terrace, made a sudden leap,

And seeing that it was a soft October night,

Curled once about the house, and fell asleep.

And indeed there will be time

For the yellow smoke that slides along the street

25   Rubbing its back upon the window-panes;

There will be time, there will be time

To prepare a face to meet the faces that you meet;

There will be time to murder and create,

And time for all the works and days of hands

30   That lift and drop a question on your plate;

Time for you and time for me,

And time yet for a hundred indecisions,

And for a hundred visions and revisions,

Before the taking of a toast and tea.

---

3. **Michelangelo:** Michelangelo Buonarroti (1475–1564), a great artist of
the Italian Renaissance.

INFER

Where does the speaker want to take his companion in lines 4–7? Who might his companion be?

_____

_____

_____

_____

_____

_____

IDENTIFY

What is the fog compared to in the **extended metaphor** in lines 15–22? Underline words and phrases that develop the comparison.

_____

_____

IDENTIFY MAIN IDEAS

In lines 23–34, circle the words that are repeated. How would you state the **main idea** of this stanza?

_____

_____

_____

_____

35 In the room the women come and go

Talking of Michelangelo.

FLUENCY

Read the boxed passage aloud twice. Focus on conveying simple meaning the first time around. During your second reading, try to bring the speaker's words to life.

DRAMATIC MONOLOGUE

What do you learn about Prufrock's **character traits** from what he says about himself in lines 37–48? *(Grade 9–10 Review)*

_____

_____

_____

_____

_____

_____

_____

_____

_____

And indeed there will be time

To wonder, "Do I dare?" and, "Do I dare?"

Time to turn back and descend the stair,

40   With a bald spot in the middle of my hair—

(They will say: "How his hair is growing thin!")

My morning coat,[4] my collar mounting firmly to the chin,

My necktie rich and modest, but asserted by a simple pin—

(They will say: "But how his arms and legs are thin!")

45   Do I dare

Disturb the universe?

In a minute there is time

For decisions and revisions which a minute will reverse.

For I have known them all already, known them all—

50   Have known the evenings, mornings, afternoons,

I have measured out my life with coffee spoons;

I know the voices dying with a dying fall[5]

Beneath the music from a farther room.

        So how should I presume?

55   And I have known the eyes already, known them all—

The eyes that fix you in a formulated[6] phrase,

And when I am formulated, sprawling on a pin,

When I am pinned and wriggling on the wall,

Then how should I begin

60   To spit out all the butt-ends of my days and ways?

        And how should I presume?

INTERPRET

How would you describe a life measured out by coffee spoons (line 51)?

_____

_____

_____

_____

_____

_____

---

4. **morning coat:** formal daytime dress for men.
5. **dying fall:** in music, notes that fade away.
6. **formulated** *v.* used as *adj.:* reduced to a formula and made insignificant.

And I have known the arms already, known them all—

Arms that are braceleted and white and bare

(But in the lamplight, downed with light brown hair!)

65   Is it perfume from a dress

That makes me so digress?

Arms that lie along a table, or wrap about a shawl.

     And should I then presume?

     And how should I begin?

    . . . . .

70   Shall I say, I have gone at dusk through narrow streets

And watched the smoke that rises from the pipes

Of lonely men in shirt-sleeves, leaning out of windows? . . .

I should have been a pair of ragged claws

Scuttling across the floors of silent seas.

    . . . . .

75   And the afternoon, the evening, sleeps so peacefully!

Smoothed by long fingers,

Asleep . . . tired . . . or it malingers,⁷

Stretched on the floor, here beside you and me.

Should I, after tea and cakes and ices,

80   Have the strength to force the moment to its crisis?

But though I have wept and fasted, wept and prayed,

Though I have seen my head (grown slightly bald)

     brought in upon a platter,⁸

I am no prophet—and here's no great matter;

I have seen the moment of my greatness flicker,

85   And I have seen the eternal Footman hold my coat,

     and snicker,

---

7. **malingers:** pretends to be sick to get out of work or duty.
8. **my head . . . a platter:** biblical allusion to the execution of John the Baptist (Mark 6:17–28; Matthew 14:3–11). The dancing of Salome so pleased Herod Antipas, ruler of ancient Galilee, that he offered her any reward she desired. Goaded by her mother, who hated John, Salome asked for John's head. Herod ordered the prophet beheaded and his head delivered on a serving plate.

INTERPRET

What does Prufrock compare himself to in lines 57–58? What does this **metaphor** tell you about him?

_____

_____

_____

_____

_____

IDENTIFY MAIN IDEAS

Prufrock wonders if he should tell his story, then decides to begin. What **main idea** about life does he express in lines 70–72?

_____

_____

_____

INTERPRET

The "eternal Footman" is a **metaphor** for death. What vision of his future does Prufrock see in line 85?

_____

_____

_____

_____

_____

_____

_____

_____

_____

_____

_____

_____

DRAMATIC
MONOLOGUE

The speaker continues to ask questions of his listener(s) in lines 99–110. Underline the question he repeats.

INTERPRET

What do you think the woman in lines 96–98 and 107–110 **symbolizes,** or represents?

_____

_____

_____

_____

_____

_____

_____

_____

And in short, I was afraid.

And would it have been worth it, after all,

After the cups, the marmalade, the tea,

Among the porcelain, among some talk of you and me,

90 Would it have been worth while,

To have bitten off the matter with a smile,

To have squeezed the universe into a ball

To roll it towards some overwhelming question,

To say: "I am Lazarus,[9] come from the dead,

95 Come back to tell you all, I shall tell you all"—

If one, settling a pillow by her head,

     Should say: "That is not what I meant at all.

     That is not it, at all."

And would it have been worth it, after all,

100 Would it have been worth while,

After the sunsets and the dooryards and the sprinkled streets,

After the novels, after the teacups, after the skirts that trail

     along the floor—

And this, and so much more?—

It is impossible to say just what I mean!

But as if a magic lantern[10] threw the nerves in patterns on a

105   screen:

Would it have been worth while

If one, settling a pillow or throwing off a shawl,

And turning toward the window, should say:

     "That is not it at all,

110   That is not what I meant, at all."

     . . . . . .

No! I am not Prince Hamlet, nor was meant to be;

Am an attendant lord, one that will do

To swell a progress,[11] start a scene or two,

---

9. **Lazarus:** In the Bible, a man that Jesus brought back from the dead (John 11: 38–44).
10. **magic lantern:** early type of projector that could magnify and project images.
11. **swell a progress:** fill out a scene in a play or pageant by serving as an extra.

115　Advise the prince; no doubt, an easy tool,
　　　Deferential, glad to be of use,
　　　Politic, cautious, and meticulous;
　　　Full of high sentence,[12] but a bit obtuse;[13]
　　　At times, indeed, almost ridiculous—
　　　Almost, at times, the Fool.

120　I grow old . . . I grow old . . .
　　　I shall wear the bottoms of my trousers rolled.

　　　Shall I part my hair behind? Do I dare to eat a peach?
　　　I shall wear white flannel trousers, and walk upon the beach.
　　　I have heard the mermaids singing, each to each.

125　I do not think that they will sing to me.

　　　I have seen them riding seaward on the waves
　　　Combing the white hair of the waves blown back
　　　When the wind blows the water white and black.

　　　We have lingered in the chambers of the sea
130　By sea-girls wreathed with seaweed red and brown
　　　Till human voices wake us, and we drown.

---

12. **high sentence:** pompous talk.
13. **obtuse:** slow to understand.

The Love Song of J. Alfred Prufrock

Reading Skills: Identifying Main Ideas The chart below lists four **main ideas** from "The Love Song of J. Alfred Prufrock." In the right column, fill in at least two passages from the poem to support each main idea.

Main Idea	Lines from the Poem
People lead lonely existences.	
People have trouble communicating their feelings.	
People have a hard time being decisive.	
Ordinary life keeps people from following their dreams.	

 Check your Standards Mastery at the back of this book.

A Rose for Emily by William Faulkner

LITERARY FOCUS: SETTING

Most works of fiction have a specific setting that is an important element of the story. The **setting** is the time and location in which a story takes place. Setting also refers to the customs and social conditions of that place and time.

You may find some of the language in "A Rose for Emily" offensive. Faulkner included it in order to portray accurately a racially segregated southern town at the turn of the last century.

Setting the Story   Knowing the setting of a story gives you certain expectations or ideas about what it will be like. For example, if the setting is a large Victorian mansion, you might expect either a murder mystery or a romance. The chart below lists several settings. In the right column, jot down what the setting leads you to expect from the story.

Setting	What the Story Might Be Like
a spaceship	
the Arctic	
a tropical island	
1800s California	

READING SKILLS: MAKING INFERENCES ABOUT CHARACTER

The personalities of literary characters are often as complicated as those of people you know in life—and just as hard to get to know. One way to learn what a character is like is by making inferences. An **inference** is a good guess that is based on information in the text and on your own knowledge and experience. To make an inference about a character, you look for clues in the character's speech, appearance, and behavior; you listen to what other characters say about him or her; and you compare the character's behavior with that of other people you know.

REVIEW SKILLS

As you read "A Rose for Emily," look for the following literary devices.

FORESHADOWING
The use of hints and clues to suggest what will happen later in a plot.

FLASHBACK
A scene that interrupts the normal chronological sequence of events in a story to show an event that took place earlier in time.

Reading Standard 3.5c
Evaluate the philosophical, political, religious, ethical, and social influences of the historical period that shaped the characters, plots, and settings.

Reading Standard 3.6 (Grade 9–10 Review)
Analyze and trace an author's development of time and sequence, including the use of complex literary devices (e.g., foreshadowing, flashbacks).

A Rose for Emily

William Faulkner

I

When Miss Emily Grierson died, our whole town went to her
funeral: the men through a sort of respectful affection for a
fallen monument, the women mostly out of curiosity to see the
inside of her house, which no one save an old manservant—a
combined gardener and cook—had seen in at least ten years.

It was a big, squarish frame house that had once been white,
decorated with cupolas[1] and spires and scrolled balconies in the
heavily lightsome style of the seventies,[2] set on what had once
been our most select street. But garages and cotton gins had
10 encroached and obliterated even the august names of that
neighborhood; only Miss Emily's house was left, lifting its
stubborn and coquettish decay above the cotton wagons and
the gasoline pumps—an eyesore among eyesores. And now
Miss Emily had gone to join the representatives of those august
names where they lay in the cedar-bemused cemetery among
the ranked and anonymous graves of Union and Confederate
soldiers who fell at the battle of Jefferson.

Alive, Miss Emily had been a tradition, a duty, and a care; a
sort of hereditary obligation upon the town, dating from that
20 day in 1894 when Colonel Sartoris, the mayor—he who fathered
the edict that no Negro woman should appear on the streets
without an apron—**remitted** her taxes, the dispensation dating
from the death of her father on into perpetuity.[3] Not that Miss
Emily would have accepted charity. Colonel Sartoris invented an

---

1. **cupolas** (kyo͞o′pə·ləz) *n. pl.*: small, dome-shaped structures built on a roof.
2. **the seventies:** the 1870s.
3. **perpetuity** (pur′pə·to͞o′ə·tē) *n.:* eternity.

Sidebar

involved tale to the effect that Miss Emily's father had loaned money to the town, which the town, as a matter of business, preferred this way of repaying. Only a man of Colonel Sartoris' generation and thought could have invented it, and only a woman could have believed it.

30   When the next generation, with its more modern ideas, became mayors and aldermen, this arrangement created some little dissatisfaction. On the first of the year they mailed her a tax notice. February came, and there was no reply. They wrote her a formal letter, asking her to call at the sheriff's office at her convenience. A week later the mayor wrote her himself, offering to call or to send his car for her and received in reply a note on paper of an **archaic** shape in a thin, flowing calligraphy in faded ink, to the effect that she no longer went out at all. The tax notice was also enclosed, without comment.

40   They called a special meeting of the Board of Aldermen. A deputation waited upon her, knocked at the door through which no visitor had passed since she ceased giving china-painting lessons eight or ten years earlier. They were admitted by the old Negro into a dim hall from which a stairway mounted into still more shadow. It smelled of dust and disuse—a close, dank smell. The Negro led them into the parlor. It was furnished in heavy, leather-covered furniture. When the Negro opened the blinds of one window they could see that the leather was cracked; and when they sat down, a faint dust rose sluggishly
50 about their thighs spinning with slow motes in the single sun-ray. On a tarnished gilt easel before the fireplace stood a crayon portrait of Miss Emily's father.

They rose when she entered—a small, fat woman in black, with a thin gold chain descending to her waist and vanishing into her belt, leaning on an ebony cane with a tarnished gold head. Her skeleton was small and spare; perhaps that was why what would have been merely plumpness in another was obesity in her. She looked bloated, like a body long submerged in motionless water, and of that pallid hue. Her eyes, lost in the fatty

INFER

Underline what the Colonel did to help Miss Emily (lines 18–23). Why do you think he helped her?

_____

_____

_____

VOCABULARY

remitted (ri·mit′id) v.: canceled; refrained from enforcing payment.

archaic (är·kā′ik) adj.: old-fashioned.

COMPARE & CONTRAST

Pause at line 39. Compare the attitudes of the younger leaders with those of Colonel Sartoris's generation.

_____

_____

_____

_____

_____

SETTING

Circle the words starting with d in lines 43–46. What do these words tell you about Miss Emily's house?

_____

_____

ridges of her face, looked like two small pieces of coal pressed into a lump of dough as they moved from one face to another while the visitors stated their errand.

She did not ask them to sit. She just stood in the door and listened quietly until the spokesman came to a stumbling halt. Then they could hear the invisible watch ticking at the end of the gold chain.

INFER

Re-read lines 52–66. What can you infer about Miss Emily's character based on her appearance and behavior?

_____

_____

_____

_____

_____

_____

_____

_____

FLUENCY

Read the boxed passage aloud twice. Try to capture in your voice Miss Emily's insistent tone. The authorities should sound important but frustrated.

WORD STUDY

The word *vanquished* (line 81) means "conquered; defeated." *Horse and foot* (line 81) is an **idiom** meaning "completely."

IDENTIFY

The author introduces a **flashback** in lines 81–89. Underline when the flashback takes place. *(Grade 9–10 Review)*

Her voice was dry and cold. "I have no taxes in Jefferson. Colonel Sartoris explained it to me. Perhaps one of you can gain access to the city records and satisfy yourselves."

70 "But we have. We are the city authorities, Miss Emily. Didn't you get a notice from the sheriff, signed by him?"

"I received a paper, yes," Miss Emily said. "Perhaps he considers himself the sheriff . . . I have no taxes in Jefferson."

"But there is nothing on the books to show that, you see. We must go by the—"

"See Colonel Sartoris. I have no taxes in Jefferson."

"But, Miss Emily—"

"See Colonel Sartoris." (Colonel Sartoris had been dead almost ten years.) "I have no taxes in Jefferson. Tobe!" The
80 Negro appeared. "Show these gentlemen out."

II

So she vanquished them, horse and foot, just as she had vanquished their fathers thirty years before about the smell. That was two years after her father's death and a short time after her sweetheart—the one we believed would marry her—had deserted her. After her father's death she went out very little; after her sweetheart went away, people hardly saw her at all. A few of the ladies had the temerity[4] to call, but were not received, and the only sign of life about the place was the Negro man—a young man then—going in and out with a market basket.

90 "Just as if a man—any man—could keep a kitchen properly,"

---

4. **temerity** *n.:* foolish boldness; rashness.

My Mother (1921) by George Wesley Bellows. Oil on canvas
(210.9 cm × 124.5 cm).

SETTING

How does the use of the racial slur in line 100 reflect the period in which the story is set?

_____

_____

_____

_____

INTERPRET

What social belief is shown in Judge Stevens's comment in lines 111–112?

_____

_____

_____

_____

PARAPHRASE

Underline the words and phrases in lines 113–118 that describe what the men do at Miss Emily's house. In your own words, tell what is happening in this episode.

_____

_____

_____

_____

_____

_____

_____

the ladies said; so they were not surprised when the smell developed. It was another link between the gross, teeming world and the high and mighty Griersons.

A neighbor, a woman, complained to the mayor, Judge Stevens, eighty years old.

"But what will you have me do about it, madam?" he said.

"Why, send her word to stop it," the woman said. "Isn't there a law?"

"I'm sure that won't be necessary," Judge Stevens said. "It's probably just a snake or a rat that nigger of hers killed in the yard. I'll speak to him about it."

The next day he received two more complaints, one from a man who came in diffident deprecation.[5] "We really must do something about it, Judge. I'd be the last one in the world to bother Miss Emily, but we've got to do something." That night the Board of Aldermen met—three graybeards and one younger man, a member of the rising generation.

"It's simple enough," he said. "Send her word to have her place cleaned up. Give her a certain time to do it in, and if she don't . . ."

"Dammit, sir," Judge Stevens said, "will you accuse a lady to her face of smelling bad?"

So the next night, after midnight, four men crossed Miss Emily's lawn and slunk about the house like burglars, sniffing along the base of the brickwork and at the cellar openings while one of them performed a regular sowing motion with his hand out of a sack slung from his shoulder. They broke open the cellar door and sprinkled lime there, and in all the outbuildings. As they recrossed the lawn, a window that had been dark was lighted and Miss Emily sat in it, the light behind her, and her upright torso motionless as that of an idol. They crept quietly across the lawn and into the shadow of the locusts that lined the street. After a week or two the smell went away.

___

5. **diffident deprecation:** timid disapproval.

That was when people had begun to feel really sorry for her. People in our town, remembering how old lady Wyatt, her great-aunt, had gone completely crazy at last, believed that the Griersons held themselves a little too high for what they really were. None of the young men were quite good enough for Miss Emily and such. We had long thought of them as a tableau,[6] Miss Emily a slender figure in white in the background, her father a spraddled silhouette in the foreground, his back to her and clutching a horsewhip, the two of them framed by the back-flung front door. So when she got to be thirty and was still single, we were not pleased exactly, but **vindicated;** even with insanity in the family she wouldn't have turned down all of her chances if they had really materialized.

When her father died, it got about that the house was all that was left to her; and in a way, people were glad. At last they could pity Miss Emily. Being left alone, and a **pauper,** she had become humanized. Now she too would know the old thrill and the old despair of a penny more or less.

The day after his death all the ladies prepared to call at the house and offer condolence and aid, as is our custom. Miss Emily met them at the door, dressed as usual and with no trace of grief on her face. She told them that her father was not dead. She did that for three days, with the ministers calling on her, and the doctors, trying to persuade her to let them dispose of the body. Just as they were about to resort to law and force, she broke down, and they buried her father quickly.

We did not say she was crazy then. We believed she had to do that. We remembered all the young men her father had driven away, and we knew that with nothing left, she would have to cling to that which had robbed her, as people will.

---

6. **tableau** *n.:* striking dramatic scene, usually motionless.

IDENTIFY

Underline the detail in lines 124–130 that explains why the townspeople thought the Griersons acted too proudly.

INFER

What can you infer about Emily's father and his relationship with Emily from the description in lines 129–133?

_____

_____

_____

_____

VOCABULARY

vindicated (vin′də·kāt′id) *v.* used as *adj.:* proved correct.
pauper (pô′pər) *n.:* extremely poor person.

INTERPRET

Pause at line 149. Emily shows no grief while denying her father's death and refusing to allow his burial. What two different meanings could the phrase *she broke down* (lines 148–149) have?

_____

_____

_____

_____

_____

III

SETTING

What do the details in lines 158–170 reveal about the historical period in which the story is set?

_____

_____

_____

_____

_____

_____

_____

_____

_____

_____

_____

INFER

Pause at line 170. Who is Homer Barron? What have you learned about his character so far?

_____

_____

_____

_____

_____

_____

_____

_____

She was sick for a long time. When we saw her again, her hair was cut short, making her look like a girl, with a vague resemblance to those angels in colored church windows—sort of tragic and serene.

The town had just let the contracts for paving the sidewalks, and in the summer after her father's death they began the work. The construction company came with niggers and mules and machinery, and a foreman named Homer Barron, a Yankee—a big, dark, ready man, with a big voice and eyes lighter than his face. The little boys would follow in groups to hear him cuss the niggers, and the niggers singing in time to the rise and fall of picks. Pretty soon he knew everybody in town. Whenever you heard a lot of laughing anywhere about the square, Homer Barron would be in the center of the group. Presently we began to see him and Miss Emily on Sunday afternoons driving in the yellow-wheeled buggy and the matched team of bays from the livery stable.

At first we were glad that Miss Emily would have an interest, because the ladies all said, "Of course a Grierson would not think seriously of a Northerner, a day laborer." But there were still others, older people, who said that even grief could not cause a real lady to forget *noblesse oblige*[7]—without calling it *noblesse oblige.* They just said, "Poor Emily. Her kinsfolk should come to her." She had some kin in Alabama; but years ago her father had fallen out with them over the estate of old lady Wyatt, the crazy woman, and there was no communication between the two families. They had not even been represented at the funeral.

And as soon as the old people said, "Poor Emily," the whispering began. "Do you suppose it's really so?" they said to one another. "Of course it is. What else could . . ." This behind their

---

7. *noblesse oblige* (nō·bles′ō·blēzh′): from the French for "nobility obliges"— that is, the supposed obligation of the upper classes to act nobly or kindly toward the lower classes.

hands; rustling of craned[8] silk and satin behind jalousies[9] closed upon the sun of Sunday afternoon as the thin, swift, clop-clop-clop of the matched team passed: "Poor Emily."

She carried her head high enough—even when we believed that she was fallen. It was as if she demanded more than ever the recognition of her dignity as the last Grierson; as if it had wanted that touch of earthiness to reaffirm her imperviousness. Like when she bought the rat poison, the arsenic. That was over a year after they had begun to say "Poor Emily," and while the two female cousins were visiting her.

"I want some poison," she said to the druggist. She was over thirty then, still a slight woman, though thinner than usual, with cold, haughty black eyes in a face the flesh of which was strained across the temples and about the eye-sockets as you imagine a lighthouse-keeper's face ought to look. "I want some poison," she said.

"Yes, Miss Emily. What kind? For rats and such? I'd recom—"

"I want the best you have. I don't care what kind."

The druggist named several. "They'll kill anything up to an elephant. But what you want is—"

"Arsenic," Miss Emily said. "Is that a good one?"

"Is . . . arsenic? Yes, ma'am. But what you want—"

"I want arsenic."

The druggist looked down at her. She looked back at him, erect, her face like a strained flag. "Why, of course," the druggist said. "If that's what you want. But the law requires you to tell what you are going to use it for."

Miss Emily just stared at him, her head tilted back in order to look him eye for eye, until he looked away and went and got the arsenic and wrapped it up. The Negro delivery boy brought her the package; the druggist didn't come back. When she opened

---

8. **craned** *v.* used as *adj:* stretched.
9. **jalousies** (jal'ə·sēz') *n. pl.:* windows, shades, or doors made of overlapping, adjustable slats.

190

200

210

CLARIFY

Pause at line 186. What two reasons do the townspeople have for thinking Miss Emily has disgraced herself with Homer Barron?

_____
_____
_____
_____
_____
_____

PREDICT

Circle Miss Emily's words to the druggist in line 194 that may **foreshadow** an important plot development. What do you think will happen? *(Grade 9–10 Review)*

_____
_____

INFER

Re-read lines 194–210. Why do you think Emily and the druggist behave the way they do?

_____
_____
_____
_____
_____

_____

_____

_____

_____

ANALYZE

Re-read lines 227–234. Underline the details that explain how the people of the town behaved. How do their actions reflect the social and ethical standards of the period?

_____

_____

_____

_____

_____

CLARIFY

Pause at line 243. Why do the townspeople think Miss Emily has gotten married?

_____

_____

_____

_____

_____

the package at home there was written on the box, under the skull and bones: "For rats."

IV

So the next day we all said, "She will kill herself"; and we said it would be the best thing. When she had first begun to be seen with Homer Barron, we had said, "She will marry him." Then we
220 said, "She will persuade him yet," because Homer himself had remarked—he liked men, and it was known that he drank with the younger men in the Elks' Club—that he was not a marrying man. Later we said, "Poor Emily," behind the jalousies as they passed on Sunday afternoon in the glittering buggy, Miss Emily with her head high and Homer Barron with his hat cocked and a cigar in his teeth, reins and whip in a yellow glove.

Then some of the ladies began to say that it was a disgrace to the town and a bad example to the young people. The men did not want to interfere, but at last the ladies forced the Baptist
230 minister—Miss Emily's people were Episcopal—to call upon her. He would never divulge what happened during that interview, but he refused to go back again. The next Sunday they again drove about the streets, and the following day the minister's wife wrote to Miss Emily's relations in Alabama.

So she had blood-kin under her roof again and we sat back to watch developments. At first nothing happened. Then we were sure that they were to be married. We learned that Miss Emily had been to the jeweler's and ordered a man's toilet set[10] in silver, with the letters H. B. on each piece. Two days later we
240 learned that she had bought a complete outfit of men's clothing, including a nightshirt, and we said, "They are married." We were really glad. We were glad because the two female cousins were even more Grierson than Miss Emily had ever been.

So we were not surprised when Homer Barron—the streets had been finished some time since—was gone. We were a little

---

10. **toilet set:** set of grooming aids, such as a hand mirror, hairbrush, and comb.

disappointed that there was not a public blowing-off, but we believed that he had gone on to prepare for Miss Emily's coming, or to give her a chance to get rid of the cousins. (By that time it was a cabal,[11] and we were all Miss Emily's allies to help **circumvent** the cousins.) Sure enough, after another week they departed. And, as we had expected all along, within three days Homer Barron was back in town. A neighbor saw the Negro man admit him at the kitchen door at dusk one evening.

And that was the last we saw of Homer Barron. And of Miss Emily for some time. The Negro man went in and out with the market basket, but the front door remained closed. Now and then we would see her at a window for a moment, as the men did that night when they sprinkled the lime, but for almost six months she did not appear on the streets. Then we knew that this was to be expected too; as if that quality of her father which had thwarted her woman's life so many times had been too **virulent** and too furious to die.

When we next saw Miss Emily, she had grown fat and her hair was turning gray. During the next few years it grew grayer and grayer until it attained an even pepper-and-salt iron-gray, when it ceased turning. Up to the day of her death at seventy-four it was still that vigorous iron-gray, like the hair of an active man.

From that time on her front door remained closed, save for a period of six or seven years, when she was about forty, during which she gave lessons in china-painting. She fitted up a studio in one of the downstairs rooms, where the daughters and grand-daughters of Colonel Sartoris' contemporaries were sent to her with the same regularity and in the same spirit that they were sent to church on Sundays with a twenty-five-cent piece for the collection plate. Meanwhile her taxes had been remitted.

Then the newer generation became the backbone and the spirit of the town, and the painting pupils grew up and fell away

---

11. **cabal** (kə·bäl') *n.*: small group involved in a secret intrigue.

INTERPRET

Re-read lines 254–262. Why are the townspeople not surprised when Homer Barron and Miss Emily are not seen?

VOCABULARY

circumvent (sur'kəm·vent') *v.*: avoid by cleverness or deceit.

virulent (vir'yoo·lənt) *adj.*: full of hate; venomous.

INTERPRET

Underline the **simile** in lines 267–269. What does it tell you about Miss Emily's character? Why is the figure of speech **ironic**?

_____

_____

_____

_____

_____

_____

_____

INFER

Re-read lines 286–292. What does this information reveal about Miss Emily's character?

_____

_____

_____

_____

_____

_____

_____

_____

_____

VOCABULARY

tranquil (traŋ′kwəl) *adj.:* calm; quiet.

perverse (pər·vʉrs′) *adj.:* odd; contrary.

280 and did not send their children to her with boxes of color and tedious brushes and pictures cut from the ladies' magazines. The front door closed upon the last one and remained closed for good. When the town got free postal delivery, Miss Emily alone refused to let them fas-ten the metal numbers above

290 her door and attach a mail-box to it. She would not lis-ten to them.

Daily, monthly, yearly we watched the Negro grow grayer and more stooped, going in and out with the market basket. Each December we sent her a tax notice, which would be

300 returned by the post office a week later, unclaimed. Now and then we would see her in one of the downstairs win-dows—she had evidently shut up the top floor of the house—like the carven torso of an idol in a niche, looking or not looking at us, we could never tell which. Thus she

310 passed from generation to generation—dear, inescapable, impervious, **tranquil,** and **perverse.**

That Which I Should Have Done I Did Not Do (1931–1941) by Ivan Le Lorraine Albright. Oil on canvas (246.5 cm × 91.5 cm).

And so she died. Fell ill in the house filled with dust and shadows, with only a doddering Negro man to wait on her. We did not even know she was sick; we had long since given up trying to get any information from the Negro. He talked to no one, probably not even to her, for his voice had grown harsh and rusty, as if from disuse.

320   She died in one of the downstairs rooms, in a heavy walnut bed with a curtain, her gray head propped on a pillow yellow and moldy with age and lack of sunlight.

V

The Negro met the first of the ladies at the front door and let them in, with their hushed, sibilant[12] voices and their quick, curious glances, and then he disappeared. He walked right through the house and out the back and was not seen again.

The two female cousins came at once. They held the funeral on the second day, with the town coming to look at Miss Emily beneath a mass of bought flowers, with the crayon face of her

330   father musing profoundly above the bier[13] and the ladies sibilant and macabre;[14] and the very old men—some in their brushed Confederate uniforms—on the porch and the lawn, talking of Miss Emily as if she had been a contemporary of theirs, believing that they had danced with her and courted her perhaps, confusing time with its mathematical progression, as the old do, to whom all the past is not a diminishing road but, instead, a huge meadow which no winter ever quite touches, divided from them now by the narrow bottle-neck of the most recent decade of years.

340   Already we knew that there was one room in that region above stairs which no one had seen in forty years, and which would have to be forced. They waited until Miss Emily was decently in the ground before they opened it.

ANALYZE

What attitudes do the towns-people show toward African Americans in lines 323–326?

_____

_____

_____

_____

_____

_____

_____

COMPARE & CONTRAST

Re-read lines 327–339. How does the scene at Miss Emily's funeral contrast with her relationship with the towns-people during her life?

_____

_____

_____

_____

PREDICT

Pause at line 343. What do you think the townspeople will find in the room?

_____

_____

_____

_____

---

12. **sibilant** (sib′ə·lənt) *adj.:* hissing.
13. **bier** (bir) *n.:* coffin and its supporting platform.
14. **macabre** (mə·käb′rə) *adj.:* focused on the gruesome; horrible.

SETTING

Re-read lines 344–354. What does this description tell you about the room?

_____

_____

_____

_____

VOCABULARY

acrid (ak′rid) *adj.:* bitter; irritating.

inextricable (in·eks′tri·kə·bəl) *adj.:* unable to be freed or disentangled from.

INFER

Pause at line 363. How do you think Homer Barron died?

_____

_____

_____

DRAW CONCLUSIONS

Re-read lines 364–367. Circle what the townspeople find on the second pillow. What horrifying conclusion can you draw from this detail?

_____

_____

_____

_____

The violence of breaking down the door seemed to fill this room with pervading dust. A thin, **acrid** pall as of the tomb seemed to lie everywhere upon this room decked and furnished as for a bridal: upon the valance curtains of faded rose color, upon the rose-shaded lights, upon the dressing table, upon the delicate array of crystal and the man's toilet things backed with
350 tarnished silver, silver so tarnished that the monogram was obscured. Among them lay a collar and tie, as if they had just been removed, which, lifted, left upon the surface a pale crescent in the dust. Upon a chair hung the suit, carefully folded; beneath it the two mute shoes and the discarded socks.

The man himself lay in the bed.

For a long while we just stood there, looking down at the profound and fleshless grin. The body had apparently once lain in the attitude of an embrace, but now the long sleep that outlasts love, that conquers even the grimace of love, had
360 cuckolded[15] him. What was left of him, rotted beneath what was left of the nightshirt, had become **inextricable** from the bed in which he lay; and upon him and upon the pillow beside him lay that even coating of the patient and biding dust.

Then we noticed that in the second pillow was the indentation of a head. One of us lifted something from it, and leaning forward, that faint and invisible dust dry and acrid in the nostrils, we saw a long strand of iron-gray hair.

---

15. **cuckolded** (kuk′əld·id) *v.:* betrayed; usually used to describe a husband whose wife has been unfaithful.

A Rose for Emily

Reading Skills: Making Inferences About Character   You make inferences about character based on clues in the text and on your own knowledge and experience. Some clues from "A Rose for Emily" are listed in the left-hand column of the chart below. In the right-hand column, fill in any inferences you can make about the character listed, based on the clue and on your own knowledge of what people are like.

Story Clue	Inferences About Character
"'But, Miss Emily—.' "'See Colonel Sartoris.' (Colonel Sartoris had been dead almost ten years.) 'I have no taxes in Jefferson. Tobe! . . . Show these gentlemen out.'" (lines 77–80)	**Miss Emily:**
". . . that day in 1894 when Colonel Sartoris, the mayor—he who fathered the edict that no Negro woman should appear on the streets without an apron—remitted [Miss Emily's] taxes . . ." (lines 19–22)	**Colonel Sartoris:**
"Whenever you heard a lot of laughing anywhere about the square, Homer Barron would be in the center of the group." (lines 165–167)	**Homer Barron:**
". . . Miss Emily a slender figure in white in the background, her father a spraddled silhouette in the foreground, his back to her and clutching a horsewhip . . ." (lines 130–132)	**Her father:**

A Rose for Emily

VOCABULARY IN CONTEXT

DIRECTIONS: Write words from the word box to complete the paragraph below. Not all words from the box will be used.

Word Box

remitted

archaic

vindicated

pauper

circumvent

virulent

tranquil

perverse

acrid

inextricable

William Faulkner never broke his binding, (1) _____ ties to the South. His decision to remain in Mississippi most of his life was (2) _____ by his brilliant literary career. However, while romantic Southern writers describe the sweet scent of magnolias, Faulkner reveals the (3) _____ odor of the society he knew so well. Many of the characters in his works have a contrary, (4) _____ love-hate relationship with their communities. While some of Faulkner's characters, such as Miss Emily, have a calm, almost (5) _____ appearance, they are burdened by angry, (6) _____ emotions below the surface.

DENOTATIONS AND CONNOTATIONS

A word's **denotation** is its literal, dictionary definition. Its **connotations** are the additional meanings, associations, and emotions suggested by the word. For example, the words *save* and *hoard* both mean "keep." However, *save* has positive connotations, while *hoard* has negative connotations of greed and secrecy.

DIRECTIONS: For each word from "A Rose for Emily" listed below that has a positive connotation, fill in a word with a similar meaning that has a negative connotation, and vice versa. The first one has been filled in for you.

Reading Standard 1.2 (Grade 9–10 Review) Distinguish between the denotative and connotative meanings of words and interpret the connotative power of words.

Positive Connotation	Negative Connotation	Positive Connotation	Negative Connotation
curiosity	nosiness	earthiness	
	dank		haughty
	bloated		stared
slender		persuade	

 Check your Standards Mastery at the back of this book.

The Jilting of Granny Weatherall by Katherine Anne Porter

LITERARY FOCUS: STREAM OF CONSCIOUSNESS

Stream of consciousness is a style of writing that portrays the sometimes chaotic workings of a character's mind. This technique presents thoughts, memories, emotions, associations, and images as they flow randomly through a character's mind. Stream-of-consciousness passages often contain **ambiguities,** or meanings that are open to more than one interpretation.

As you read this story, notice how Granny Weatherall's thoughts of the present mingle with her memories of the past. Also, be sure to look out for ambiguities.

Record Your Thoughts   Record some of your own thoughts in a stream-of-consciousness style. First, find a photograph in this book or in a magazine. Look at the image, and record your thoughts, associations, memories, and feelings in the chart below. A sample has been provided for you.

Image	Thoughts About Photograph
burning building	fire in my neighborhood—flames shooting in the sky—how a burn hurts—firefighters covered with soot—flames of hell

READING SKILLS: READING CLOSELY

Stories written in a stream-of-consciousness style require you to **read closely**. Here are some suggestions to make your reading easier:

* Notice **details** about people and events. Ask questions as you read.
* Pay attention to **verb tenses** to help you distinguish past from present.
* Look for **quotation marks,** which enclose words that are spoken aloud. Unspoken words and thoughts have no quotation marks.
* Find **context clues** that tell you which character is speaking.
* Re-read if you are puzzled about something.

Reading Standard 1.3
Discern the meaning of analogies encountered.

Reading Standard 3.3
Analyze the ways in which irony, tone, mood, the author's style, and the "sound" of language achieve specific rhetorical or aesthetic purposes or both.

Reading Standard 3.8 (Grade 9–10 Review)
Interpret and evaluate the impact of ambiguities, subtleties, contradictions, ironies, and incongruities in a text.

The Jilting of Granny Weatherall

Katherine Anne Porter

STREAM OF CONSCIOUSNESS

In lines 2–5, underline Granny Weatherall's unspoken thoughts, which have no quotation marks. Circle what she says aloud, which is in quotation marks.

INFER

Underline what Granny Weatherall says to the doctor in lines 10–12. What can you infer about her character from this dialogue?

_____

_____

_____

_____

INTERPRET

Why does it seem to Granny Weatherall that her bones and the doctor are floating (lines 19–22)?

_____

_____

_____

She flicked her wrist neatly out of Doctor Harry's pudgy careful fingers and pulled the sheet up to her chin. The brat ought to be in knee breeches. Doctoring around the country with spectacles on his nose! "Get along now, take your schoolbooks and go. There's nothing wrong with me."

Doctor Harry spread a warm paw like a cushion on her forehead where the forked green vein danced and made her eyelids twitch. "Now, now, be a good girl, and we'll have you up in no time."

10 "That's no way to speak to a woman nearly eighty years old just because she's down. I'd have you respect your elders, young man."

"Well, Missy, excuse me." Doctor Harry patted her cheek. "But I've got to warn you, haven't I? You're a marvel, but you must be careful or you're going to be good and sorry."

"Don't tell me what I'm going to be. I'm on my feet now, morally speaking. It's Cornelia. I had to go to bed to get rid of her."

Her bones felt loose, and floated around in her skin, and 20 Doctor Harry floated like a balloon around the foot of the bed. He floated and pulled down his waistcoat and swung his glasses on a cord. "Well, stay where you are, it certainly can't hurt you."

"Get along and doctor your sick," said Granny Weatherall. "Leave a well woman alone. I'll call for you when I want you. . . . Where were you forty years ago when I pulled through milk leg[1] and double pneumonia? You weren't even born. Don't let

---

1. **milk leg:** painful swelling of the leg, usually as a result of an infection during childbirth.

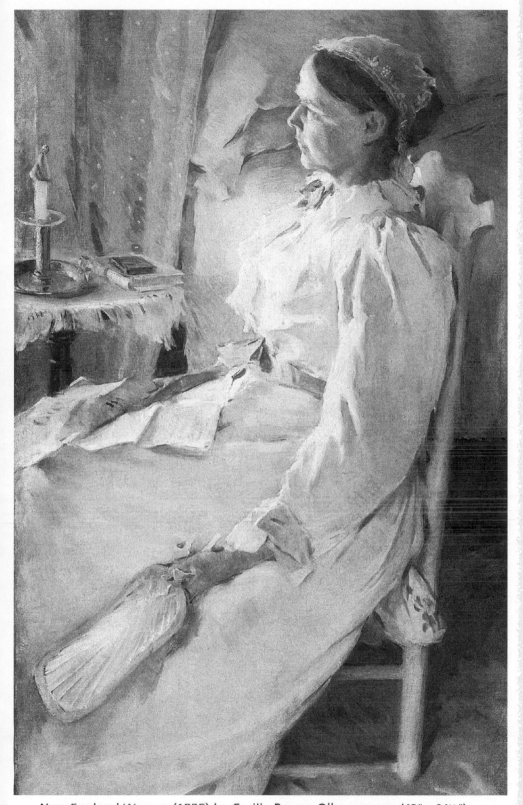

New England Woman (1895) by Cecilia Beaux. Oil on canvas (43″ × 24¼″).
The Pennsylvania Academy of the Fine Arts, Philadelphia. Joseph E. Temple Fund.

READING CLOSELY

Who is speaking in lines 37–38?

_____

_____

VOCABULARY

tactful (takt′fəl) _adj._: skilled in saying the right thing.

IRONY

Circle the adjectives Granny Weatherall uses to describe Cornelia in lines 39–44. What is **ironic** about this passage? _(Grade 9–10 Review)_

_____

_____

_____

AMBIGUITY

Lines 51–55 can be understood in two ways. What is ambiguous about Granny Weatherall's thoughts of her children and her day? _(Grade 9–10 Review)_

_____

_____

_____

_____

_____

_____

_____

Cornelia lead you on," she shouted, because Doctor Harry appeared to float up to the ceiling and out. "I pay my own bills, and I don't throw my money away on nonsense!"

30   She meant to wave goodbye, but it was too much trouble. Her eyes closed of themselves, it was like a dark curtain drawn around the bed. The pillow rose and floated under her, pleasant as a hammock in a light wind. She listened to the leaves rustling outside the window. No, somebody was swishing newspapers: No, Cornelia and Doctor Harry were whispering together. She leaped broad awake, thinking they whispered in her ear.

"She was never like this, never like this!" "Well, what can we expect?" "Yes, eighty years old. . . ."

Well, and what if she was? She still had ears. It was like
40 Cornelia to whisper around doors. She always kept things secret in such a public way. She was always being **tactful** and kind. Cornelia was dutiful; that was the trouble with her. Dutiful and good: "So good and dutiful," said Granny, "that I'd like to spank her." She saw herself spanking Cornelia and making a fine job of it.

"What'd you say, Mother?"

Granny felt her face tying up in hard knots.

"Can't a body think, I'd like to know?"

"I thought you might want something."

"I do. I want a lot of things. First off, go away and don't
50 whisper."

She lay and drowsed, hoping in her sleep that the children would keep out and let her rest a minute. It had been a long day. Not that she was tired. It was always pleasant to snatch a minute now and then. There was always so much to be done, let me see: tomorrow.

Tomorrow was far away and there was nothing to trouble about. Things were finished somehow when the time came; thank God there was always a little margin over for peace: Then a person could spread out the plan of life and tuck in the edges
60 orderly. It was good to have everything clean and folded away, with the hairbrushes and tonic bottles sitting straight on the

white embroidered linen: the day started without fuss and the pantry shelves laid out with rows of jelly glasses and brown jugs and white stone-china jars with blue whirligigs and words painted on them: coffee, tea, sugar, ginger, cinnamon, allspice: and the bronze clock with the lion on top nicely dusted off. The dust that lion could collect in twenty-four hours! The box in the attic with all those letters tied up, well, she'd have to go through that tomorrow. All those letters—George's letters and John's let-

70 ters and her letters to them both—lying around for the children to find afterward made her uneasy. Yes, that would be tomorrow's business. No use to let them know how silly she had been once.

While she was rummaging around she found death in her mind and it felt **clammy** and unfamiliar. She had spent so much time preparing for death there was no need for bringing it up again. Let it take care of itself now. When she was sixty she had felt very old, finished, and went around making farewell trips to see her children and grandchildren, with a secret in her mind: This is the very last of your mother, children! Then she made

80 her will and came down with a long fever. That was all just a notion like a lot of other things, but it was lucky too, for she had once for all got over the idea of dying for a long time. Now she couldn't be worried. She hoped she had better sense now. Her father had lived to be one hundred and two years old and had drunk a noggin[2] of strong hot toddy[3] on his last birthday. He told the reporters it was his daily habit, and he owed his long life to that. He had made quite a scandal and was very pleased about it. She believed she'd just **plague** Cornelia a little.

90 "Cornelia! Cornelia!" No footsteps, but a sudden hand on her cheek. "Bless you, where have you been?"

"Here, Mother."

"Well, Cornelia, I want a noggin of hot toddy."

"Are you cold, darling?"

---

2. **noggin** *n.:* mug.
3. **hot toddy** *n.:* drink made of liquor mixed with hot water, sugar, and spices.

READING CLOSELY

Underline the details in lines 60–66 that help you picture Granny Weatherall's orderly life.

READING CLOSELY

Pause at line 73. Who do you think the letter writers George and John are?

_____

_____

_____

_____

_____

_____

IDENTIFY

In lines 74–83, underline what Granny Weatherall did at age sixty.

VOCABULARY

clammy (klam'ē) *adj.:* cold and damp.
plague (plāg) *v.:* annoy.

FLUENCY

Read the boxed passage aloud twice. Focus on conveying meaning the first time. During your second reading, try to bring Granny Weatherall's thoughts to life.

INFER

Based on lines 97–107, what do you think Granny Weatherall's relationship with her children is like?

_____

_____

_____

_____

_____

_____

_____

STREAM OF CONSCIOUSNESS

In lines 108–137, Granny Weatherall's mind wanders between the past and the present. What do you learn about her life in this long paragraph?

_____

_____

_____

_____

_____

_____

_____

"I'm chilly, Cornelia. Lying in bed stops the circulation. I must have told you that a thousand times."

Well, she could just hear Cornelia telling her husband that Mother was getting a little childish and they'd have to humor her. The thing that most annoyed her was that Cornelia thought 100 she was deaf, dumb, and blind. Little hasty glances and tiny gestures tossed around her and over her head saying, "Don't cross her, let her have her way, she's eighty years old," and she sitting there as if she lived in a thin glass cage. Sometimes Granny almost made up her mind to pack up and move back to her own house where nobody could remind her every minute that she was old. Wait, wait, Cornelia, till your own children whisper behind your back!

In her day she had kept a better house and had got more work done. She wasn't too old yet for Lydia to be driving eighty 110 miles for advice when one of the children jumped the track, and Jimmy still dropped in and talked things over: "Now, Mammy, you've a good business head, I want to know what you think of this? . . ." Old. Cornelia couldn't change the furniture around without asking. Little things, little things! They had been so sweet when they were little. Granny wished the old days were back again with the children young and everything to be done over. It had been a hard pull, but not too much for her. When she thought of all the food she had cooked, and all the clothes she had cut and sewed, and all the gardens she had made—well, 120 the children showed it. There they were, made out of her, and they couldn't get away from that. Sometimes she wanted to see John again and point to them and say, Well, I didn't do so badly, did I? But that would have to wait. That was for tomorrow. She used to think of him as a man, but now all the children were older than their father, and he would be a child beside her if she saw him now. It seemed strange and there was something wrong in the idea. Why, he couldn't possibly recognize her. She had fenced in a hundred acres once, digging the postholes herself and clamping the wires with just a Negro boy to help. That

130 changed a woman. John would be looking for a young woman with the peaked Spanish comb in her hair and the painted fan. Digging postholes changed a woman. Riding country roads in the winter when women had their babies was another thing: sitting up nights with sick horses and sick Negroes and sick children and hardly ever losing one. John, I hardly ever lost one of them! John would see that in a minute, that would be something he could understand, she wouldn't have to explain anything!

It made her feel like rolling up her sleeves and putting the whole place to rights again. No matter if Cornelia was deter-
140 mined to be everywhere at once, there were a great many things left undone on this place. She would start tomorrow and do them. It was good to be strong enough for everything, even if all you made melted and changed and slipped under your hands, so that by the time you finished you almost forgot what you were working for. What was it I set out to do? she asked herself intently, but she could not remember. A fog rose over the valley, she saw it marching across the creek swallowing the trees and moving up the hill like an army of ghosts. Soon it would be at the near edge of the orchard, and then it was time to go in and light the lamps.
150 Come in, children, don't stay out in the night air.

Lighting the lamps had been beautiful. The children huddled up to her and breathed like little calves waiting at the bars in the twilight. Their eyes followed the match and watched the flame rise and settle in a blue curve, then they moved away from her. The lamp was lit, they didn't have to be scared and hang on to mother any more. Never, never, never more. God, for all my life I thank Thee. Without Thee, my God, I could never have done it. Hail, Mary, full of grace.

I want you to pick all the fruit this year and see that nothing
160 is wasted. There's always someone who can use it. Don't let good things rot for want of using. You waste life when you waste good food. Don't let things get lost. It's bitter to lose things. Now, don't let me get to thinking, not when I am tired and taking a little nap before supper. . . .

IRONY

Dramatic irony occurs when the reader knows something a character doesn't. What is the dramatic irony in lines 138–142? *(Grade 9–10 Review)*

_____

_____

_____

_____

STREAM OF CONSCIOUSNESS

What is the progression of Granny Weatherall's thoughts in lines 146–150?

_____

_____

_____

_____

AMBIGUITY

Re-read lines 159–162. Underline the phrase that shows how strongly Granny Weatherall feels about losing things. What might she be thinking about losing besides food? *(Grade 9–10 Review)*

_____

_____

_____

_____

_____

_____

The pillow rose about her shoulders and pressed against her heart and the memory was being squeezed out of it: Oh, push down the pillow, somebody: It would smother her if she tried to hold it. Such a fresh breeze blowing and such a green day with no threats in it. But he had not come, just the same. What does a
170 woman do when she has put on the white veil and set out the white cake for a man and he doesn't come? She tried to remember. No, I swear he never harmed me but in that. He never harmed me but in that . . . and what if he did? There was the day, the day, but a whirl of dark smoke rose and covered it, crept up and over into the bright field where everything was planted so carefully in orderly rows. That was hell, she knew hell when she saw it. For sixty years she had prayed against remembering him and against losing her soul in the deep pit of hell, and now the two things were mingled in one and the thought of him was
180 a smoky cloud from hell that moved and crept in her head when she had just got rid of Doctor Harry and was trying to rest a minute. Wounded **vanity,** Ellen, said a sharp voice in the top of her mind. Don't let your wounded vanity get the upper hand of you. Plenty of girls get **jilted.** You were jilted, weren't you? Then stand up to it. Her eyelids wavered and let in streamers of blue-gray light like tissue paper over her eyes. She must get up and pull the shades down or she'd never sleep. She was in bed again and the shades were not down. How could that happen? Better turn over, hide from the light, sleeping in the light gave you
190 nightmares. "Mother, how do you feel now?" and a stinging wetness on her forehead. But I don't like having my face washed in cold water!

Hapsy? George? Lydia? Jimmy? No, Cornelia, and her features were swollen and full of little puddles. "They're coming, darling, they'll all be here soon." Go wash your face, child, you look funny.

Instead of obeying, Cornelia knelt down and put her head on the pillow. She seemed to be talking but there was no sound.

"Well, are you tongue-tied? Whose birthday is it? Are you going to give a party?"

Cornelia's mouth moved urgently in strange shapes. "Don't do that, you bother me, daughter."

"Oh, no, Mother. Oh, no . . ."

Nonsense. It was strange about children. They **disputed** your every word. "No what, Cornelia?"

"Here's Doctor Harry."

"I won't see that boy again. He just left five minutes ago."

"That was this morning, Mother. It's night now. Here's the nurse."

"This is Doctor Harry, Mrs. Weatherall. I never saw you look so young and happy!"

"Ah, I'll never be young again—but I'd be happy if they'd let me lie in peace and get rested."

She thought she spoke up loudly, but no one answered. A warm weight on her forehead, a warm bracelet on her wrist, and a breeze went on whispering, trying to tell her something. A shuffle of leaves in the everlasting hand of God, He blew on them and they danced and rattled. "Mother, don't mind, we're going to give you a little hypodermic."[4] "Look here, daughter, how do ants get in this bed? I saw sugar ants yesterday." Did you send for Hapsy too?

It was Hapsy she really wanted. She had to go a long way back through a great many rooms to find Hapsy standing with a baby on her arm. She seemed to herself to be Hapsy also, and the baby on Hapsy's arm was Hapsy and himself and herself, all at once, and there was no surprise in the meeting. Then Hapsy melted from within and turned flimsy as gray gauze and the baby was a gauzy shadow, and Hapsy came up close and said, "I thought you'd never come," and looked at her very searchingly and said, "You haven't changed a bit!" They leaned forward to kiss, when Cornelia began whispering from a long way off,

---

4. **hypodermic** n.: injection of medicine.

READING CLOSELY

Re-read lines 194–213 carefully. Circle the words Cornelia says. Underline what Granny Weatherall says aloud. Put two lines under the words Granny thinks she says aloud but doesn't.

VOCABULARY

disputed (di·spyoot'id) v.: contested.

READING CLOSELY

Underline the **images** in lines 214–216. What do these images describe?

_____

_____

_____

_____

_____

_____

STREAM OF CONSCIOUSNESS

Granny Weatherall thinks about her daughter Hapsy in lines 222–231. Underline how Granny finds Hapsy. Circle Hapsy's words. What do you learn here about Hapsy?

_____

_____

_____

_____

IDENTIFY

Re-read lines 233–239. Who is George?

_____

_____

_____

READING CLOSELY

What do you think was not given back to Granny Weatherall (lines 240–243)?

_____

_____

_____

_____

_____

_____

_____

_____

_____

_____

Evening Light (1908) by Frank Benson. Oil on canvas (25¼″ × 30½″).
Cincinnati Art Museum, Kate Banning Fund.

"Oh, is there anything you want to tell me? Is there anything I can do for you?"

Yes, she had changed her mind after sixty years and she would like to see George. I want you to find George. Find him and be sure to tell him I forgot him. I want him to know I had my husband just the same and my children and my house like any other woman. A good house too and a good husband that I loved and fine children out of him. Better than I hoped for even.

240 Tell him I was given back everything he took away and more. Oh, no, oh, God, no, there was something else besides the house and the man and the children. Oh, surely they were not all?

What was it? Something not given back. . . .
Her breath crowded down under her ribs and
grew into a monstrous frightening shape with
cutting edges; it bored up into her head, and
the agony was unbelievable: Yes, John, get the
Doctor now, no more talk, my time has come.

When this one was born it should be the
250 last. The last. It should have been born first,
for it was the one she had truly wanted.
Everything came in good time. Nothing left
out, left over. She was strong, in three days she
would be as well as ever. Better. A woman
needed milk in her to have her full health.

"Mother, do you hear me?"

"I've been telling you—"

"Mother, Father Connolly's here."

"I went to Holy Communion only last
260 week. Tell him I'm not so sinful as all that."

"Father just wants to speak to you."

He could speak as much as he pleased. It
was like him to drop in and inquire about her
soul as if it were a teething baby, and then stay on for a cup of
tea and a round of cards and gossip. He always had a funny
story of some sort, usually about an Irishman who made his little mistakes and confessed them, and the point lay in some
absurd thing he would blurt out in the confessional showing his
struggles between native piety and original sin.[5] Granny felt easy
270 about her soul. Cornelia, where are your manners? Give Father
Connolly a chair. She had her secret comfortable understanding
with a few favorite saints who cleared a straight road to God for
her. All as surely signed and sealed as the papers for the new

---

5. **original sin:** in Christian theology, the sin of disobedience committed
   by Adam and Eve, the first man and first woman, which is passed on
   to all persons.

READING CLOSELY

Re-read lines 244–255.
Underline what Granny
Weatherall thinks about saying. What does her deathbed
pain remind her of?

_____

_____

_____

_____

_____

_____

_____

_____

_____

_____

_____

_____

STREAM OF
CONSCIOUSNESS

Re-read lines 258–274. Father
Connolly's visit reminds
Granny Weatherall of visits
by the priest in the past.
Underline what happened
during a different visit (lines
262–265). This memory leads
her to think about God.
Circle how Granny feels
about religion (lines
269–274).

IDENTIFY

In lines 274–275, Granny remembers another day the priest was there. What happened that day?

_____

_____

AMBIGUITY

Re-read lines 275–283. Who do you think catches Granny Weatherall when she almost faints? Who threatens to kill George? *(Grade 9–10 Review)*

_____

_____

_____

STREAM OF CONSCIOUSNESS

Granny Weatherall's thoughts wander through time in lines 284–290. What periods of her life is she imagining?

_____

_____

_____

_____

_____

Forty Acres. Forever . . . heirs and assigns forever. Since the day the wedding cake was not cut, but thrown out and wasted. The whole bottom dropped out of the world, and there she was blind and sweating with nothing under her feet and the walls falling away. His hand had caught her under the breast, she had not
280 fallen, there was the freshly polished floor with the green rug on it, just as before. He had cursed like a sailor's parrot and said, "I'll kill him for you." Don't lay a hand on him, for my sake leave something to God. "Now, Ellen, you must believe what I tell you. . . ."

So there was nothing, nothing to worry about any more, except sometimes in the night one of the children screamed in a nightmare, and they both hustled out shaking and hunting for the matches and calling, "There, wait a minute, here we are!" John, get the doctor now, Hapsy's time has come. But there was Hapsy standing by the bed in a white cap. "Cornelia, tell Hapsy
290 to take off her cap. I can't see her plain."

Her eyes opened very wide and the room stood out like a picture she had seen somewhere. Dark colors with the shadows rising toward the ceiling in long angles. The tall black dresser gleamed with nothing on it but John's picture, enlarged from a little one, with John's eyes very black when they should have been blue. You never saw him, so how do you know how he looked? But the man insisted the copy was perfect, it was very rich and handsome. For a picture, yes, but it's not my husband. The table by the bed had a linen cover and a candle and a cruci-
300 fix. The light was blue from Cornelia's silk lampshades. No sort of light at all, just frippery. You had to live forty years with kerosene lamps to appreciate honest electricity. She felt very strong and she saw Doctor Harry with a rosy **nimbus** around him.

"You look like a saint, Doctor Harry, and I vow that's as near as you'll ever come to it."

"She's saying something."

"I heard you, Cornelia. What's all this carrying-on?"

"Father Connolly's saying—"

310 Cornelia's voice staggered and bumped like a cart in a bad road. It rounded corners and turned back again and arrived nowhere. Granny stepped up in the cart very lightly and reached for the reins, but a man sat beside her and she knew him by his hands, driving the cart. She did not look in his face, for she knew without seeing, but looked instead down the road where the trees leaned over and bowed to each other and a thousand birds were singing a Mass. She felt like singing too, but she put her hand in the bosom of her dress and pulled out a rosary, and Father Connolly murmured Latin in a very solemn voice and

320 tickled her feet.[6] My God, will you stop that nonsense? I'm a married woman. What if he did run away and leave me to face the priest by myself? I found another a whole world better. I wouldn't have exchanged my husband for anybody except St. Michael[7] himself, and you may tell him that for me with a thank you in the bargain.

Light flashed on her closed eyelids, and a deep roaring shook her. Cornelia, is that lightning? I hear thunder. There's going to be a storm. Close all the windows. Call the children in. . . . "Mother, here we are, all of us." "Is that you, Hapsy?" "Oh, no,

330 I'm Lydia. We drove as fast as we could." Their faces drifted above her, drifted away. The rosary fell out of her hands and Lydia put it back. Jimmy tried to help, their hands fumbled together, and Granny closed two fingers around Jimmy's thumb. Beads wouldn't do, it must be something alive. She was so amazed her thoughts ran round and round. So, my dear Lord,

---

6. **murmured . . . feet:** The priest is performing the sacramental last rites of the Roman Catholic Church, which include anointing the dying person's feet with oil.

7. **Michael:** most powerful of the four archangels in Jewish and Christian doctrine. In Christian art he is usually depicted as a handsome knight in white armor.

AMBIGUITY

Re-read lines 310–317. Granny Weatherall doesn't say who is in the cart beside her. Who do you think he is? *(Grade 9–10 Review)*

_____

_____

_____

_____

_____

READING CLOSELY

Re-read lines 320–325. Granny Weatherall says she greatly loves her husband, John, so why does she keep thinking about George?

_____

_____

_____

_____

_____

_____

READING CLOSELY

In lines 326–330, Granny Weatherall's mind moves from the present to the past. Circle details that take place in the present. Underline details that Granny imagines from the past.

READING CLOSELY

Re-read lines 335–346. Granny Weatherall realizes that she is dying. Why doesn't she want to die yet?

_____

_____

_____

_____

_____

IDENTIFY

In line 350, underline what reconciles Granny Weatherall to dying.

VOCABULARY

dwindled (dwin'dəld) *v.*: diminished.

AMBIGUITY

Lines 361–365 can be interpreted several ways. Once again Granny Weatherall has been left alone without a sign from God. What sorrow do you think has wiped away all others? *(Grade 9–10 Review)*

_____

_____

_____

_____

_____

_____

this is my death and I wasn't even thinking about it. My children have come to see me die. But I can't, it's not time. Oh, I always hated surprises. I wanted to give Cornelia the amethyst[8] set—Cornelia, you're to have the amethyst set, but Hapsy's to wear it when she wants, and, Doctor Harry, do shut up. Nobody sent for you. Oh, my dear Lord, do wait a minute. I meant to do something about the Forty Acres, Jimmy doesn't need it and Lydia will later on, with that worthless husband of hers. I meant to finish the altar cloth and send six bottles of wine to Sister Borgia for her dyspepsia.[9] I want to send six bottles of wine to Sister Borgia, Father Connolly, now don't let me forget.

Cornelia's voice made short turns and tilted over and crashed. "Oh, Mother, oh, Mother, oh, Mother . . ."

"I'm not going, Cornelia. I'm taken by surprise. I can't go."

You'll see Hapsy again. What about her? "I thought you'd never come." Granny made a long journey outward, looking for Hapsy. What if I don't find her? What then? Her heart sank down and down, there was no bottom to death, she couldn't come to the end of it. The blue light from Cornelia's lampshade drew into a tiny point in the center of her brain, it flickered and winked like an eye, quietly it fluttered and **dwindled.** Granny lay curled down within herself, amazed and watchful, staring at the point of light that was herself; her body was now only a deeper mass of shadow in an endless darkness and this darkness would curl around the light and swallow it up. God, give a sign!

For the second time there was no sign. Again no bridegroom and the priest in the house. She could not remember any other sorrow because this grief wiped them all away. Oh, no, there's nothing more cruel than this—I'll never forgive it. She stretched herself with a deep breath and blew out the light.

---

8. **amethyst** (am'i·thist) *n.*: purple or violet quartz gemstone, used in jewelry.
9. **dyspepsia** (dis·pep'sē·ə) *n.*: indigestion.

The Jilting of Granny Weatherall

Reading Skills: Reading Closely   The chart below lists some of the people in Granny Weatherall's life. In the right-hand column, fill in what you learned about each of the characters as Granny spoke or thought about them in this stream-of-consciousness narrative.

Character	What I Learned About the Character
George	
John	
Cornelia	
Hapsy	
Father Connolly	

The Jilting of Granny Weatherall

VOCABULARY DEVELOPMENT

VOCABULARY IN CONTEXT

DIRECTIONS: Write vocabulary words from the word box to complete the paragraph below. Not all words from the box will be used.

Word Box

tactful

clammy

plague

vanity

jilted

disputed

nimbus

dwindled

That Katherine Anne Porter's fame is well deserved cannot be

(1) _____. Who would contest that her use of language

to create character and mood is the sign of a great literary talent? In this

famous short story, she is able to draw readers into the personal, inner world

of a dying grandmother who was (2) _____ by her lover

on her wedding day sixty years before. This rejection in Granny Weatherall's

early life would (3) _____ her until she died. Porter cre-

ates a vibrant portrait of a strong-willed woman, who is blunt rather than

(4) _____ in her dealings with her family.

ANALOGIES: USING SYNONYMS AND ANTONYMS

In a **word analogy,** two pairs of words have the same relationship. Often
the words in each pair are **synonyms**—words with similar meanings—or
antonyms—words with opposite meanings. In the analogy below, the words
in each pair are synonyms.

ANGRY : FURIOUS :: humorous : funny

DIRECTIONS: Study each word analogy below to determine if the words in the
complete pair are antonyms or synonyms. Then, fill in each blank with the
appropriate word from the word box above. In the blank following each analogy, write "A" if the word pairs are antonyms or "S" if they are synonyms.

1. DESTROYED : CREATED :: _____ : increased   _____

2. _____ : HALO :: ocean : sea   _____

3. ARID : DRY :: _____ : damp   _____

4. _____ : MODESTY :: sanity : madness   _____

**Reading
Standard 1.3**
Discern the
meaning of
analogies
encountered,
analyzing
specific
comparisons as
well as
relationships
and inferences.

 Check your Standards Mastery at the back of this book.

The Death of the Hired Man by Robert Frost

BEFORE YOU READ

LITERARY FOCUS: A NARRATIVE POEM AND BLANK VERSE

A **narrative poem** is a poem that tells a story. As with a short story or novel, the story in a narrative poem includes a series of events with a beginning, a middle, and an end. A narrative poem also includes characters and, often, dialogue. Most of "The Death of the Hired Man" consists of a dialogue between a husband and wife as they discuss Silas, the hired man.

"The Death of a Hired Man" is written in **blank verse**, which is unrhymed iambic pentameter. An **iamb** is an unaccented syllable followed by an accented syllable: da DUM (˘ ′), as in the word *confess*. In iambic pentameter, there are five iambs in each line.

A poem that is written to follow a more or less regular pattern of stressed and unstressed syllables is written in **meter.** If you try to beat out the meter in Frost's poem, you will find that Frost often varies the metric pattern. He does this so that his poem will not sound sing-song and become monotonous.

READING SKILLS: DRAWING INFERENCES

An **inference** is a guess based on information in the text and on your own knowledge and experience. When you draw inferences about characters, you make intelligent guesses about what the characters are like, what their feelings are, and why they do the things they do. You base your inferences on a character's appearance, behavior, and words, as well as on the comments and responses of other characters.

Use the Skill   In "The Death of the Hired Man," Silas never speaks. You learn about Silas's character from what the husband and wife say about him. As you read, look for clues to his character, and make inferences about him.

REVIEW SKILLS

As you read "The Death of the Hired Man," look for the following literary element.

CHARACTERIZATION
The way a writer reveals the personality of a character. In **direct characterization,** the writer tells us directly what a character is like. In **indirect characterization,** the writer reveals character through the person's appearance, actions, words, thoughts, and effect on other people.

Reading Standard 3.1
Analyze characteristics of subgenres that are used in poetry.

Reading Standard 3.3
Analyze the ways in which the author's style and the "sound" of language achieve specific rhetorical or aesthetic purposes.

Reading Standard 3.9 (Grade 9–10 Review)
Explain how voice, persona, and the choice of a narrator affect characterization and the tone, plot, and credibility of a text.

Photograph of an old man asleep on a porch (1936). His cane is between his legs. Photo by Dorothea Lange.

The Death of the Hired Man

Robert Frost

Mary sat musing on the lamp-flame at the table,
Waiting for Warren. When she heard his step,
She ran on tiptoe down the darkened passage
To meet him in the doorway with the news

5   And put him on his guard. "Silas is back."
She pushed him outward with her through the door
And shut it after her. "Be kind," she said.
She took the market things from Warren's arms
And set them on the porch, then drew him down

10 To sit beside her on the wooden steps.

"When was I ever anything but kind to him?
But I'll not have the fellow back," he said.
"I told him so last haying, didn't I?
If he left then, I said, that ended it.

15 What good is he? Who else will harbor[1] him
At his age for the little he can do?
What help he is there's no depending on.
Off he goes always when I need him most.
He thinks he ought to earn a little pay,

20 Enough at least to buy tobacco with,
So he won't have to beg and be beholden.[2]
'All right,' I say, 'I can't afford to pay
Any fixed wages, though I wish I could.'
'Someone else can.' 'Then someone else will have to.'

25 I shouldn't mind his bettering himself

---

1. **harbor** v.: provide safe shelter for.
2. **beholden** adj.: indebted.

IDENTIFY

A **narrative poem** tells a story and includes characters and, often, dialogue. In lines 1–7, circle the names of the characters. Underline the dialogue.

ANALYZE

Lines 7–10 are a good example of **blank verse**. Mark the five iambs in each line by putting the symbols ˘ over the unstressed syllables and ' over the stressed syllables.

CLARIFY

Pause at line 18. Why is Warren angry at Silas?

_____

_____

_____

_____

_____

INFER

In lines 19–24, circle what Silas wanted. Underline why Warren couldn't give it to him. What do you think Warren *does* give Silas in exchange for his labor?

_____

_____

Pause at line 30. What have
you learned about Silas and
Warren so far?

_____

_____

_____

_____

_____

_____

FLUENCY

Read the boxed passage
aloud at least twice. Be
aware of the beat of the
lines, but read naturally. Try
to bring the characters of
Mary and Warren to life by
reading the speech of each
character somewhat differently.

INFER

Re-read lines 39–43.
Underline the details that
describe how Mary tries to
help Silas. What inference
can you draw about Mary
from these actions?

_____

_____

_____

_____

_____

_____

If that was what it was. You can be certain,
When he begins like that, there's someone at him
Trying to coax him off with pocket money—
In haying time, when any help is scarce.
30   In winter he comes back to us. I'm done."

"Sh! not so loud: He'll hear you," Mary said.

"I want him to: He'll have to soon or late."

"He's worn out. He's asleep beside the stove.
When I came up from Rowe's I found him here,
35   Huddled against the barn door fast asleep,
A miserable sight, and frightening, too—
You needn't smile—I didn't recognize him—
I wasn't looking for him—and he's changed.
Wait till you see."

           "Where did you say he'd been?"

40   "He didn't say. I dragged him to the house,
And gave him tea and tried to make him smoke.
I tried to make him talk about his travels.
Nothing would do: He just kept nodding off."

"What did he say? Did he say anything?"

"But little."

45   "Anything? Mary, confess
He said he'd come to ditch³ the meadow for me."

"Warren!"

_____

3. **ditch** *v.:* dig drainage channels in.

"But did he? I just want to know."

"Of course he did. What would you have him say?
Surely you wouldn't grudge the poor old man
50 Some humble way to save his self-respect.
He added, if you really care to know,
He meant to clear the upper pasture, too.
That sounds like something you have heard before?
Warren, I wish you could have heard the way
55 He jumbled everything. I stopped to look
Two or three times—he made me feel so queer[4]—
To see if he was talking in his sleep.
He ran on[5] Harold Wilson—you remember—
The boy you had in haying four years since.
60 He's finished school, and teaching in his college.
Silas declares you'll have to get him back.
He says they two will make a team for work:
Between them they will lay this farm as smooth!
The way he mixed that in with other things.
65 He thinks young Wilson a likely lad, though daft
On education—you know how they fought
All through July under the blazing sun,
Silas up on the cart to build the load,
Harold along beside to pitch it on."

70 "Yes, I took care to keep well out of earshot."

"Well, those days trouble Silas like a dream.
You wouldn't think they would. How some things linger!
Harold's young college-boy's assurance piqued[6] him.
After so many years he still keeps finding
75 Good arguments he sees he might have used.

---

4. **queer** *adj.:* uncomfortable; ill at ease.
5. **ran on:** kept talking in a rambling way about.
6. **piqued** *v.:* provoked.

IDENTIFY

Pause at line 50. What has Silas said he's come back to do?

_____

_____

_____

INFER

Re-read lines 54–57. Circle the detail that describes Silas's behavior. What inference can you draw about his character based on this detail?

_____

_____

_____

PARAPHRASE

In your own words, retell the story events narrated in lines 65–75.

_____

_____

_____

_____

_____

_____

_____

_____

Re-read lines 78–95. How are
Silas and Harold alike, and
how are they different?

_____

_____

_____

_____

_____

_____

_____

_____

_____

_____

_____

_____

INFER

What can you infer about
Silas's character based on
lines 99–102?

_____

_____

_____

_____

_____

_____

_____

I sympathize. I know just how it feels

To think of the right thing to say too late.

Harold's associated in his mind with Latin.

He asked me what I thought of Harold's saying

80   He studied Latin, like the violin,

Because he liked it—that an argument!

He said he couldn't make the boy believe

He could find water with a hazel prong[7]—

Which showed how much good school had ever done him.

85   He wanted to go over that. But most of all

He thinks if he could have another chance

To teach him how to build a load of hay—"

"I know, that's Silas' one accomplishment.

He bundles every forkful in its place,

90   And tags and numbers it for future reference,

So he can find and easily dislodge it

In the unloading. Silas does that well.

He takes it out in bunches like big birds' nests.

You never see him standing on the hay

95   He's trying to lift, straining to lift himself."

"He thinks if he could teach him that, he'd be

Some good perhaps to someone in the world.

He hates to see a boy the fool of books.

Poor Silas, so concerned for other folk,

100   And nothing to look backward to with pride,

And nothing to look forward to with hope,

So now and never any different."

Part of a moon was falling down the west,

Dragging the whole sky with it to the hills.

105   Its light poured softly in her lap. She saw it

And spread her apron to it. She put out her hand

---

7. **hazel prong:** forked branch used to find water underground.

Silhouette of man in barn.

Among the harplike morning-glory strings,
Taut with the dew from garden bed to eaves,
As if she played unheard some tenderness

110   That wrought[8] on him beside her in the night.
"Warren," she said, "he has come home to die:
You needn't be afraid he'll leave you this time."

"Home," he mocked gently.

                              "Yes, what else but home?
It all depends on what you mean by home.

115   Of course he's nothing to us, any more
Than was the hound that came a stranger to us
Out of the woods, worn out upon the trail."

---

8. **wrought** *v.:* worked.

INTERPRET

Lines 103–110 switch from dialogue to narration that uses beautiful **imagery.** What senses do these images appeal to?

IDENTIFY

In lines 111–112, circle what Mary says Silas has come home to do.

In lines 118–120, underline
Warren's definition of home,
and circle Mary's definition
of home. What differences
do you see in their two
points of view?

_____

_____

_____

_____

_____

_____

_____

_____

_____

_____

CLARIFY

Re-read lines 124–129. Where
does Warren think that Silas
should go to get help?

_____

_____

_____

_____

_____

_____

_____

_____

"Home is the place where, when you have to go there,
They have to take you in."

          "I should have called it
120   Something you somehow haven't to deserve."

Warren leaned out and took a step or two,
Picked up a little stick, and brought it back
And broke it in his hand and tossed it by.
"Silas has better claim on us you think
125   Than on his brother? Thirteen little miles
As the road winds would bring him to his door.
Silas has walked that far no doubt today.
Why doesn't he go there? His brother's rich,
A somebody—director in the bank."

    "He never told us that."

130   "We know it, though."

"I think his brother ought to help, of course.
I'll see to that if there is need. He ought of right
To take him in, and might be willing to—
He may be better than appearances.
135   But have some pity on Silas. Do you think
If he had any pride in claiming kin
Or anything he looked for from his brother,
He'd keep so still about him all this time?"

"I wonder what's between them."

             "I can tell you.
140   Silas is what he is—we wouldn't mind him—
But just the kind that kinsfolk can't abide.
He never did a thing so very bad.

He don't know why he isn't quite as good

As anybody. Worthless though he is,

145 He won't be made ashamed to please his brother."

"*I* can't think Si ever hurt anyone."

"No, but he hurt my heart the way he lay

And rolled his old head on that sharp-edged chair-back.

He wouldn't let me put him on the lounge.

150 You must go in and see what you can do.

I made the bed up for him there tonight.

You'll be surprised at him—how much he's broken.

His working days are done; I'm sure of it."

"I'd not be in a hurry to say that."

155 "I haven't been. Go, look, see for yourself.

But, Warren, please remember how it is:

He's come to help you ditch the meadow.

He has a plan. You mustn't laugh at him.

He may not speak of it, and then he may.

160 I'll sit and see if that small sailing cloud

Will hit or miss the moon."

                      It hit the moon.

Then there were three there, making a dim row,

The moon, the little silver cloud, and she.

Warren returned—too soon, it seemed to her—

165 Slipped to her side, caught up her hand and waited.

"Warren?" she questioned.

                      "Dead," was all he answered.

INFER

What inferences can you make about why Silas and his brother don't get along (lines 131–145)?

_____

_____

_____

INFER

In lines 153–154, circle what Mary says about Silas's ability to work, and underline Warren's reply. What can you infer about Mary's and Warren's characters from their reactions?

_____

_____

_____

INTERPRET

The narration again includes a beautiful image in lines 160–163. Why do you think the poet includes this image of the moon, cloud, and woman?

_____

_____

_____

_____

_____

_____

_____

The Death of the Hired Man

Reading Skills: Drawing Inferences   You can draw inferences about characters based on what they say, on what they do, and on what others say about them. The chart below lists some of the things Mary and Warren say in "The Death of the Hired Man." In the right-hand column, write what you infer about Mary, Warren, and Silas, based on the dialogue quoted here.

Dialogue from the Poem	Inference About Character
"'But I'll not have the fellow back,' he said. / 'I told him so last haying, didn't I? / If he left then, I said, that ended it.'" (lines 12–14)	Warren:
"'Surely you wouldn't grudge the poor old man / Some humble way to save his self-respect.'" (lines 49–50)	Mary:
"'He never did a thing so very bad. / He don't know why he isn't quite as good / As anybody. Worthless though he is, / He won't be made ashamed to please his brother.'" (lines 142–145)	Silas:

✔ Check your Standards Mastery at the back of this book.

Harlem by Langston Hughes

BEFORE YOU READ

LITERARY FOCUS: MOOD

The general feeling created in a piece of writing is called its **mood**. This mood, or atmosphere, is created by all the elements of the text: diction, or word choice; sounds; images; and figures of speech. Often, the mood of a text can be summed up in one word—gloomy, joyful, fearful, ominous, mysterious.

Setting the Mood   Sometimes just the setting of a text is enough to establish a mood. The chart below lists three settings. In the right column, fill in the mood you would expect from each setting.

Setting	Mood
A dark castle	
A sunny beach	
High mountain peaks	

READING SKILLS: IDENTIFYING HISTORICAL THEMES

Certain themes occur again and again during certain historical periods. During the American revolutionary period, for example, writers often explored themes of freedom or identity. These themes reflected the optimistic, rational views of the time.

"Harlem," on the other hand, was written during the Great Depression of the 1930s, when millions of Americans faced severe economic problems. The number of people without jobs rose from four million to twelve million between 1930 and 1932. Many people who still had jobs worked fewer hours for less pay. It was a time when even a one-cent price increase meant that many people couldn't afford bread. Harlem, a neighborhood in New York City inhabited primarily by African Americans, was hit hard by the Depression. As you read the following poem, notice how it relates to the concerns of that historical period.

REVIEW SKILLS

As you read "Harlem," think about the following literary element.

THEME
The insight about human life revealed in a work of literature. Writers rarely state themes directly. Readers must infer the theme by thinking carefully about all the details in the text: diction, mood, sounds, images, figures of speech.

Reading Standard 3.3
Analyze the ways in which irony, tone, mood, the author's style, and the sound of language achieves specific rhetorical or aesthetic purposes or both.

Reading Standard 3.12 (Grade 9–10 Review)
Analyze the way in which a work of literature is related to the themes and issues of its historical period. (Historical approach)

Harlem

Langston Hughes

INTERPRET

Underline details that help create the **mood** in lines 1–6. Describe this mood in your own words.

_____

_____

IDENTIFY

In lines 7–15, underline details that show the economic effects of the Depression. Circle details that show the effects of discrimination.

INTERPRET

Circle the **metaphor** in line 17 that repeats the metaphor in line 1. What does this figure of speech tell you about life in Harlem during this historical period?

_____

_____

ANALYZE

How would you state the **theme** of this poem? *(Grade 9–10 Review)*

_____

_____

_____

Here on the edge of hell
Stands Harlem—
Remembering the old lies,
The old kicks in the back,
5   The old "Be patient"
They told us before.

Sure, we remember.
Now when the man at the corner store
Says sugar's gone up another two cents,
10   And bread one,
And there's a new tax on cigarettes—
We remember the job we never had,
Never could get,
And can't have now
15   Because we're colored.

So we stand here
On the edge of hell
In Harlem
And look out on the world
20   And wonder
What we're gonna do
In the face of what
We remember.

"Harlem" from *The Collected Poems of Langston Hughes.* Copyright © 1944 by the Estate of Langston Hughes. Reprinted by permission of **Alfred A. Knopf, a division of Random House, Inc.** Electronic format by permission of **Harold Ober Associates.**

Harlem

Reading Skills: Identifying Historical Themes   The poem "Harlem" reflects the themes and issues of the historical period we call the Great Depression. The chart below lists details from the poem. In the right-hand column, fill in the historical themes or issues these details illustrate.

Details from "Harlem"	Historical Theme or Issue
"Remembering the old lies, / The old kicks in the back, / The old 'Be patient' / They told us before." (lines 3–6)	
". . . the man at the corner store / Says sugar's gone up another two cents, / And bread one," (lines 8–10)	
"We remember the job we never had, / Never could get, / And can't have now / Because we're colored." (lines 12–15)	

✓ Check your Standards Mastery at the back of this book.

from **Dust Tracks on a Road** by Zora Neale Hurston

LITERARY FOCUS: AUTOBIOGRAPHY

An **autobiography** is the life story of a person that is written by that same person. (The word is made up of the prefix *auto–,* meaning "self," and the word *biography,* meaning "story of a life.") Since *Dust Tracks on a Road* is an autobiography of a writer, you can expect to learn about Hurston's literary roots. Because this is a personal piece of writing, you will also find **subjective details** that describe how Hurston felt about her experiences.

READING SKILLS: IDENTIFYING HISTORICAL ISSUES

Most fiction and nonfiction writing is set in a specific historical period. In one way or another, the writing of a particular era reflects concerns and convictions and even prejudices of that era. As you read this excerpt from Zora Neale Hurston's autobiography, notice the issues that were important in the historical time and place she is writing about: the early 1900s in the South. What themes—or revelations about human experience—would you expect to find in literature written during that time and place?

Zora Neale Hurston.

from Dust Tracks on a Road

Zora Neale Hurston

I used to take a seat on top of the gatepost and watch the world go by. One way to Orlando ran past my house, so the carriages and cars would pass before me. The movement made me glad to see it. Often the white travelers would **hail** me, but more often I hailed them, and asked, "Don't you want me to go a piece of the way with you?"

They always did. I know now that I must have caused a great deal of amusement among them, but my self-assurance must have carried the point, for I was always invited to come along. I'd
10 ride up the road for perhaps a half-mile, then walk back. I did not do this with the permission of my parents, nor with their fore-knowledge. When they found out about it later, I usually got a whipping. My grandmother worried about my forward ways a great deal. She had known slavery and to her my **brazenness** was unthinkable.

"Git down offa dat gatepost! You li'l sow, you! Git down! Setting up dere looking dem white folks right in de face! They's gowine[1] to lynch you, yet. And don't stand in dat doorway gazing out at 'em neither. Youse too brazen to live long."

20 Nevertheless, I kept right on gazing at them, and "going a piece of the way" whenever I could make it. The village seemed dull to me most of the time. If the village was singing a chorus, I must have missed the tune.

Perhaps a year before the old man[2] died, I came to know two other white people for myself. They were women.

It came about this way. The whites who came down from the

---

1. **gowine:** dialect for "going."
2. **old man:** white farmer who knew Hurston's family, took her fishing, and gave her advice.

AUTOBIOGRAPHY

An **autobiography** is the story of a person's life written by that person. Circle the pronoun in the first line that indicates who is telling the story.

VOCABULARY

hail (hāl) *v.:* greet.
brazenness (brā′zən·nis) *n.:* boldness.

IDENTIFY

This autobiography takes place in the segregated South of the early 1900s. What **historical issue** can you identify in the grandmother's speech in lines 16–19? (*Lynch* means "murder without a trial.") (*Grade 9–10 Review*)

_____

_____

_____

_____

INTERPRET

Circle the **figurative language** in lines 22–23. How did the writer feel about the village where she lived?

_____

_____

_____

_____

_____

_____

VOCABULARY

caper (kā′pər) *n.:* foolish prank.

INFER

Pause at line 42. Why were the children so well-behaved when the visitors came to the school?

_____

_____

_____

_____

_____

INFER

Re-read lines 43–51. Why do you think Mr. Calhoun was so nervous?

_____

_____

_____

_____

_____

North were often brought by their friends to visit the village school. A Negro school was something strange to them, and while they were always sympathetic and kind, curiosity must
30 have been present, also. They came and went, came and went. Always, the room was hurriedly put in order, and we were threatened with a prompt and bloody death if we cut one **caper** while the visitors were present. We always sang a spiritual, led by Mr. Calhoun himself. Mrs. Calhoun always stood in the back, with a palmetto switch[3] in her hand as a squelcher. We were all little angels for the duration, because we'd better be. She would cut her eyes[4] and give us a glare that meant trouble, then turn her face toward the visitors and beam as much as to say it was a great privilege and pleasure to teach lovely children like us. They
40 couldn't see that palmetto hickory in her hand behind all those benches, but we knew where our angelic behavior was coming from.

Usually, the visitors gave warning a day ahead and we would be cautioned to put on shoes, comb our heads, and see to ears and fingernails. There was a close inspection of every one of us before we marched in that morning. Knotty heads, dirty ears, and fingernails got hauled out of line, strapped, and sent home to lick the calf[5] over again.

This particular afternoon, the two young ladies just popped
50 in. Mr. Calhoun was flustered, but he put on the best show he could. He dismissed the class that he was teaching up at the front of the room, then called the fifth grade in reading. That was my class.

So we took our readers and went up front. We stood up in the usual line, and opened to the lesson. It was the story of Pluto

---

3. **palmetto switch:** whip made from the stem of a large, fanlike leaf of a kind of palm tree. Teachers sometimes used these switches to discipline students.
4. **cut her eyes:** slang for "look scornfully."
5. **lick the calf:** slang for "wash up."

and Persephone.[6] It was new and hard to the class in general, and Mr. Calhoun was very uncomfortable as the readers stumbled along, spelling out words with their lips, and in mumbling undertones before they exposed them experimentally to the teacher's ears.

Then it came to me. I was fifth or sixth down the line. The story was not new to me, because I had read my reader through from lid to lid, the first week that Papa had bought it for me.

That is how it was that my eyes were not in the book, working out the paragraph which I knew would be mine by counting the children ahead of me. I was observing our visitors, who held a book between them, following the lesson. They had shiny hair, mostly brownish. One had a looping gold chain around her neck. The other one was dressed all over in black and white with a pretty finger ring on her left hand. But the thing that held my eyes were their fingers. They were long and thin, and very white, except up near the tips. There they were baby pink. I had never seen such hands. It was a fascinating discovery for me. I wondered how they felt. I would have given those hands more attention, but the child before me was almost through. My turn next, so I got on my mark, bringing my eyes back to the book and made sure of my place. Some of the stories I had reread several times, and this Greco-Roman myth was one of my favorites. I was **exalted** by it, and that is the way I read my paragraph.

"Yes, Jupiter[7] had seen her (Persephone). He had seen the maiden picking flowers in the field. He had seen the chariot of the dark monarch pause by the maiden's side. He had seen him when he seized Persephone. He had seen the black horses leap down Mount Aetna's[8] fiery throat. Persephone was now in Pluto's dark **realm** and he had made her his wife."

---

6. **Pluto and Persephone** (pər·sef′ə·nē): In classical mythology, Pluto, or Hades, is the god who rules the underworld; Persephone, also known as Proserpina, is his wife, queen of the underworld. In this version of the origin of the seasons, Hurston uses the names of Roman and Greek gods interchangeably.
7. **Jupiter:** in Roman mythology, king of the gods.
8. **Mount Aetna's:** Mount Aetna (also spelled *Etna*) is a volcanic mountain in eastern Sicily.

IDENTIFY

Pause at line 63. Why was Zora familiar with the story?

_____

_____

_____

_____

_____

_____

_____

_____

_____

AUTOBIOGRAPHY

Re-read lines 70–73. Underline the **subjective details** that reveal Zora's reactions to the visitors.

VOCABULARY

exalted (eg·zôlt′id) *v.:* lifted up.
realm (relm) *n.:* kingdom.

FLUENCY

Read the boxed passage aloud twice. On your second read, try to bring the scene to life by reading the myth with the expression and enthusiasm that Zora must have used to impress and delight her teacher and the visitors.

WORD STUDY

The word *pomegranate* (päm′gran′it) in line 94 refers to a type of fruit that has a tough, red rind; juicy, rich red flesh; and many small seeds. This fruit tastes both sweet and sour.

The two women looked at each other and then back to me. Mr. Calhoun broke out with a proud smile beneath his bristly moustache, and instead of the next child taking up where I had ended, he nodded to me to go on. So I read the story to the end,

90 where flying Mercury, the messenger of the Gods, brought Persephone back to the sunlit earth and restored her to the arms of Dame Ceres, her mother, that the world might have springtime and summer flowers, autumn and harvest. But because she had bitten the pomegranate while in Pluto's kingdom, she must return to him for three months of each year, and be his queen. Then the world had winter, until she returned to earth.

The class was dismissed and the visitors smiled us away and went into a low-voiced conversation with Mr. Calhoun for a few

Dunbar High School, Quincy, Florida.
Florida State Archives.

IDENTIFY

Pause at line 104. Why does Zora think that she is in trouble?

INFER

Underline Zora's behavior in lines 109–110. What can you infer about her character based on this behavior?

100 minutes. They glanced my way once or twice and I began to worry. Not only was I barefooted, but my feet and legs were dusty. My hair was more uncombed than usual, and my nails were not shiny clean. Oh, I'm going to catch it now. Those ladies saw me, too. Mr. Calhoun is promising to 'tend to me. So I thought.

Then Mr. Calhoun called me. I went up thinking how awful it was to get a whipping before company. Furthermore, I heard a snicker run over the room. Hennie Clark and Stell Brazzle did it out loud, so I would be sure to hear them. The smart aleck was going to get it. I slipped one hand behind me and switched my
110 dress tail at them, indicating scorn.

IDENTIFY

What do the Northern women do in lines 115–117 that most Southern whites would not do in this **historical period**? *(Grade 9–10 Review)*

_____

_____

INFER

In lines 122–123, underline what Zora says she hated. What does this detail tell you about her character?

_____

_____

_____

_____

PARAPHRASE

Re-read lines 130–136. Restate the information in this passage in your own words.

_____

_____

_____

_____

_____

_____

_____

_____

"Come here, Zora Neale," Mr. Calhoun cooed as I reached the desk. He put his hand on my shoulder and gave me little pats. The ladies smiled and held out those flower-looking fingers toward me. I seized the opportunity for a good look.

"Shake hands with the ladies, Zora Neale," Mr. Calhoun prompted and they took my hand one after the other and smiled. They asked me if I loved school, and I lied that I did. There was some truth in it, because I liked geography and read-ing, and I liked to play at recess time. Whoever it was invented
120   writing and arithmetic got no thanks from me. Neither did I like the arrangement where the teacher could sit up there with a pal-metto stem and lick me whenever he saw fit. I hated things I couldn't do anything about. But I knew better than to bring that up right there, so I said yes, I *loved* school.

"I can tell you do," Brown Taffeta gleamed. She patted my head, and was lucky enough not to get sandspurs in her hand. Children who roll and tumble in the grass in Florida are apt to get sandspurs in their hair. They shook hands with me again and I went back to my seat.

130   When school let out at three o'clock, Mr. Calhoun told me to wait. When everybody had gone, he told me I was to go to the Park House, that was the hotel in Maitland, the next afternoon to call upon Mrs. Johnstone and Miss Hurd. I must tell Mama to see that I was clean and brushed from head to feet, and I must wear shoes and stockings. The ladies liked me, he said, and I must be on my best behavior.

The next day I was let out of school an hour early, and went home to be stood up in a tub of suds and be scrubbed and have my ears dug into. My sandy hair sported a red ribbon to match
140   my red and white checked gingham dress, starched until it could stand alone. Mama saw to it that my shoes were on the right feet, since I was careless about left and right. Last thing, I was given a handkerchief to carry, warned again about my behavior, and sent off, with my big brother John to go as far as the hotel gate with me.

First thing, the ladies gave me strange things, like stuffed dates and preserved ginger, and encouraged me to eat all that I wanted. Then they showed me their Japanese dolls and just talked. I was then handed a copy of *Scribner's Magazine,* and asked to read a place that was pointed out to me. After a paragraph or two, I was told with smiles, that that would do.

I was led out on the grounds and they took my picture under a palm tree. They handed me what was to me then a heavy cylinder done up in fancy paper, tied with a ribbon, and they told me goodbye, asking me not to open it until I got home.

My brother was waiting for me down by the lake, and we hurried home, eager to see what was in the thing. It was too heavy to be candy or anything like that. John insisted on toting it for me.

My mother made John give it back to me and let me open it. Perhaps, I shall never experience such joy again. The nearest thing to that moment was the telegram accepting my first book. One hundred goldy-new pennies rolled out of the cylinder. Their gleam lit up the world. It was not **avarice** that moved me. It was the beauty of the thing. I stood on the mountain. Mama let me play with my pennies for a while, then put them away for me to keep.

That was only the beginning. The next day I received an Episcopal hymnbook bound in white leather with a golden cross stamped into the front cover, a copy of *The Swiss Family Robinson,* and a book of fairy tales.

I set about to commit the song words to memory. There was no music written there, just the words. But there was to my consciousness music in between them just the same. "When I survey the Wondrous Cross" seemed the most beautiful to me, so I committed that to memory first of all. Some of them seemed dull and without life, and I pretended they were not there. If white people liked trashy singing like that, there must be something funny about them that I had not noticed before. I stuck to the pretty ones where the words marched to a throb I could feel.

EVALUATE

Re-read lines 146–151. Underline what the women did during Zora's visit. How would you describe their treatment of her?

_____

_____

_____

_____

_____

_____

_____

_____

VOCABULARY

avarice (av′ə·ris) *n.:* greed.

INTERPRET

Circle the **metaphor** in line 164. What does this figure of speech tell you about Zora's feelings when she received her gift?

_____

_____

AUTOBIOGRAPHY

What **subjective details** does Zora reveal in lines 171–179?

_____

_____

_____

_____

_____

_____

_____

_____

_____

In lines 194–195, Zora says she doesn't know why she likes the Norse tales so much. How would you explain her admiration?

_____

_____

_____

_____

_____

_____

_____

tread (tred) *n.:* step; walk.

profoundly (prō·found′lē) *adv.:* deeply.

resolved (rē·zälvd′) *v.:* made a decision; determined.

conceive (kən·sēv′) *v.:* think; imagine.

180   A month or so after the two young ladies returned to Minnesota, they sent me a huge box packed with clothes and books. The red coat with a wide circular collar and the red tam pleased me more than any of the other things. My chums pretended not to like anything that I had, but even then I knew that they were jealous. Old Smarty had gotten by them again. The clothes were not new, but they were very good. I shone like the morning sun.

    But the books gave me more pleasure than the clothes. I had never been too keen on dressing up. It called for hard scrubbings
190 with Octagon soap suds getting in my eyes, and none too gentle fingers scrubbing my neck and gouging in my ears.

    In that box were *Gulliver's Travels, Grimm's Fairy Tales, Dick Whittington, Greek and Roman Myths,* and best of all, *Norse Tales.* Why did the Norse tales strike so deeply into my soul? I do not know, but they did. I seemed to remember seeing Thor swing his mighty short-handled hammer as he sped across the sky in rumbling thunder, lightning flashing from the **tread** of his steeds and the wheels of his chariot. The great and good Odin, who went down to the well of knowledge to drink, and was told
200 that the price of a drink from that fountain was an eye. Odin drank deeply, then plucked out one eye without a murmur and handed it to the grizzly keeper, and walked away. That held majesty for me.

    Of the Greeks, Hercules moved me most. I followed him eagerly on his tasks. The story of the choice of Hercules as a boy when he met Pleasure and Duty, and put his hand in that of Duty and followed her steep way to the blue hills of fame and glory, which she pointed out at the end, moved me **profoundly.** I **resolved** to be like him. The tricks and turns of the other gods
210 and goddesses left me cold. There were other thin books about this and that sweet and gentle little girl who gave up her heart to Christ and good works. Almost always they died from it, preaching as they passed. I was utterly indifferent to their deaths. In the first place I could not **conceive** of death, and in the next place

they never had any funerals that amounted to a hill of beans, so I didn't care how soon they rolled up their big, soulful, blue eyes and kicked the bucket. They had no meat on their bones.

But I also met Hans Andersen[9] and Robert Louis Stevenson.[10] They seemed to know what I wanted to hear and said it in a way that tingled me. Just a little below these friends was Rudyard Kipling in his Jungle Books.[11] I loved his talking snakes as much as I did the hero.

I came to start reading the Bible through my mother. She gave me a licking one afternoon for repeating something I had overheard a neighbor telling her. She locked me in her room after the whipping, and the Bible was the only thing in there for me to read. I happened to open to the place where David was doing some mighty smiting, and I got interested. David went here and he went there, and no matter where he went, he smote 'em hip and thigh. Then he sung songs to his harp awhile, and went out and smote some more. Not one time did David stop and preach about sins and things. All David wanted to know from God was who to kill and when. He took care of the other details himself. Never a quiet moment. I liked him a lot. So I read a great deal more in the Bible, hunting for some more active people like David. Except for the beautiful language of Luke and Paul, the New Testament still plays a poor second to the Old Testament for me. The Jews had a God who laid about Him[12] when they needed Him. I could see no use waiting till Judgment Day to see a man who was just crying for a good killing, to be told to go and roast.[13] My idea was to give him a good killing first, and then if he got roasted later on, so much the better.

---

9. **Hans Andersen:** Hans Christian Andersen (1805–1875), Danish writer known primarily for his fairy tales.
10. **Robert Louis Stevenson** (1850–1894): Scottish writer of adventure stories such as *Kidnapped* and *Treasure Island.*
11. **Rudyard Kipling . . . Books:** Kipling (1865–1936) was an English writer born in India. His *Jungle Book* and *Second Jungle Book* contain stories of the adventures of Mowgli, a boy raised by animals in the jungles of India.
12. **laid about Him:** slang for "struck blows in every direction."
13. **roast:** slang for "burn in hell."

INFER

Re-read lines 223–236. Why do you think Zora liked the Biblical character David?

_____

_____

_____

WORD STUDY

In lines 227–228, David is smiting someone. *Smite* (smīt) means "to destroy or kill." *Smote* is its past tense.

AUTOBIOGRAPHY

Underline the sentence in lines 236–238 in which the writer describes her point of view as an adult. How does this detail indicate that this story is the **autobiography** of a writer?

_____

_____

_____

_____

_____

_____

_____

_____

_____

from Dust Tracks on a Road

Reading Skills: Identifying Historical Issues   Most nonfiction texts are set in a specific historical period and therefore reveal the issues that were important during that period. The chart below lists three passages from Zora Neale Hurston's autobiography. In the right-hand column, fill in the historical issues alluded to by the passages.

Passage from Autobiography	Historical Issue
"'Setting up dere looking dem white folks right in de face! They's gowine to lynch you, yet. And don't stand in dat doorway gazing out at 'em neither. Youse too brazen to live long.'" (lines 17–19)	
"The whites who came down from the North were often brought by their friends to visit the village school. A Negro school was something strange to them. . . ." (lines 26–28)	
"Neither did I like the arrangement where the teacher could sit up there with a palmetto stem and lick me whenever he saw fit." (lines 120–122)	

from **Dust Tracks on a Road**

VOCABULARY IN CONTEXT

DIRECTIONS: Write words from the word box to complete the paragraph below. Not all words will be used.

Word Box

- hail
- brazenness
- caper
- exalted
- realm
- avarice
- tread
- profoundly
- resolved
- conceive

The young girl was determined. She was (1) _____ to read her short story aloud to the visiting famous writer. She boldly raised her hand and waved it in the air. Her (2) _____ was rewarded as the teacher called on her. As the words of her own story filled the classroom, the girl seemed to enter another (3) _____. She lost herself in the special kingdom of her imagination. When the girl finished reading, the visitor was deeply and (4) _____ moved by her story. He praised her, and so was the first to (5) _____ her as the great writer she was destined to become.

WORDS FROM GREEK AND ROMAN MYTHOLOGY

DIRECTIONS: In the first column of the chart below are three sentences with underlined words. In the second column is a list of figures from Greek and Roman mythology from whom those words are derived. Use clues in both columns to guess at the meaning of each word. If you are not certain, check your answer in the dictionary.

Sentence	Figure from Myths	Word Meaning
1. The <u>narcissistic</u> actor looked in every mirror he passed.	Narcissus, a beautiful Greek youth who fell in love with his own reflection	
2. The military band played <u>martial</u> music at the parade.	Mars, the Roman god of war	
3. Clearing the field of heavy rocks is a <u>Herculean</u> task.	Hercules, a Greek hero known for his great strength	

Reading Standard 1.3 (Grade 9–10 Review) Identify Greek, Roman, and Norse mythology and use the knowledge to understand the origin and meaning of new words (e.g., the word *narcissistic* drawn from the myth of Narcissus and Echo).

 Check your Standards Mastery at the back of this book.

Contemporary Literature (1939 to Present)

Contemporary Literature
(1939 to Present)

John Leggett, Susan Allen Toth, John Malcolm Brinnin, and Thomas Hernacki

The following essay provides highlights of the historical period.
For a more detailed version of this essay,
see *Holt Literature and Language Arts,* pages 796–809.

Reading Standard 2.3 (Grade 9–10 Review) Generate relevant questions about readings on issues that can be researched.

Reading Standard 3.5 Analyze recognized works of American literature representing a variety of genres and traditions.

On August 6, 1945, at 8:15 A.M., an atomic bomb was dropped on the Japanese city of Hiroshima from the U.S. airplane *Enola Gay*. Within seconds the center of Hiroshima had disappeared. The bomb in effect ended World War II, and its mushroom cloud has cast a shadow over every generation since.

Although many Americans disapproved of the use of the atomic bomb to end World War II, most agreed with the purpose of the war itself. They were fighting against tyranny, against regimes that would destroy the American way of life.
10 Only twenty years later, however, the United States became deeply involved in another overseas war—this time in Vietnam—that would sharply divide the nation.

IDENTIFY

Re-read lines 1–9. What was the main purpose of America's involvement in World War II? Underline the answer.

CLARIFY

Pause at line 12. What war did not have the popular support among American citizens that World War II had?

_____

_____

_____

_____

_____

_____

_____

_____

Nuclear explosion in the Nevada desert (1955).

WORD STUDY

Gallows (line 16) are an upright frame with a crossbar and rope, used for hanging condemned criminals. Thus, the term *gallows humor* refers to a morbid joke that might be uttered in the midst of an execution—or in any other place where humor is unexpected.

INTERPRET

Pause at line 40. Underline the words that tell you the purpose of science and technology. Why do you think the purpose is described as **ironic,** or the opposite of what you might expect?

_____

_____

_____

_____

_____

_____

_____

_____

_____

_____

_____

_____

_____

_____

To some writers the madness of the war-torn world was an inescapable condition of modern life, and the only appropriate response was hard-edged laughter at life's tragic ironies. The term *gallows humor*—ironic humor arising from an acknowledgment of the absurd or grotesque— was often used to describe the work of writers who flourished after World War II.

The 1970s saw the winding down of the Vietnam War, but
20 another focus of disillusionment filled the news: The Watergate scandal, which in 1974 forced the only resignation of a U.S. president, Richard M. Nixon.

Then came the 1980s, when individual enjoyment and material success seemed to overshadow other concerns. As the 1980s ended, so did the cold war, the struggle between the United States and the Soviet Union that had dominated international politics since shortly after the end of World War II. The Soviet Union collapsed as its republics and satellite nations
30 declared independence. The end of the cold war reduced but did not end the threat of nuclear violence.

In many ways the nuclear bomb is the dramatic symbol of the last half of the twentieth century. Its infamous mushroom cloud represents the triumph of science and technology, the purpose of

Peace Today by Rube Goldberg.
The Granger Collection, New York.

which was, ironically enough, to benefit humankind, to make
40 life richer and easier for us all.

The Promise and Peril of Technology

In some ways, science and technology have fulfilled their promise. They have increased the life spans of many people and have better fed and housed many. They have moved us faster from place to place—even allowing a few of us to stroll on the surface of the moon.

Counter Intelligence (1996) by Mark Kostabi. Oil on canvas (84″ × 132″).
© Mark Kostabi.

Large segments of our society still live in poverty, however. Computer technology has wiped out many jobs, making them obsolete, especially in the manufacturing sector, even though it
50 has opened up employment in the white-collar and service sectors. Many Americans feel that they have become anonymous consumers, known only by a computer password or credit card number. They worry, too, that their privacy is unprotected and that their thoughts and even their dreams are being shaped by mass advertising, mass journalism, and mass entertainment.

Contemporary Fiction: Diversity and Vitality

One of the words most commonly used to describe contemporary American culture is **postmodern,** a term that, like our age, is still in the process of being defined. Postmodernism sees
60 contemporary culture as a change—a development or a departure—from modernism, the dominant movement in the arts from about 1890 to 1945. In literature the great American modernists—notably Ezra Pound, T. S. Eliot, William Carlos

IDENTIFY CAUSE & EFFECT

Re-read lines 42–55. Underline the details that describe the positive ways that technology has affected everyday life. Then, circle details that describe the negative effects of technology.

WORD STUDY

Look at the word *obsolete* in line 49. Based on **context clues** provided in the surrounding words and phrases, what do you think *obsolete* means?

_____

_____

_____

_____

_____

_____

_____

_____

_____

_____

_____

_____

IDENTIFY

Pause at line 55, and skim the rest of the introduction. Underline the main headings that tell you which three **genres,** or types of literature, it will cover.

Williams, Marianne Moore, Wallace Stevens, Katherine Anne Porter, William Faulkner, and Ernest Hemingway—forged new styles and new forms with which to express the sensibility of the early twentieth century. Postmodern writers build with many of the tools the modernists provided, but they are constructing a body of literature that is strikingly different from that produced

70 by the modernists.

■ Perspectives in Postmodern Fiction

Postmodern writers of fiction allow for multiple meanings and multiple worlds in their works. Realistic and literal worlds, past worlds, and dreamlike metaphorical worlds may merge. Narrators and characters may tell different versions of a story, or a story may lend itself to several valid interpretations. The postmodernist asks, "Why choose only one version? Why limit ourselves?"

Student with poster of Václav Havel, celebrating the arrival of democracy in Czechoslovakia (1989).

Writers of our time do not abide by conventional rules for shaping fiction. Donald Barthelme's story "Sentence," for example, is a nine-page tale that consists entirely of one sentence. In Walter Abish's novel *Alphabetical Africa* (1974), every word in the first chapter begins with the letter *a,* every word in the second chapter begins with *a* or *b,* and so on through the alphabet to *z* and then, in reverse, all the way back to *a.*

Some postmodern works are also intensely self-conscious. They comment on themselves, criticize themselves, take themselves apart, and encourage us to put them back together again. In his novel *Operation Shylock* (1993), the author Philip Roth meets a character named Philip Roth and wonders which one of them is real. In other words, postmodern literature is aware of itself as literature and encourages the reader's self-awareness as well.

The vitality of contemporary fiction lies in its cultural diversity, in its enthusiasm for blending fiction with nonfiction, and its extraordinary sense of play. It also demonstrates a typically American ability to invigorate the old by means of the new.

Contemporary Nonfiction: Breaking the Barriers

Until fairly recently *nonfiction* meant whatever was *not* fiction—suggesting that nonfiction was not a literary form and not art. Nonfiction writers were lumped together with journalists, who in turn were defined as nonliterary folk whose work was quickly written, read, and discarded. Critics tended to concentrate on the search for the elusive Great American Novel, which was thought to be more important than anything a nonfiction writer could produce.

Since the 1970s, however, nonfiction has come into its own. Lists of bestsellers, which have always included self-help books, cookbooks, and exercise manuals, now regularly feature memoirs, biographies, and histories as well.

WORD STUDY

When you think of the term *self-conscious,* you might think of a person who is shy or lacking in confidence. In a more general sense, however, *self-conscious* can also mean "self-aware." The use of the phrase *self-conscious* to describe postmodern writing (line 86) refers to a literary approach in which writers are fully aware of the fragility and artificiality of their craft. Self-conscious writing is a playful way of encouraging readers to look past the trappings of style and content in order to get to a higher truth.

COMPARE & CONTRAST

Re-read lines 101–112. In your own words, compare the role of nonfiction then and now.

IDENTIFY

Pause at line 120. What problems do critics generally face when discussing nonfiction?

_____

_____

_____

_____

_____

_____

_____

_____

_____

_____

_____

_____

_____

_____

_____

FLUENCY

Read the boxed passage aloud twice. In your first reading, read for understanding, or comprehension. What words or phrases should be emphasized? Then, in your second reading, try to improve the speed and flow of your delivery.

■ Does It Have to Be Accurate?

Critics, however, are still uncertain about the terminology we should apply to nonfiction. For instance, when discussing fiction, we can talk about point of view, character, plot, theme, and setting; in discussing more complex fiction, we can analyze irony, metaphors, symbols, and levels of meaning. These traditional literary terms don't always apply to nonfiction,

120 however.

More troubling is the problem of accuracy. Truth or accuracy is often a test applied to nonfiction, with frequently unsatisfactory results. For example, a class read Peter Matthiessen's *The Snow Leopard* (1978) about wildlife in the Himalayas and the writer's search for the meaning of life. The class praised the book for its penetrating observations, philosophical depth, and narrative technique. Students were then asked

130 whether they would like it just as much if they learned that it was fiction, that Matthiessen had never gone to the Himalayas at all. (This, of course, is *not* the case.) No, many students said; they would not like the book as well. It would no longer be true. Wasn't truth what distinguished nonfiction from fiction?

■ The New Journalism

This question was often raised in the 1960s, when the new

140 journalism (also called literary journalism) began to appear. Truman Capote, Tom Wolfe, Joan Didion, Norman Mailer, and others attracted attention by describing contemporary culture and actual events in strongly individual voices. They used many of the devices of fiction, including complex characterization, plot, suspense, setting, symbolism, and irony.

A new journalist did not feel obliged to keep his or her opinion and presence out of the writing; in fact, presence and participation were often crucial. Joan Didion bought a dress for a defendant in a trail she was covering as a journalist. Truman Capote befriended the murderers he was writing about in *In Cold Blood,* which he called a nonfiction novel—a perfect example of the overlapping of genres. Readers wanted to know just what the writer was thinking or feeling about the subject, and so the tone of a book became nearly as important as its facts.

If facts alone do not distinguish nonfiction from fiction, what does? No one is sure. What readers *are* sure about is their interest in nonfiction that uses the traditional attractions of accomplished fiction: characters to care about, suspense, and compelling use of language. Many readers, eager for literature that will illuminate their lives, enrich their knowledge, and entertain them, have become as willing to turn to nonfiction as fiction.

Contemporary Poetry: Varied and Intensely Personal

In recent years more Americans have been writing poetry than ever before. It is a special challenge to determine which poets and movements will last.

■ The Decline of Modernism

There are a number of clear, significant differences between American poetry written before World War II and poetry written in the decades since. The twenty years between the two world wars marked the flowering and near monopoly of modernist poetry. That was the kind of poetry defined, by and large, by the theories and practices of T. S. Eliot, Ezra Pound, and W. H. Auden.

In 1917, Eliot had called for an impersonal, objective poetry that was not concerned with the private or personal emotions of the poet. The poem, said Eliot, should be

ANALYZE

Re-read lines 138–154. What is new journalism, and how is it different from earlier forms of journalism?

_____

_____

_____

_____

_____

_____

_____

_____

_____

_____

_____

_____

_____

_____

_____

_____

_____

IDENTIFY

Pause at line 175. Which poets helped define poetry between the two world wars? Circle their names.

180

impersonal, allusive (it should make references, or allusions, to other works), and intellectually challenging. Modernist writers followed Pound's insistence that the image was all-important and that any unnecessary words should be omitted; but in doing this, they often eliminated material that could have made their poetry more understandable to more people.

By the early 1950s, there was a growing sense that modernism was somehow played out, that it was no longer appropriate for the times. The era itself may have had something to do with the shift away from modernism. A generation had returned from war to a country where conformity and material

190

success were the main values. The Soviet Union and the atomic bomb worried Americans in the late 1940s and 1950s, but acquiring a house and a car and making money were generally of more immediate importance.

■ The Beat Poets

In 1956, a long poem called *Howl* was published by Allen Ginsberg. A cry of outrage against the conformity of the 1950s, *Howl* was far removed from the safe confines of

200

modernism. *Howl* begins, "I saw the best minds of my generation destroyed by madness, starving hysterical naked," and it continues at the same intense pitch for hundreds of lines.

Beatnik poet reading to the accompaniment of a musician in New York's Greenwich Village (1959).

Together with *On the Road* (1957), Jack Kerouac's novel celebrating the bohemian life, *Howl* quickly became a kind

210

of bible for the young nonconformists who made up what became known as the beat generation. Beat poetry and the beat lifestyle—marked by poetry readings, jazz performances, and the appearance of late-night coffeehouses in San Francisco and New York's Greenwich Village—had an immediate impact on American popular culture. Moreover, *Howl* addressed the concerns of contemporary life. Many of Ginsberg's concerns—the injustices of modern life, the importance of the imagination—would become the principal themes of the next decade's poetry.

220 ■ **Poetry and Personal Experience**

In 1959, Robert Lowell published *Life Studies,* one of the most important and influential volumes of verse to appear since World War II. These poems are about intensely personal experiences that modernist poets have avoided dealing with directly: emotional distress, alcoholism, illness, and depression.

Shortly after *Life Studies* appeared, a critic described Lowell's poems as "confessional." The label stuck, and the **confessional school** of poets, mostly friends or students of Lowell's, was officially born. Those poets—including Sylvia

230 Plath, Anne Sexton, and John Berryman—wrote frank, sometimes brutal poems about their private lives. They used poetry to confess their most personal problems.

■ **History of the Human Heart**

Today American poetry is characterized by diversity. The extraordinary variety in style and attitude has attracted large new audiences. Poetry performances have sprung up throughout America, with live poetry slams at such places as the Nuyorican Poets Café in New York City. Technology has made available thousands of readings on audiotape and videotape, and

240 television broadcasts and numerous Web sites are devoted to poetry.

Much contemporary poetry reflects a democratic quality. Poetry lives in the people, contemporary poets seem to say, and any walk of life, any experience, any style of expression, can result in authentic poetry. Contemporary poets often write in

IDENTIFY

Pause at line 232. What was the **confessional school** of poets?

_____

_____

_____

_____

_____

_____

_____

_____

_____

_____

_____

_____

_____

_____

_____

_____

ANALYZE

Re-read lines 242–245. Underline the words or phrases that describe how contemporary poetry has a "democratic quality."

the language of common speech, and they do not hesitate to surprise or even shock with their language, their attitudes, and the details of their private lives. Poetry today is anything but impersonal.

250   Will today's poetry reach audiences a hundred years from now? The answer by the poet laureate Billy Collins suggests that it will: "It's the only history of the human heart we have," he says.

Where the Present Meets the Past on the Way to the Future

The literature that captures a wide audience often does so by offering a fresh voice and a new attitude. Nevertheless, much of contemporary American literature deals with the same themes

that concerned our greatest writers of the
nineteenth century: Poe, Hawthorne,
260 Whitman, Dickinson, Melville, Emerson,
and Thoreau. The characters created by the
novelist John Updike, for example, seek
spiritual revelations in ordinary life. "The
invariable mark of wisdom," Emerson wrote,
"is to find the miraculous in the common."
It is more difficult, however, to find spiritual
values in the cheap clutter of modern life
than it was in the woods around Emerson's
Concord. Still, Updike's characters continue
270 the search. "I find myself . . . circling back to
man's religious nature," Updike has written
of his own work, "and the real loss of man
and art alike when that nature has nowhere
to plug itself in." Those words would serve
to describe the work of a great number of
contemporary writers whose intellectual
roots can be traced to the Transcendentalists
of the nineteenth century and perhaps even
further back, to those hardy, practical
280 Puritans who braved the two-month voyage
across the Atlantic in small wooden ships.

Poetry reading at
Nuyorican Poets
Café in New York
City (1995).

CONNECT

Pause at line 270. What questions about Emerson or Concord do you have? What sources would you look in to find answers to your questions? (Grade 9–10 Review)

_____

_____

_____

_____

_____

_____

_____

COMPARE & CONTRAST

Re-read lines 255–281. What is one thing that contemporary American literature has in common with nineteenth-century writing?

_____

_____

_____

_____

_____

_____

_____

_____

_____

_____

The Death of the Ball Turret Gunner by Randall Jarrell

BEFORE YOU READ

LITERARY FOCUS: IMPLIED METAPHOR

An **implied metaphor** is a figure of speech that compares two unlike things by suggesting the two things that are being compared instead of directly naming them. For example, Emily Dickinson begins a poem about a train like this:

> "I like to see it lap the Miles—
>
> And lick the Valleys up"

Dickinson doesn't directly tell us that she is comparing a train with an animal. Instead, she uses words that apply to an animal's actions—*lap* and *lick*—and trusts us to catch the comparison with the way a train eats up the miles.

The Power of Suggestion   The left-hand column of the chart below contains **implied metaphors**—figures of speech that suggest a comparison between two things. Read the implied metaphors. Then, in the right-hand column, describe what two things are being compared in each case.

Implied Metaphor	Two Things Compared
Popularity blooms in gorgeous color, but it quickly fades.	
She was feathered in bright colors from head to toe.	

READING SKILLS: VISUALIZING

Visualizing means using your imagination to picture what is happening in a text. When you read a poem, take the time to allow the figures of speech and images to create pictures in your mind. For example, when you read Emily Dickinson's lines about the train, above, you might pause at the words *lap* and *lick* and visualize the train moving rapidly through the valleys, as if it is devouring them.

Use the Skill   As you read this poem, let the images help you visualize what is happening. Then, go back and underline or highlight words and phrases that make you think of *birth* and *death*.

The Death of the Ball Turret Gunner

Randall Jarrell

> **BACKGROUND**
> This famous poem describes a crew member in one of the B-17
> or B-24 bombers used in World War II. The "ball turret" was a
> sphere, a "ball" set into the belly of the plane. The gunner
> inside the turret fired a machine gun. Both the turret and the
> gunner revolved as the gunner tracked his targets.

From my mother's sleep I fell into the State,
And I hunched in its belly till my wet fur froze.
Six miles from earth, loosed from its dream of life,
I woke to black flak and the nightmare fighters.
5   When I died they washed me out of the turret with a hose.

A Czech fighter pilot in England (1940).

IDENTIFY

Jarrell's poem is based on a powerful **implied metaphor**. Underline details in the poem that suggest a comparison between the death of the airman and the process of being born.

INTERPRET

How is a gunner inside a ball turret like a fetus inside its mother's womb?

_____

_____

_____

INTERPRET

What is horrible about the "birth" in this poem?

_____

_____

The Death of the Ball Turret Gunner

Reading Skills: Visualizing   When you read a text, you should try to visualize actions, characters, and settings. To practice visualizing, fill out the chart below with descriptions of what each line in the poem makes you see (or hear, touch, feel, taste).

Line from Poem	What I Visualize
"From my mother's sleep I fell into the State,"	I visualize . . .
"And I hunched in its belly till my wet fur froze."	I visualize . . .
"Six miles from the earth, loosed from its dream of life,"	I visualize . . .
"I woke to the black flak and the nightmare fighters."	I visualize . . .
"When I died they washed me out of the turret with a hose."	I visualize . . .

Check your Standards Mastery at the back of this book.

The Handsomest Drowned Man in the World

by Gabriel García Márquez

BEFORE YOU READ

LITERARY FOCUS: MAGIC REALISM

Magic realism is a style of writing that blends ordinary reality with fantastic elements in a matter-of-fact way. As you read this story, you will encounter references to religion in words like *relics, scapular,* and *holy water.* You will see a reference to magic in the phrase *sea charms.* You will find references to Greek myths in words like *labyrinth* and *sirens.* All of these elements exist side by side with down-to-earth details about chickens, clothes, furniture, food, and so on.

READING SKILLS: ANALYZING ARCHETYPES

Archetype (är′kə·tīp) means "an original model" or "a basic pattern." Archetypes can be characters, things, or plots. For example, the archetype of the superhuman hero appears in the *Odyssey,* as well as in comic strips and movies about Superman. The archetype of metamorphosis—magical transformation from one thing to another—appears in ancient myths and in the fairy tale about Cinderella. The archetype of the heroic quest or the perilous journey occurs in *Moby-Dick* and in movies about Indiana Jones.

Use the Skill   As you read "The Handsomest Drowned Man in the World," watch especially for the archetype of the superhuman hero. Underline or highlight details that help you recognize the hero's larger-than-life qualities.

Reading Standard 3.6
Analyze the way in which authors through the centuries have used archetypes drawn from myth and tradition in literature, film, political speeches, and religious writings.

Reading Standard 3.7 (Grade 9–10 Review)
Recognize and understand the significance of various literary devices, including figurative language, imagery, allegory, and symbolism, and explain their appeal.

Reading Standard 3.7
Analyze recognized works of world literature from a variety of authors.

The Handsomest Drowned Man in the World

Gabriel García Márquez, *translated by* Gregory Rabassa

IDENTIFY

Re-read lines 1–4. Circle the words that tell you that what the children are seeing must be huge.

COMPARE & CONTRAST

Pause at line 15. How do the children treat the drowned man? How do the adult men treat him?

_____

_____

_____

_____

_____

_____

_____

_____

_____

_____

_____

_____

A Tale for Children

The first children who saw the dark and slinky bulge approaching through the sea let themselves think it was an enemy ship. Then they saw it had no flags or masts and they thought it was a whale. But when it was washed up on the beach, they removed the clumps of seaweed, the jellyfish tentacles, and the remains of fish and flotsam, and only then did they see that it was a drowned man.

They had been playing with him all afternoon, burying him
10 in the sand and digging him up again, when someone chanced to see them and spread the alarm in the village. The men who carried him to the nearest house noticed that he weighed more than any dead man they had ever known, almost as much as a horse, and they said to each other that maybe he'd been floating too long and the water had got into his bones. When they laid him on the floor they said he'd been taller than all other men because there was barely enough room for him in the house, but they thought that maybe the ability to keep on growing after death was part of the nature of certain drowned
20 men. He had the smell of the sea about him and only his shape gave one to suppose that it was the corpse of a human being, because the skin was covered with a crust of mud and scales.

They did not even have to clean off his face to know that the dead man was a stranger. The village was made up of only twenty-odd wooden houses that had stone courtyards with no flowers and which were spread about on the end of a desertlike

cape. There was so little land that mothers always went about
with the fear that the wind would carry off their children and
the few dead that the years had caused among them had to be
thrown off the cliffs. But the sea was calm and **bountiful** and all
the men fit into seven boats. So when they found the drowned
man they simply had to look at one another to see that they
were all there.

   That night they did not go out to work at sea. While
the men went to find out if anyone was missing in neighboring
villages, the women stayed behind to care for the drowned man.
They took the mud off with grass swabs, they removed the
underwater stones entangled in his hair, and they scraped the
crust off with tools used for scaling fish. As they were doing that
they noticed that the vegetation on him came from faraway

Sergio Bustamente/Photos
by Clint Clemens.

30

40

VOCABULARY

bountiful (bɔun'tə·fəl) *adj.:*
generous.

CLARIFY

Re-read lines 24–35. How do
the villagers know right
away that the dead man is a
stranger?

Notes _____

_____

_____

_____

_____

_____

_____

_____

VOCABULARY

haggard (hag′ərd) *adj.:*
gaunt; worn out.

virile (vir′əl) *adj.:* manly;
masculine.

WORD STUDY

The word *labyrinths* in line
44 comes from a Greek myth
about a maze built for King
Minos of Crete. Today we call
any complicated maze or net-
work a *labyrinth*. What
would happen to a body that
"sailed through labyrinths of
coral"?

_____

_____

_____

_____

_____

_____

_____

oceans and deep water and that his clothes were in tatters, as if
he had sailed through labyrinths of coral. They noticed too that
he bore his death with pride, for he did not have the lonely look
of other drowned men who came out of the sea or that **haggard,**
needy look of men who drowned in rivers. But only when they
finished cleaning him off did they become aware of the kind of
man he was and it left them breathless. Not only was he the

50   tallest, strongest, most **virile,** and best-built man they had ever
seen, but even though they were looking at him there was no
room for him in their imagination.

     They could not find a bed in the village large enough to lay
him on nor was there a table solid enough to use for his wake.
The tallest men's holiday pants would not fit him, not the fattest
ones' Sunday shirts, nor the shoes of the one with the biggest
feet. Fascinated by his huge size and his beauty, the women then
decided to make him some pants from a large piece of sail and a

shirt from some bridal brabant linen[1] so that he could continue
60   through his death with dignity. As they sewed, sitting in a circle
and gazing at the corpse between stitches, it seemed to them that
the wind had never been so steady nor the sea so restless as on
that night and they supposed that the change had something to
do with the dead man. They thought that if that magnificent
man had lived in the village, his house would have had the
widest doors, the highest ceiling, and the strongest floor, his
bedstead would have been made from a midship frame held
together by iron bolts, and his wife would have been the happi-
est woman. They thought that he would have had so much
70   authority that he could have drawn fish out of the sea simply by
calling their names and that he would have put so much work
into his land that springs would have burst forth from among
the rocks so that he would have been able to plant flowers on the
cliffs. They secretly compared him to their own men, thinking
that for all their lives theirs were incapable of doing what he
could do in one night, and they ended up dismissing them deep
in their hearts as the weakest, meanest, and most useless creatures on earth. They were wandering through that maze of fantasy when the oldest woman, who as the oldest had looked upon
80   the drowned man with more compassion than passion, sighed:

"He has the face of someone called Esteban."[2]

It was true. Most of them had only to take another look
at him to see that he could not have any other name. The more
stubborn among them, who were the youngest, still lived for a
few hours with the illusion that when they put his clothes on
and he lay among the flowers in patent leather shoes his name
might be Lautaro.[3] But it was a vain illusion. There had not been
enough canvas, the poorly cut and worse sewn pants were too

---

1. **brabant** (brə·bant′) **linen:** linen from Brabant, a province of Belgium known for its fine lace and cloth.
2. **Esteban** (es·te′bän): Spanish equivalent of "Stephen." In Christian tradition, Stephen was the first martyr. He was stoned to death because of his beliefs.
3. **Lautaro** (lou·tä′rô): leader of the Araucanian Indian people who resisted the Spanish conquistadors entering their land, in what is now Chile, during the sixteenth century. Lautaro is now seen as a Chilean national hero.

Pause at line 64. How is the description of the sea and the wind's change typical of **magic realism**?

_____

_____

_____

_____

_____

_____

Read the footnotes about the two names the women consider for the man, Esteban and Lautaro. How do both possibilities **symbolize** someone who stands far above ordinary men—someone who is an archetypal superhero? *(Grade 9–10 Review)*

_____

_____

_____

_____

_____

_____

_____

_____

_____

_____

_____

_____

_____

_____

_____

_____

_____

_____

_____

_____

_____

_____

_____

_____

_____

_____

**COMPARE &
CONTRAST**

Re-read lines 92–112. Up
until now, Esteban, the
drowned man, has seemed
heroic. Here, the women
begin to imagine down-to-
earth problems the living
Esteban must have faced.
Circle the very long sentence
that humorously summarizes
these problems.

90 tight, and the hidden strength of his heart popped the buttons
on his shirt. After midnight the whistling of the wind died down
and the sea fell into its Wednesday drowsiness.[4] The silence put
an end to any last doubts: he was Esteban. The women who had
dressed him, who had combed his hair, had cut his nails and
shaved him were unable to hold back a shudder of pity when
they had to resign themselves to his being dragged along the
ground. It was then that they understood how unhappy he must
have been with that huge body since it bothered him even after
death. They could see him in life, condemned to going through
doors sideways, cracking his head on crossbeams, remaining on

100 his feet during visits, not knowing what to do with his soft, pink,
sea lion hands while the lady of the house looked for her most
resistant chair and begged him, frightened to death, sit here,
Esteban, please, and he, leaning against the wall, smiling, don't
bother, ma'am, I'm fine where I am, his heels raw and his back
roasted from having done the same thing so many times whenever he paid a visit, don't bother, ma'am, I'm fine where I am,
just to avoid the embarrassment of breaking up the chair, and
never knowing perhaps that the ones who said don't go, Esteban,
at least wait till the coffee's ready, were the ones who later on

110 would whisper the big boob finally left, how nice, the handsome
fool has gone. That was what the women were thinking beside
the body a little before dawn. Later, when they covered his face
with a handkerchief so that the light would not bother him, he
looked so forever dead, so defenseless, so much like their men
that the first furrows of tears opened in their hearts. It was one
of the younger ones who began the weeping. The others, coming
to, went from sighs to wails, and the more they sobbed the more
they felt like weeping, because the drowned man was becoming

---

4. **Wednesday drowsiness** (and later **Wednesday meat** and **Wednesday
dead body**): *Wednesday* is a colloquial expression for "tiresome."
In many fishing villages, fishers returned from the sea on Thursday,
so by Wednesday, people began running out of food and were
generally weary and bored.

all the more Esteban for them, and so they wept so much, for he

120 was the most **destitute,** most peaceful, and most obliging man
on earth, poor Esteban. So when the men returned with the
news that the drowned man was not from the neighboring
villages either, the women felt an opening of jubilation in the
midst of their tears.

      "Praise the Lord," they sighed, "he's ours!"

      The men thought the fuss was only womanish **frivolity.**
Fatigued because of the difficult nighttime inquiries, all they
wanted was to get rid of the bother of the newcomer once and
for all before the sun grew strong on that arid, windless day.

130 They improvised a litter with the remains of foremasts and
gaffs,[5] tying it together with rigging so that it would bear the
weight of the body until they reached the cliffs. They wanted to
tie the anchor from a cargo ship to him so that he would sink
easily into the deepest waves, where fish are blind and divers die
of nostalgia, and bad currents would not bring him back to
shore, as had happened with other bodies. But the more they
hurried, the more the women thought of ways to waste time.
They walked about like startled hens, pecking with the sea
charms[6] on their breasts, some interfering on one side to put a

140 scapular[7] of the good wind on the drowned man, some on the
other side to put a wrist compass on him, and after a great deal
of *get away from there, woman, stay out of the way, look, you
almost made me fall on top of the dead man,* the men began to
feel mistrust in their livers and started grumbling about why so
many main-altar decorations for a stranger, because no matter
how many nails and holy-water jars he had on him, the sharks
would chew him all the same, but the women kept piling on

---

5. **gaffs** *n. pl.:* poles used on a boat to support a sail.
6. **sea charms:** magic charms worn to protect the wearer from dangers
   at sea.
7. **scapular** (skap′yə · lər) *n.:* pair of small cloth squares showing images
   of saints, joined by string and worn under clothing by some Roman
   Catholics as a symbol of religious devotion.

VOCABULARY

destitute (des′tə · tōōt′) *adj.:*
poverty-stricken.
frivolity (fri · văl′ə · tē) *n.:*
silliness.

CLARIFY

Pause at line 125. Why are
the women happy to learn
that Esteban didn't come
from a neighboring village?

_____

_____

_____

_____

_____

_____

_____

_____

_____

WORD STUDY

The word *nostalgia* in line
135 usually means "a longing
for things of the past." Here,
though, the author plays
with the original meaning
of the Greek word root
nostos, "to return home."
In that sense, a diver might
"die of nostalgia" if he went
so deep that he couldn't
return to the surface.

COMPARE & CONTRAST

Review lines 126–154. Contrast what the men want to accomplish with the approach the women take.

_____

_____

_____

_____

_____

_____

CLARIFY

Pause at line 177. What personality traits do the townspeople attribute to Estaban?

_____

_____

_____

_____

_____

FLUENCY

Read the boxed passage aloud twice. Pause at commas, and come to a stop at periods. Try to bring to life this vivid description of the drowned man the villagers call Esteban.

their junk relics, running back and forth, stumbling, while they released in sighs what they did not in tears, so that the men
150 finally exploded with *since when has there ever been such a fuss over a drifting corpse, a drowned nobody, a piece of cold Wednesday meat.* One of the women, **mortified** by so much lack of care, then removed the handkerchief from the dead man's face and the men were left breathless too.

He was Esteban. It was not necessary to repeat it for them to recognize him. If they had been told Sir Walter Raleigh, even they might have been impressed with his gringo accent, the macaw[8] on his shoulder, his cannibal-killing blunderbuss,[9] but there could be only one Esteban in the world and there he was,
160 stretched out like a sperm whale, shoeless, wearing the pants of an undersized child, and with those stony nails that had to be cut with a knife. They only had to take the handkerchief off his face to see that he was ashamed, that it was not his fault that he was so big or so heavy or so handsome, and if he had known that this was going to happen, he would have looked for a more discreet place to drown in, seriously, I even would have tied the anchor off a galleon around my neck and staggered off a cliff like someone who doesn't like things in order not to be upsetting people now with this Wednesday dead body, as you people
170 say, in order not to be bothering anyone with this filthy piece of cold meat that doesn't have anything to do with me. There was so much truth in his manner that even the most mistrustful men, the ones who felt the bitterness of endless nights at sea fearing that their women would tire of dreaming about them and begin to dream of drowned men, even they and others who were harder still shuddered in the marrow of their bones at Esteban's sincerity.

_____

8. **macaw** *n.:* large, brightly colored parrot.
9. **blunderbuss** *n.:* now-outdated gun with a short, flaring muzzle.

That was how they came to hold the most splendid funeral they could conceive of for an abandoned drowned man. Some women who had gone to get flowers in the neighboring villages returned with other women who could not believe what they had been told, and those women went back for more flowers when they saw the dead man, and they brought more and more until there were so many flowers and so many people that it was hard to walk about. At the final moment it pained them to return him to the waters as an orphan and they chose a father and mother from among the best people, and aunts and uncles and cousins, so that through him all the inhabitants of the village became kinsmen. Some sailors who heard the weeping from a distance went off course and people heard of one who had himself tied to the mainmast, remembering ancient fables about sirens.[10] While they fought for the privilege of carrying him on their shoulders along the steep escarpment by the cliffs, men and women became aware for the first time of the desolation of their streets, the dryness of their courtyards, the narrowness of their dreams as they faced the splendor and beauty of their drowned man. They let him go without an anchor so that he could come back if he wished and whenever he wished, and they all held their breath for the fraction of centuries the body took to fall into the abyss. They did not need to look at one another to realize that they were no longer all present, that they would never be. But they also knew that everything would be different from then on, that their houses would have wider doors, higher ceilings, and stronger floors so that Esteban's memory could go everywhere without bumping into beams and so that no one in the future would dare whisper the big boob finally died, too bad,

10. **sirens** *n. pl.*: In Greek mythology, the sirens are sea maidens whose seductive singing lures men to wreck their boats on coastal rocks. Odysseus, hero of Homer's *Odyssey*, fills his crew's ears with wax so that they can pass the sirens safely. Odysseus, however, has his crew tie him to the ship's mast so that he can listen to the sirens' songs without plunging into the sea.

INTERPRET

Why do the villagers make the drowned man a member of their own extended families (lines 185–189)?

_____

_____

_____

_____

_____

_____

ANALYZE

Re-read lines 189–192. What characteristics of **magic realism** do you notice in this description of what happens to the sailors?

_____

_____

_____

_____

_____

_____

_____

_____

_____

_____

_____

_____

_____

_____

_____

_____

_____

_____

_____

_____

_____

_____

_____

_____

_____

_____

_____

_____

_____

_____

_____

_____

_____

CLARIFY

Re-read lines 200–220. What do the men and women realize about their lives at this point? Underline the details that give you this information.

the handsome fool has finally died, because they were going to paint their house fronts gay colors to make Esteban's memory eternal and they were going to break their backs digging for
210   springs among the stones and planting flowers on the cliffs so that in future years at dawn the passengers on great liners would awaken, suffocated by the smell of gardens on the high seas, and the captain would have to come down from the bridge in his dress uniform, with his astrolabe,[11] his polestar, and his row of war medals and, pointing to the promontory of roses on the horizon, he would say in fourteen languages, look there, where the wind is so peaceful now that it's gone to sleep beneath the beds, over there, where the sun's so bright that the sunflowers don't know which way to turn, yes, over there, that's Esteban's
220   village.

_____

11. astrolabe (as′trō·lāb′) *n.:* instrument used to find a star's altitude and to help navigators determine their position at sea.

The Handsomest Drowned Man in the World

Reading Skills: Analyzing Archetypes   Recall that **archetypes** are age-old models or patterns that involve characters, images, or plots. One important archetype in this story is the superhuman hero. Review the story details in the left-hand column that describe characteristics of a superhero. In the right-hand column, list details from the story that support each characteristic.

Characteristics of a Superhuman Hero	Details from the Story
His origins are mysterious.	
He is a larger-than-life figure—handsome, powerful, and impossible to comprehend in ordinary human terms.	
He has special powers. He can do marvelous things.	
He often saves people or changes their lives in some significant way.	
People hope for the hero's return someday.	

The Handsomest Drowned Man in the World

VOCABULARY IN CONTEXT

DIRECTIONS: Write vocabulary words from the Word Box to complete the paragraph below. Not all words from the box will be used.

Word Box

- bountiful
- haggard
- virile
- destitute
- frivolity
- mortified

Magic realism combines incredible events with down-to-earth details. Sometimes, characters and settings symbolize ideal conditions. For example, the hero may be incredibly handsome and (1) _____.
The sea may yield (2)_____ harvests of fish. However, everyday realities also appear. Some people may be so poor that they are practically (3)_____. Even a hero might have a tired, (4)_____ look about him. Elements like these make magical realism an alternate universe where the humdrum co-exists with the fantastic.

WORD DERIVATIONS

Some English words have interesting and colorful histories. To us a *dandelion* is just a common weed. Yet the word *dandelion* has an interesting derivation. It comes from French words for "tooth of the lion." At one time, the spikes on dandelion blossoms must have reminded people of lions' teeth.

DIRECTIONS: The chart below gives derivations for three words from "The Handsomest Drowned Man in the World." Study the information. Write in column 3 a connection you see between the word's origin and its meaning.

Reading Standard 1.1 (Grade 9–10 Review) Identify and use the literal and figurative meanings of words and understand word derivations.

Origin	Meaning	Connection
mortify: from the Latin for "to make dead"	to embarrass or humiliate deeply	
bountiful: from the French for "goodness"	giving in abundance	
nostalgia: from the Greek for "return home"	longing for some past condition	

 Check your Standards Mastery at the back of this book.

Rules of the Game by Amy Tan

LITERARY FOCUS: MOTIVATION

Motivation refers to the underlying reasons for a character's behavior. Characters may act out of pride, ambition, sibling rivalry, or some other combination of reasons. For example, winning the hand of a princess often motivates young men in fairy tales. Honor and the love of a woman motivates Sydney Carton to sacrifice his life at the end of Charles Dickens's *A Tale of Two Cities.*

What Makes People Tick? The left-hand side of the chart below lists the actions of two different people. With one or two classmates, brainstorm some possible motivations for their actions—why they acted as they did. Then, fill in the right-hand side of the chart with a motive (or a mixture of motives) that explains the behavior.

Person's Action	Motivation
An outstanding athlete starts fumbling the ball and fighting with his teammates.	
A young woman keeps up her grades, but she also takes on a part-time job after school and on the weekends.	

READING SKILLS: MAKING INFERENCES

Sometimes a writer directly tells us what makes a character tick. More often, however, writers give us the pleasure of inferring motivation for ourselves. We must sift through the details of what the characters say and do in order to figure out why they act that way.

Use the Skill   As you read "Rules of the Game," highlight or underline details that help you to **infer** the motivations of the two main characters, Waverly and her mother, Mrs. Jong.

REVIEW SKILLS

As you read "Rules of the Game," look for characters' motivations.

MOTIVATION
The underlying reasons for a character's behavior.

Reading Standard 3.3 (Grade 9–10 Review) Analyze interactions between main and subordinate characters in a literary text (e.g., internal and external conflicts, motivations, relationships, influences) and explain the way those interactions affect the plot.

Rules of the Game

from The Joy Luck Club

Amy Tan

PARAPHRASE

What do you think the mother's sayings about the wind mean (lines 10–12)? Restate the sayings in your own words.

_____

_____

_____

_____

_____

_____

_____

INFER

Re-read lines 17–18. What is the mother's **motivation** for sharing daily truths with her children? Underline the clue that helps you make this inference. *(Grade 9–10 Review)*

I was six when my mother taught me the art of invisible strength. It was a strategy for winning arguments, respect from others, and eventually, though neither of us knew it at the time, chess games.

"Bite back your tongue," scolded my mother when I cried loudly, yanking her hand toward the store that sold bags of
10 salted plums. At home, she said, "Wise guy, he not go against wind. In Chinese we say, Come from South, blow with wind—poom!—North will follow. Strongest wind cannot be seen."

The next week I bit back my tongue as we entered the store with the forbidden candies. When my mother finished her shopping, she quietly plucked a small bag of plums from the rack and put it on the counter with the rest of the items.

My mother imparted her daily truths so she could help my older brothers and me rise above our circumstances. We lived in San Francisco's Chinatown. Like most of the other Chinese chil-
20 dren who played in the back alleys of restaurants and curio shops, I didn't think we were poor. My bowl was always full, three five-course meals every day, beginning with a soup full of mysterious things I didn't want to know the names of.

We lived on Waverly Place, in a warm, clean, two-bedroom flat that sat above a small Chinese bakery specializing in steamed pastries and dim sum. In the early morning, when the alley was still quiet, I could smell fragrant red beans as they were cooked

down to a pasty sweetness. By daybreak, our flat was heavy with
the odor of fried sesame balls and sweet curried chicken cres-
cents. From my bed, I would listen as my father got ready for
work, then locked the door behind him, one-two-three clicks.

At the end of our two-block alley was a small sandlot playground with swings and slides well-shined down the middle
with use. The play area was bordered by wood-slat benches
where old-country people sat cracking roasted watermelon seeds
with their golden teeth and scattering the husks to an impatient
gathering of gurgling pigeons. The best playground, however,
was the dark alley itself. It was crammed with daily mysteries
and adventures. My brothers and I would peer into the medici-
nal herb shop, watching old Li dole out onto a still sheet of
white paper the right amount of insect shells, saffron-colored
seeds, and pungent leaves for his ailing customers. It was said
that he once cured a woman dying of an **ancestral** curse that
had eluded the best of American doctors. Next to the pharmacy
was a printer who specialized in gold-embossed wedding invita-
tions and festive red banners.

Farther down the street was Ping Yuen Fish Market. The
front window displayed a tank crowded with doomed fish and
turtles struggling to gain footing on the slimy green-tiled sides.
A handwritten sign informed tourists, "Within this store, is all
for food, not for pet." Inside, the butchers with their blood-
stained white smocks deftly gutted the fish while customers
cried out their orders and shouted, "Give me your freshest," to
which the butchers always protested, "All are freshest." On less
crowded market days, we would inspect the crates of live frogs
and crabs which we were warned not to poke, boxes of dried
cuttlefish, and row upon row of iced prawns, squid, and slippery
fish. The sanddabs made me shiver each time; their eyes lay on
one flattened side and reminded me of my mother's story of a
careless girl who ran into a crowded street and was crushed by a
cab. "Was smash flat," reported my mother.

30

40

50

60

WORD STUDY

Context often helps define
a word or term you do not
recognize. The first sentence
of the story's fifth paragraph
(lines 24–26) mentions
steamed pastries and *dim
sum*." Circle the details in the
rest of the paragraph that
name some of the ingredi-
ents that go into these foods.

VOCABULARY

ancestral (an·ses′trəl) *adj.:*
inherited.

CLARIFY

Pause at line 46. What made
the dark alley a favorite
place for Waverly and her
brothers to play in?

_____

_____

_____

_____

_____

_____

_____

_____

_____

_____

_____

_____

_____

_____

IDENTIFY

Pause at line 79. Circle the narrator's legal American name. Draw a box around the name she is called at home and its meaning.

INFER

Pause at line 92. Why do you think the narrator is being "wicked"?

_____

_____

_____

_____

_____

_____

INFER

Pause at line 95. Based on what you've read so far, what can you infer about the character of the mother?

_____

_____

_____

_____

_____

_____

_____

_____

At the corner of the alley was Hong Sing's, a four-table café with a recessed stairwell in front that led to a door marked "Tradesmen." My brothers and I believed the bad people emerged from this door at night. Tourists never went to Hong Sing's, since the menu was printed only in Chinese. A Caucasian man with a big camera once posed me and my playmates in front of the restaurant. He had us move to the side of the picture window so the photo would capture the roasted duck with
70 its head dangling from a juice-covered rope. After he took the picture, I told him he should go into Hong Sing's and eat dinner. When he smiled and asked me what they served, I shouted, "Guts and duck's feet and octopus gizzards!" Then I ran off with my friends, shrieking with laughter as we scampered across the alley and hid in the entryway grotto of the China Gem Company, my heart pounding with hope that he would chase us.

My mother named me after the street that we lived on: Waverly Place Jong, my official name for important American documents. But my family called me Meimei, "Little Sister."
80 I was the youngest, the only daughter. Each morning before school, my mother would twist and yank on my thick black hair until she had formed two tightly wound pigtails. One day, as she struggled to weave a hard-toothed comb through my disobedi-ent hair, I had a sly thought.

I asked her, "Ma, what is Chinese torture?" My mother shook her head. A bobby pin was wedged between her lips. She wetted her palm and smoothed the hair above my ear, then pushed the pin in so that it nicked sharply against my scalp.

"Who say this word?" she asked without a trace of knowing
90 how wicked I was being. I shrugged my shoulders and said, "Some boy in my class said Chinese people do Chinese torture."

"Chinese people do many things," she said simply. "Chinese people do business, do medicine, do painting. Not lazy like American people. We do torture. Best torture."

My older brother Vincent was the one who actually got the chess set. We had gone to the annual Christmas party held at the First Chinese Baptist Church at the end of the alley. The missionary ladies had put together a Santa bag of gifts donated by members of another church. None of the gifts had names on them. There were separate sacks for boys and girls of different ages.

One of the Chinese parishioners had donned a Santa Claus costume and a stiff paper beard with cotton balls glued to it. I think the only children who thought he was the real thing were too young to know that Santa Claus was not Chinese. When my turn came up, the Santa man asked me how old I was. I thought it was a trick question; I was seven according to the American formula and eight by the Chinese calendar. I said I was born on March 17, 1951. That seemed to satisfy him. He then solemnly asked if I had been a very, very good girl this year and did I believe in Jesus Christ and obey my parents. I knew the only answer to that. I nodded back with equal solemnity.

Having watched the other children opening their gifts, I already knew that the big gifts were not necessarily the nicest ones. One girl my age got a large coloring book of biblical characters, while a less greedy girl who selected a smaller box received a glass vial of lavender toilet water.[1] The sound of the box was also important. A ten-year-old boy had chosen a box that jangled when he shook it. It was a tin globe of the world with a slit for inserting money. He must have thought it was full of dimes and nickels, because when he saw that it had just ten pennies, his face fell with such undisguised disappointment that

---

1. **toilet water:** perfumed after-bath skin freshener.

CLARIFY

Pause at line 114. Americans determine their age according to the year they reached on their last birthday. Chinese determine their age by naming the year that began at that last birthday. Thus, someone who turned 7 on her last birthday is said to be 8 in the Chinese way of speaking. How old are you, in Chinese terms?

_____

_____

_____

INFER

Re-read lines 118–125. Based on these descriptions of Christmas gifts, what can you infer about Waverly's character?

_____

_____

_____

_____

_____

_____

_____

_____

_____

_____

VOCABULARY

intricate (in'tri·kit) *adj.:*
complicated; detailed.

INFER

Re-read lines 141–151.
Compare what the mother
says about the chess set at
the church with what she
says about it at home. What
motivates her each time?
(Grade 9–10 Review)

his mother slapped the side of his head and led him out of the
church hall, apologizing to the crowd for her son who had such
130 bad manners he couldn't appreciate such a fine gift.

As I peered into the sack, I quickly fingered the remaining
presents, testing their weight, imagining what they contained. I
chose a heavy, compact one that was wrapped in shiny silver foil
and a red satin ribbon. It was a twelve-pack of Life Savers and I
spent the rest of the party arranging and rearranging the candy
tubes in the order of my favorites. My brother Winston chose
wisely as well. His present turned out to be a box of **intricate**
plastic parts; the instructions on the box proclaimed that when
they were properly assembled he would have an authentic
140 miniature replica of a World War II submarine.

Vincent got the chess set, which would have been a very
decent present to get at a church Christmas party, except it was
obviously used and, as we discovered later, it was missing a black
pawn and a white knight. My mother graciously thanked the
unknown benefactor, saying, "Too good. Cost too much." At
which point, an old lady with fine white, wispy hair nodded
toward our family and said with a whistling whisper, "Merry,
merry Christmas."

When we got home, my mother told Vincent to throw the
150 chess set away. "She not want it. We not want it," she said, toss-
ing her head stiffly to the side with a tight, proud smile. My
brothers had deaf ears. They were already lining up the chess
pieces and reading from the dog-eared instruction book.

I watched Vincent and Winston play during Christmas
week. The chessboard seemed to hold elaborate secrets waiting
to be untangled. The chessmen were more powerful than Old
Li's magic herbs that cured ancestral curses. And my brothers
wore such serious faces that I was sure something was at stake
that was greater than avoiding the tradesmen's door to Hong
160 Sing's.

"Let me! Let me!" I begged between games when one
brother or the other would sit back with a deep sigh of relief

Scene from the movie *The Joy Luck Club.*
© Buena Vista Distribution, Inc.

Notes

INFER

Pause at line 166. Why do
you think Waverly wants to
play chess so badly?

and victory, the other annoyed, unable to let go of the outcome.
Vincent at first refused to let me play, but when I offered my Life
Savers as replacements for the buttons that filled in for the missing pieces, he relented. He chose the flavors: wild cherry for the
black pawn and peppermint for the white knight. Winner could
eat both.

170   As our mother sprinkled flour and rolled out small doughy
circles for the steamed dumplings that would be our dinner that
night, Vincent explained the rules, pointing to each piece. "You
have sixteen pieces and so do I. One king and queen, two
bishops, two knights, two castles, and eight pawns. The pawns
can only move forward one step, except on the first move. Then

IDENTIFY

Re-read lines 169–177. Underline the rules Vincent explains to his sister.

INTERPRET

Underline lines 192–197, where Waverly's mother applies the rules of chess to learning your way in a new country. How might her words relate to the story's title?

they can move two. But they can only take men by moving crossways like this, except in the beginning, when you can move ahead and take another pawn."

"Why?" I asked as I moved my pawn. "Why can't they move more steps?"

180 "Because they're pawns," he said.

"But why do they go crossways to take other men? Why aren't there any women and children?"

"Why is the sky blue? Why must you always ask stupid questions?" asked Vincent. "This is a game. These are the rules. I didn't make them up. See. Here. In the book." He jabbed a page with a pawn in his hand. "Pawn. P-A-W-N. Pawn. Read it yourself."

My mother patted the flour off her hands. "Let me see book," she said quietly. She scanned the pages quickly, not read-
190 ing the foreign English symbols, seeming to search deliberately for nothing in particular.

"This American rules," she concluded at last. "Every time people come out from foreign country, must know rules. You not know, judge say, Too bad, go back. They not telling you why so you can use their way go forward. They say, Don't know why, you find out yourself. But they knowing all the time. Better you take it, find out why yourself." She tossed her head back with a satisfied smile.

I found out about all the whys later. I read the rules and
200 looked up all the big words in a dictionary. I borrowed books from the Chinatown library. I studied each chess piece, trying to absorb the power each contained.

I learned about opening moves and why it's important to control the center early on; the shortest distance between two points is straight down the middle. I learned about the middle game and why tactics between two adversaries are like clashing ideas; the one who plays better has the clearest plans for both attacking and getting out of traps. I learned why it is essential in the endgame to have foresight, a mathematical understanding of

210 all possible moves, and patience; all weaknesses and advantages become evident to a strong adversary and are **obscured** to a tiring opponent. I discovered that for the whole game one must gather invisible strengths and see the endgame before the game begins.

I also found out why I should never reveal "why" to others. A little knowledge withheld is a great advantage one should store for future use. That is the power of chess. It is a game of secrets in which one must show and never tell.

I loved the secrets I found within the sixty-four black and
220 white squares. I carefully drew a handmade chessboard and pinned it to the wall next to my bed, where at night I would stare for hours at imaginary battles. Soon I no longer lost any games or Life Savers, but I lost my adversaries. Winston and Vincent decided they were more interested in roaming the streets after school in their Hopalong Cassidy[2] cowboy hats.

On a cold spring afternoon, while walking home from school, I detoured through the play- ground at the end of our alley.
230 I saw a group of old men, two seated across a folding table playing a game of chess, others smoking pipes, eating peanuts, and watching. I ran home and grabbed Vincent's chess set, which was bound in a cardboard box with rubber bands. I also carefully selected two prized rolls of Life Savers. I came back to the park and approached a man who was observing the game.

"Want to play?" I asked him. His face widened with sur-
240 prise and he grinned as he looked at the box under my arm.

---

2. **Hopalong Cassidy:** cowboy hero of movies and television from the 1930s through the early 1950s.

VOCABULARY

obscured (əb·skyo͞ord′) v.: concealed; hidden.

INFER

Re-read lines 203–218, which tell you what Waverly learned from chess. What do these details tell you about her character?

_____

_____

_____

_____

_____

_____

_____

_____

_____

_____

_____

_____

_____

_____

IDENTIFY

Whom does Waverly see in the park (lines 230–234)? Underline details that describe these people and what they are doing.

IDENTIFY

Re-read lines 253–260. Underline details that reveal what Waverly learned from chess.

INFER

Pause at line 265. "Proper Chinese humility" requires Waverly's mother not to boast about her daughter's skill. How does she really feel about Waverly's success?

_____

_____

_____

_____

INTERPRET

Pause at line 273. What **motivates** Waverly to pretend she doesn't want to play? *(Grade 9–10 Review)*

_____

_____

_____

_____

_____

_____

_____

_____

"Little sister, been a long time since I play with dolls," he said, smiling benevolently. I quickly put the box down next to him on the bench and displayed my **retort.**

Lau Po, as he allowed me to call him, turned out to be a much better player than my brothers. I lost many games and many Life Savers. But over the weeks, with each diminishing roll of candies, I added new secrets. Lau Po gave me the names. The Double Attack from the East and West Shores. Throwing Stones on the Drowning Man. The Sudden Meeting of the Clan. The

250 Surprise from the Sleeping Guard. The Humble Servant Who Kills the King. Sand in the Eyes of Advancing Forces. A Double Killing Without Blood.

There were also the fine points of chess etiquette. Keep captured men in neat rows, as well-tended prisoners. Never announce "Check" with vanity, lest someone with an unseen sword slit your throat. Never hurl pieces into the sandbox after you have lost a game, because then you must find them again, by yourself, after apologizing to all around you. By the end of the

260 summer, Lau Po had taught me all he knew, and I had become a better chess player.

A small weekend crowd of Chinese people and tourists would gather as I played and defeated my opponents one by one. My mother would join the crowds during these outdoor exhibition games. She sat proudly on the bench, telling my admirers with proper Chinese humility, "Is luck."

A man who watched me play in the park suggested that my mother allow me to play in local chess tournaments. My mother smiled graciously, an answer that meant nothing. I desperately wanted to go, but I bit back my tongue. I knew she would not let

270 me play among strangers. So as we walked home I said in a small voice that I didn't want to play in the local tournament. They would have American rules. If I lost, I would bring shame on my family.

"Is shame you fall down nobody push you," said my mother.

During my first tournament, my mother sat with me in the front row as I waited for my turn. I frequently bounced my legs to unstick them from the cold metal seat of the folding chair. When my name was called, I leapt up. My mother unwrapped something in her lap. It was her *chang,* a small tablet of red jade which held the sun's fire. "Is luck," she whispered, and tucked it into my dress pocket. I turned to my opponent, a fifteen-year-old boy from Oakland. He looked at me, wrinkling his nose.

As I began to play, the boy disappeared, the color ran out of the room, and I saw only my white pieces and his black ones waiting on the other side. A light wind began blowing past my ears. It whispered secrets only I could hear.

"Blow from the South," it murmured. "The wind leaves no trail." I saw a clear path, the traps to avoid. The crowd rustled. "Shhh! Shhh!" said the corners of the room. The wind blew stronger. "Throw sand from the East to distract him." The knight came forward ready for the sacrifice. The wind hissed, louder and louder. "Blow, blow, blow. He cannot see. He is blind now. Make him lean away from the wind so he is easier to knock down."

"Check," I said, as the wind roared with laughter. The wind died down to little puffs, my own breath.

My mother placed my first trophy next to a new plastic chess set that the neighborhood Tao society had given to me. As she wiped each piece with a soft cloth, she said, "Next time win more, lose less."

"Ma, it's not how many pieces you lose," I said. "Sometimes you need to lose pieces to get ahead."

"Better to lose less, see if you really need."

FLUENCY

Read the boxed passage aloud twice. On your second reading, use your voice to capture first the softness, and then the increasing loudness of the "wind" voices that only Waverly can hear.

IDENTIFY

What advice does Waverly's mother give her about improving her game (lines 298–309)? What doesn't the mother understand?

_____

_____

_____

_____

_____

_____

_____

_____

_____

_____

_____

_____

_____

_____

_____

_____

280

290

300

_____

_____

_____

_____

_____

_____

_____

_____

_____

_____

_____

_____

_____

_____

_____

_____

_____

_____

310   At the next tournament, I won again, but it was my mother who wore the triumphant grin.

"Lost eight piece this time. Last time was eleven. What I tell you? Better off lose less!" I was annoyed, but I couldn't say anything.

I attended more tournaments, each one farther away from home. I won all games, in all divisions. The Chinese bakery downstairs from our flat displayed my growing collection of trophies in its window, amidst the dust-covered cakes that were never picked up. The day after I won an important regional

320   tournament, the window encased a fresh sheet cake with whipped-cream frosting and red script saying, "Congratulations, Waverly Jong, Chinatown Chess Champion." Soon after that, a flower shop, headstone engraver, and funeral parlor offered to sponsor me in national tournaments. That's when my mother decided I no longer had to do the dishes. Winston and Vincent had to do my chores.

"Why does she get to play and we do all the work," complained Vincent.

"Is new American rules," said my mother. "Meimei play,

330   squeeze all her brains out for win chess. You play, worth squeeze towel."

By my ninth birthday, I was a national chess champion. I was still some 429 points away from grand-master status,[3] but I was **touted** as the Great American Hope, a child **prodigy** and a girl to boot. They ran a photo of me in *Life* magazine next to a quote in which Bobby Fischer[4] said, "There will never be a woman grand master." "Your move, Bobby," said the caption.

The day they took the magazine picture I wore neatly plaited braids clipped with plastic barrettes trimmed with rhine-

340   stones. I was playing in a large high school auditorium that

3. **grand-master status:** top rank in international chess competition.
4. **Bobby Fischer** (1943–   ): American chess master, the youngest player in the world to attain the rank of grand master, in 1958.

IDENTIFY

What has happened to Waverly by her ninth birthday (lines 332–337)? Underline the details that describe how her life has changed.

VOCABULARY

touted (tout′id) *v.:* highly praised.

prodigy (präd′ə·jē) *n.:* extremely gifted person.

echoed with phlegmy coughs and the squeaky rubber knobs of chair legs sliding across freshly waxed wooden floors. Seated across from me was an American man, about the same age as Lau Po, maybe fifty. I remember that his sweaty brow seemed to weep at my every move. He wore a dark, **malodorous** suit. One of his pockets was stuffed with a great white kerchief on which he wiped his palm before sweeping his hand over the chosen chess piece with great flourish.

350 In my crisp pink-and-white dress with scratchy lace at the neck, one of two my mother had sewn for these special occasions, I would clasp my hands under my chin, the delicate points of my elbows poised lightly on the table in the manner my mother had shown me for posing for the press. I would swing my patent leather shoes back and forth like an impatient child riding on a school bus. Then I would pause, suck in my lips, twirl my chosen piece in midair as if undecided, and then firmly plant it in its new threatening place, with a triumphant smile thrown back at my opponent for good measure.

I no longer played in the alley of Waverly Place. I never 360 visited the playground where the pigeons and old men gathered. I went to school, then directly home to learn new chess secrets, cleverly concealed advantages, more escape routes.

But I found it difficult to concentrate at home. My mother had a habit of standing over me while I plotted out my games. I think she thought of herself as my protective ally. Her lips would be sealed tight, and after each move I made, a soft "Hmmmmph" would escape from her nose.

"Ma, I can't practice when you stand there like that," I said one day. She retreated to the kitchen and made loud noises with 370 the pots and pans. When the crashing stopped, I could see out of the corner of my eye that she was standing in the doorway. "Hmmmph!" Only this one came out of her tight throat.

My parents made many **concessions** to allow me to practice. One time I complained that the bedroom I shared was so noisy that I couldn't think. Thereafter, my brothers slept in a bed

IDENTIFY

Re-read lines 338–348. Underline the details showing how Waverly's appearance contrasts with that of her opponent.

VOCABULARY

malodorous (mal·ō′dər·əs) *adj.:* bad-smelling.
concessions (kən·sesh′ənz) *n. pl.:* acts of giving in.

ANALYZE

Pause at line 372. How would you describe the relationship between Waverly and her mother?

_____

_____

_____

_____

_____

_____

_____

_____

_____

_____

_____

_____

INFER

Underline details in lines 384–392 that show that Waverly is cruel to her mother. How is Waverly's mother probably feeling?

_____

_____

_____

_____

_____

_____

_____

_____

_____

_____

_____

_____

_____

_____

_____

_____

_____

_____

_____

_____

VOCABULARY

careened (kə·rēnd') v.: lurched sideways.

in the living room facing the street. I said I couldn't finish my rice; my head didn't work right when my stomach was too full. I left the table with half-finished bowls and nobody complained. But there was one duty I couldn't avoid. I had to
380 accompany my mother on Saturday market days when I had no tournament to play. My mother would proudly walk with me, visiting many shops, buying very little. "This my daughter Waverly Jong," she said to whoever looked her way.

One day, after we left a shop I said under my breath, "I wish you wouldn't do that, telling everybody I'm your daughter." My mother stopped walking. Crowds of people with heavy bags pushed past us on the sidewalk, bumping into first one shoulder, then another.

"Aiii-ya. So shame be with mother?" She grasped my hand
390 even tighter as she glared at me.

I looked down. "It's not that, it's just so obvious. It's just so embarrassing."

"Embarrass you be my daughter?" Her voice was cracking with anger.

"That's not what I meant. That's not what I said."

"What you say?"

I knew it was a mistake to say anything more, but I heard my voice speaking. "Why do you have to use me to show off? If you want to show off, then why don't you learn to play chess?"
400 My mother's eyes turned into dangerous black slits. She had no words for me, just sharp silence.

I felt the wind rushing around my hot ears. I jerked my hand out of my mother's tight grasp and spun around, knocking into an old woman. Her bag of groceries spilled to the ground.

"Aii-ya! Stupid girl!" my mother and the woman cried. Oranges and tin cans **careened** down the sidewalk. As my mother stooped to help the old woman pick up the escaping food, I took off.

I raced down the street, dashing between people, not look-
410 ing back as my mother screamed shrilly, "Meimei! Meimei!" I

fled down an alley, past dark, curtained shops and merchants washing the grime off their windows. I sped into the sunlight, into a large street crowded with tourists examining trinkets and souvenirs. I ducked into another dark alley, down another street, up another alley. I ran until it hurt and I realized I had nowhere to go, that I was not running from anything. The alleys contained no escape routes.

My breath came out like angry smoke. It was cold. I sat down on an upturned plastic pail next to a stack of empty
420 boxes, cupping my chin with my hands, thinking hard. I imagined my mother, first walking briskly down one street or another looking for me, then giving up and returning home to await my arrival. After two hours, I stood up on creaking legs and slowly walked home.

The alley was quiet and I could see the yellow lights shining from our flat like two tiger's eyes in the night. I climbed the sixteen steps to the door, advancing quietly up each so as not to make any warning sounds. I turned the knob; the door was locked. I heard a chair moving, quick steps, the locks turning—
430 click! click! click!—and then the door opened.

"About time you got home," said Vincent. "Boy, are you in trouble."

He slid back to the dinner table. On a platter were the remains of a large fish, its fleshy head still connected to bones swimming upstream in vain escape. Standing there waiting for my punishment, I heard my mother speak in a dry voice.

"We not concerning this girl. This girl not have concerning for us."

Nobody looked at me. Bone chopsticks clinked against the
440 inside of bowls being emptied into hungry mouths.

I walked into my room, closed the door, and lay down on my bed. The room was dark, the ceiling filled with shadows from the dinnertime lights of neighboring flats.

In my head, I saw a chessboard with sixty-four black and white squares. Opposite me was my opponent, two angry black

IDENTIFY CAUSE & EFFECT

Re-read lines 402–424. What motivates Waverly to run away, and what causes her to go home again? *(Grade 9–10 Review)*

_____
_____
_____
_____
_____
_____
_____
_____

PARAPHRASE

Restate in your own words what Waverly's mother says about Waverly in lines 437–438.

_____
_____
_____
_____
_____
_____
_____
_____

Re-read lines 444–456. How does Waverly's imaginary chess game relate to the battle with her mother that has run through the entire story?

_____

_____

_____

_____

_____

_____

_____

_____

_____

_____

_____

_____

_____

_____

_____

_____

_____

_____

_____

slits. She wore a triumphant smile. "Strongest wind cannot be seen," she said.

Her black men advanced across the plane, slowly marching to each **successive** level as a single unit. My white pieces
450   screamed as they scurried and fell off the board one by one. As her men drew closer to my edge, I felt myself growing light. I rose up into the air and flew out the window. Higher and higher, above the alley, over the tops of tiled roofs, where I was gathered up by the wind and pushed up toward the night sky until everything below me disappeared and I was alone.

I closed my eyes and pondered my next move.

Rules of the Game

Reading Skills: Making Inferences   What **motivates** Waverly and her mother—why do they act as they do? Complete the chart below by listing two details from the story that support the inferences listed at the top of each column.

Inference: Mrs. Jong wants to practice proper Chinese values. She rejects or fears American values.	Inference: Waverly loves her mother but resists her efforts to control her.	Inference: Waverly likes chess because, unlike life, it has rules which you can master and win.

Rules of the Game

VOCABULARY DEVELOPMENT

VOCABULARY IN CONTEXT

DIRECTIONS: Write vocabulary words from the Word Box to complete the paragraph below. Not all words from the box will be used.

Word Box

- ancestral
- intricate
- obscured
- retort
- touted
- prodigy
- malodorous
- concessions
- careened
- successive

"Rules of the Game" takes place in the Chinatown district of San Francisco during the 1950s. This small district makes up a city-within-a-city. Tearooms, schools, theaters, temples, and tiny shops cram every corner of an (1)_____ maze of streets and alleys. In shop after shop, Chinatown offers (2)_____ wonders. Visitors find their vision (3)_____ by towering piles of clothing heaped on the sidewalks. Their noses twitch at aromas wafting from musty herb stores and (4)_____ butcher shops. They soon realize they can buy everything here, from clothing, incense, food, and fine jewelry to valuable, old (5)_____ treasures brought over from China.

ANALOGIES

In an **analogy** the words in one pair relate to each other in the same way as the words in a second pair. For example, a pair of words can be synonyms or antonyms, or one word in the pair may describe a characteristic of the other.

In analogies, colons stand for words. A single colon (:) should be read as "is to." A double colon (::) should be read as "as."

DIRECTIONS: Study the first pair in each analogy to analyze the relationship between the words. Then, complete the analogy by filling in the word from the box above that completes the second pair.

Reading Standard 1.3
Discern the meaning of analogies encountered, analyzing specific comparisons as well as relationships and inferences.

1. SWEET : PLEASANT :: stinky : _____

2. THROW : CATCH :: displayed : _____

3. CONDEMNED : PRAISED :: downplayed : _____

4. SOUR : LEMON :: talented : _____

5. WALKED : STUMBLED :: glided : _____

 Check your Standards Mastery at the back of this book.

from In Search of Our Mothers' Gardens by Alice Walker

BEFORE YOU READ

LITERARY FOCUS: PERSONAL ESSAY

A **personal essay** is a short piece of nonfiction writing that explores a topic in a personal way. The topic can be anything at all that interests the writer; the best personal essays often show how the writer's own experiences and emotional life connect with more universal concerns. Mark Twain, Virginia Woolf, and George Orwell are noted for their personal essays.

READING SKILLS: IDENTIFYING THE MAIN IDEA

Unlike formal essays, personal essays are often casual and conversational. They may even ramble and get off the subject for a brief time. But a good personal essay, no matter how informally it is written, is always focused on at least one main idea.

Use the Skill As you read this famous essay, mark the beginning of each new topic. When you have finished, go back and make a list of all the topics you have marked. Check to see if the writer has provided a one-sentence generalization that covers *all* of the topics. If you can't find such a sentence, then you must look at all the topics, think about the essay's title, and then infer the main idea that unifies the essay. Your statement of the main idea should be broad enough to cover all the topics in the essay.

Alice Walker.

> ### REVIEW SKILLS
>
> As you read this essay, analyze the author's use of **metaphor,** a type of figurative language.
>
> #### FIGURATIVE LANGUAGE
> Words or phrases that describe one thing in terms of another.

Reading Standard 2.5 Analyze an author's implicit and explicit philosophical assumptions and beliefs about a subject.

Reading Standard 3.1 Analyze characteristics of subgenres (e.g., satire, parody, allegory, pastoral) that are used in poetry, prose, plays, novels, short stories, essays, and other basic genres.

Reading Standard 3.7 (Grade 9–10 Review) Recognize and understand the significance of various literary devices, including figurative language, imagery, allegory, and symbolism, and explain their appeal.

from IN SEARCH OF
Our Mothers' Gardens

Alice Walker

IDENTIFY

Skim the essay, and find the page on which a poem appears. Then, count the number of footnotes in the essay that identify *specific people.* Jot down what you discover.

_____

_____

_____

_____

IDENTIFY

Underline details that describe the personality of Walker's mother (lines 5–8).

CLARIFY

Pause at line 24. What does Walker want to discover?

_____

_____

_____

VOCABULARY

vibrant (vī′brənt) *adj.:* full of energy.

In the late 1920s my mother ran away from home to marry my father. Marriage, if not running away, was expected of seventeen-year-old girls. By the time she was twenty, she had two children and was pregnant with a third. Five children later, I was born. And this is how I came to know my mother: She seemed a large, soft, loving-eyed woman who was rarely impatient in our home. Her quick, violent temper was on view only a few times a year, when she battled with the white landlord who had the misfortune to suggest to her that her children did not
10   need to go to school.

She made all the clothes we wore, even my brothers' overalls. She made all the towels and sheets we used. She spent the summers canning vegetables and fruits. She spent the winter evenings making quilts enough to cover all our beds.

During the "working" day, she labored beside—not behind—my father in the fields. Her day began before sunup, and did not end until late at night. There was never a moment for her to sit down, undisturbed, to unravel her own private thoughts; never a time free from interruption— by work or the
20   noisy inquiries of her many children. And yet, it is to my mother—and all our mothers who were not famous—that I went in search of the secret of what has fed that muzzled and often mutilated, but **vibrant,** creative spirit that the black woman has inherited, and that pops out in wild and unlikely places to this day.

But when, you will ask, did my overworked mother have time to know or care about feeding the creative spirit?

Notes _____

_____
_____
_____
_____
_____
_____
_____
_____
_____
_____
_____
_____
_____
_____
_____
_____
_____
_____
_____
_____
_____

IDENTIFY

Go back and circle words and passages in the first four paragraphs (lines 1–26) that show how Walker's mother was "overworked."

VOCABULARY

medium (mē′dē·əm) *n.:* material for an artist.

INTERPRET

Pause at line 44. Why is Walker so impressed with the quilt she saw in the Smithsonian?

_____

_____

_____

_____

_____

_____

_____

_____

_____

ANALYZE

Notice Walker's bracketed editorial changes in Woolf's essay, in lines 46–60. What do Walker's suggested changes reveal about her beliefs?

_____

_____

_____

_____

_____

_____

The answer is so simple that many of us have spent years discovering it. We have constantly looked high, when we should have looked high—and low.

30 For example: In the Smithsonian Institution in Washington, D.C., there hangs a quilt unlike any other in the world. In fanciful, inspired, and yet simple and identifiable figures, it portrays the story of the Crucifixion. It is considered rare, beyond price. Though it follows no known pattern of quilt-making, and though it is made of bits and pieces of worthless rags, it is obviously the work of a person of powerful imagination and deep spiritual feeling. Below this quilt I saw a note that says it was made by "an anonymous Black woman in Alabama, a hundred years ago."

40 If we could locate this "anonymous" black woman from Alabama, she would turn out to be one of our grandmothers— an artist who left her mark in the only materials she could afford, and in the only **medium** her position in society allowed her to use.

As Virginia Woolf[1] wrote further, in *A Room of One's Own:*

Yet genius of a sort must have existed among women as it must have existed among the working class. [Change this to "slaves" and "the wives and daughters of share-croppers."] Now and again an Emily Brontë[2] or a Robert

50 Burns[3] [change this to "a Zora Hurston or a Richard Wright"] blazes out and proves its presence. But certainly it never got itself on to paper. When, however, one reads of a witch being ducked, of a woman possessed by devils [or "Sainthood"[4]], of a wise woman selling herbs [our

---

1. **Virginia Woolf:** English novelist and critic. In *A Room of One's Own* (1929), Woolf says that, in order to write, a woman must have a room of her own (privacy) and the means to support herself (money).
2. **Emily Brontë:** English novelist and poet, best known for her novel *Wuthering Heights* (1847).
3. **Robert Burns:** eighteenth-century Scottish poet.
4. **"Sainthood":** In the early part of this essay, Walker talks about certain black women in the South called Saints. Intensely spiritual, these women were driven to madness by their creativity, for which they could find no release.

root workers], or even a very remarkable man who had a mother, then I think we are on the track of a lost novelist, a suppressed poet, of some mute and inglorious Jane Austen. . . .[5] Indeed, I would venture to guess that Anon, who wrote so many poems without signing them, was

60 often a woman. . . .

And so our mothers and grandmothers have, more often than not anonymously, handed on the creative spark, the seed of the flower they themselves never hoped to see: or like a sealed letter they could not plainly read.

And so it is, certainly, with my own mother. Unlike "Ma" Rainey's[6] songs, which retained their creator's name even while blasting forth from Bessie Smith's[7] mouth, no song or poem will bear my mother's name. Yet so many of the stories that I write, that we all write, are my mother's stories. Only recently did I

70 fully realize this: that through years of listening to my mother's stories of her life, I have absorbed not only the stories themselves, but something of the manner in which she spoke, something of the urgency that involves the knowledge that her stories—like her life—must be recorded. It is probably for this reason that so much of what I have written is about characters whose counterparts in real life are so much older than I am.

But the telling of these stories, which came from my mother's lips as naturally as breathing, was not the only way my mother showed herself as an artist. For stories, too, were subject

80 to being distracted, to dying without conclusion. Dinners must be started, and cotton must be gathered before the big rains. The artist that was and is my mother showed itself to me only after many years. This is what I finally noticed:

---

5. **Jane Austen:** English novelist, best known for *Pride and Prejudice* (1813).
6. **"Ma" Rainey:** nickname of Gertrude Malissa Nix Pridgett Rainey. She was the first great African American professional blues vocalist and is considered to be the mother of the blues.
7. **Bessie Smith:** One of the greatest of blues singers, Smith was helped to professional status by Ma Rainey. She became known in her lifetime as "Empress of the Blues."

IDENTIFY

Re-read lines 61–64. What is the **main idea** of this sentence? Underline it.

IDENTIFY

Re-read lines 65–76. What qualities of a **personal essay** do you notice in this passage?

_____

_____

_____

_____

_____

_____

_____

_____

_____

_____

_____

_____

_____

_____

_____

_____

_____

VOCABULARY

profusely (prō · fyoos′lē) *adv.:*
in great quantities.

conception (kən · sep′shən) *n.:*
mental formation of ideas.

ANALYZE

In lines 84–94, Walker
describes her mother's
creativity with her flowers.
How do these details support
Walker's topic—that black
women have inherited a
"vibrant, creative spirit"?

_____

_____

_____

_____

_____

_____

_____

IDENTIFY
CAUSE & EFFECT

Re-read lines 100–107. How
do passersby react to the
mother's garden? Why do
they have this reaction?

_____

_____

_____

_____

_____

_____

_____

Like Mem, a character in *The Third Life of Grange
Copeland,*[8] my mother adorned with flowers whatever shabby
house we were forced to live in. And not just your typical strag-
gly country stand of zinnias, either. She planted ambitious gardens—and still does—with over fifty different varieties of plants
that bloom **profusely** from early March until late November.

90   Before she left home for the fields, she watered her flowers,
chopped up the grass, and laid out new beds. When she returned
from the fields she might divide clumps of bulbs, dig a cold pit,[9]
uproot and replant roses, or prune branches from her taller
bushes or trees—until night came and it was too dark to see.

Whatever she planted grew as if by magic, and her fame as
a grower of flowers spread over three counties. Because of her
creativity with her flowers, even my memories of poverty are seen
through a screen of blooms—sunflowers, petunias, roses, dahlias,
forsythia, spirea, delphiniums, verbena . . . and on and on.

100   And I remember people coming to my mother's yard
to be given cuttings from her flowers; I hear again the praise
showered on her because whatever rocky soil she landed on, she
turned into a garden. A garden so brilliant with colors, so original in its design, so magnificent with life and creativity, that to
this day people drive by our house in Georgia—perfect strangers
and imperfect strangers—and ask to stand or walk among my
mother's art.

I notice that it is only when my mother is working in her
flowers that she is radiant, almost to the point of being invis-
110   ible—except as Creator: hand and eye. She is involved in work
her soul must have. Ordering the universe in the image of her
personal **conception** of Beauty.

Her face, as she prepares the Art that is her gift, is a
legacy of respect she leaves to me, for all that illuminates and

---

8. ***The Third Life of Grange Copeland:*** Alice Walker's first novel,
   published in 1970.
9. **cold pit:** shallow pit, usually covered with glass, that is used for
   rooting plants or sheltering young plants from temperature
   variations in the spring.

cherishes life. She has handed down respect for the possibilities—and the will to grasp them.

For her, so hindered and intruded upon in so many ways,
being an artist has still been a daily part of her life. This ability
to hold on, even in very simple ways, is work black women have
120   done for a very long time.

This poem is not enough, but it is something, for the
woman who literally covered the holes in our walls with
sunflowers:

They were women then
My mama's generation
Husky of voice—Stout of
Step
With fists as well as
Hands
130   How they battered down
Doors
And ironed
Starched white
Shirts
How they led
Armies
Headragged Generals
Across mined
Fields
140   Booby-trapped
Kitchens
To discover books
Desks
A place for us
How they knew what we
Must know
Without knowing a page
Of it
Themselves.

Alice Walker.

Re-read lines 150–151. What "garden" do you think Walker has found?

ingenious (in·jēn′yəs) *adj.:* clever.

150   Guided by my heritage of a love of beauty and a respect for strength—in search of my mother's garden, I found my own.

    And perhaps in Africa over two hundred years ago, there was just such a mother; perhaps she painted vivid and daring decorations in oranges and yellows and greens on the walls of her hut; perhaps she sang—in a voice like Roberta Flack's[10]— *sweetly* over the compounds of her village; perhaps she wove the most stunning mats or told the most **ingenious** stories of all the village storytellers. Perhaps she was herself a poet—though only her daughter's name is signed to the poems that we know.

160   Perhaps Phillis Wheatley's[11] mother was also an artist.

    Perhaps in more than Phillis Wheatley's biological life is her mother's signature made clear.

---

10. **Roberta Flack:** popular African American singer-songwriter.
11. **Phillis Wheatley** (1753?–1783): American poet, born in Africa and brought to America in slavery. Wheatley is often referred to as the first African American poet.

from In Search of Our Mothers' Gardens

Reading Skills: Identifying the Main Idea   A **main idea** is the controlling idea that unifies an essay or any other piece of nonfiction writing. When you state the main idea of a text, you must be sure your statement covers all the key details in the text. In most texts, the overall main idea is not stated directly. Instead, as the reader, you have to consider all the key details in the essay and decide on a statement that covers them all.

Your first step in determining the main idea of an essay or of any other text is to list the text's main points or topics. Use the following informal outline form to list the main topics in Walker's essay.

Once you have listed the main topics, state, in one or two sentences, a main idea that covers all these topics. You will often find that the work's title gives you a clue to the main idea the writer wants to communicate. Be sure to consider Walker's title in your statement of the main idea.

Main Points in Essay	
Main Point #1	
Main Point #2	
Main Point #3	
Main Point #4	
Statement of Main Idea of Entire Essay:	

from In Search of Our Mothers' Gardens

VOCABULARY IN CONTEXT

DIRECTIONS: Write vocabulary words from the Word Box to complete the paragraph below. Use each word only once.

Word Box

vibrant

medium

profusely

conception

ingenious

Alice Walker's (1)_____ is words. Walker's poems, essays, and stories burst with lively, (2)_____ characters, much like the flowers in her mother's (3)_____ blooming garden. In this essay, Walker supports her (4)_____ of black women as exceptionally creative, with examples taken from the life of her own mother. Walker views her mother as a talented, (5)_____ woman who created beauty out of next to nothing.

WORD ORIGINS

DIRECTIONS: An **etymology** refers to the history and development of a word. Use the information in this chart to help you identify the meaning and history of each boldface word. Write the letter of the correct definition on the line in front of the word.

Vocabulary Word	Latin Origin	Related Words
vibrant	*vibrare:* "to quiver; shake"	vibration
medium	*medius:* "between"	median strip; mediate
profusely	*profundere:* "to pour out"	profusion
conception	*conceptus:* "take in; receive"	concept; conceive
ingenious	*ingeniosus:* "gifted with genius"	ingenuity

___ 1. **vibration** (a) repeated motion (b) stillness (c) noise

___ 2. **mediate** (a) to work with two sides to come to an agreement (b) to pray very seriously (c) to give medicine to

___ 3. **profusion** (a) small amount (b) lavish supply (c) confusion

___ 4. **concept** (a) a process (b) an argument (c) an idea

___ 5. **ingenuity** (a) meanness (b) cleverness (c) goodness

 Check your Standards Mastery at the back of this book.

Straw into Gold by Sandra Cisneros

LITERARY FOCUS: ALLUSION

An **allusion** is a reference to a well-known person, place, event, or quotation from history, literature, religion, politics, sports, science, or some other branch of culture. If you say "Joe is the Einstein of my physics class," people know you are saying Joe is brilliant, because they catch your allusion to the most famous physicist of the twentieth century.

Writers expect us to catch their allusions, too. They base their confidence on the fact that many people share a large body of knowledge. That knowledge includes the folktale "Rumpelstiltskin," in which a young woman must spin a roomful of straw into gold. Sandra Cisneros alludes to the story in the title of her essay, and twice within her essay.

What's the Allusion? Complete the chart below by writing a brief paraphrase or explanation of each allusion in the left column.

Allusion	Paraphrase or Explanation
Wipe that Mona Lisa smile off your face!	
He is such a Romeo.	
Julia has a Cinderella complex.	

READING SKILLS: UNDERSTANDING A WRITER'S BACKGROUND

Personal experience is an important resource for writers. In fact, Cisneros builds this essay on her own experiences from childhood, school, and travels abroad. Here are a few of the many things that make up a writer's background:

• where and when the writer grew up

• religious traditions and ethnic values of the writer's family

• when and where the writer acquired an education

• experiences that influenced the writer's career

Use the Skill   As you read "Straw into Gold," underline or highlight details that reveal Cisneros's background and the influences on her writing.

REVIEW SKILLS

As you read "Straw into Gold," look for the use of allusion.

ALLUSION
A reference to a well-known person, place, event, or quotation from history, literature, or some other branch of culture.

Reading Standard 3.5b Contrast the major periods, themes, styles, and trends and describe how works by members of different cultures relate to one another.

Reading Standard 3.7 (Grade 9–10 Review) Recognize and understand the significance of various literary devices, including figurative language, imagery, allegory, and symbolism, and explain their appeal.

STRAW into GOLD

Sandra Cisneros

When I was living in an artists' colony in the south of France,
some fellow Latin-Americans who taught at the university in
Aix-en-Provence invited me to share a home-cooked meal with
them. I had been living abroad almost a year then on an NEA[1]
grant, **subsisting** mainly on French bread and lentils so that my
money could last longer. So when the invitation to dinner
arrived, I accepted without hesitation. Especially since they had
promised Mexican food.

What I didn't realize when they made this invitation was
10   that I was supposed to be involved in preparing the meal. I guess
they assumed I knew how to cook Mexican food because I am
Mexican. They wanted specifically tortillas, though I'd never
made a tortilla in my life.

It's true I had witnessed my mother rolling the little armies
of dough into perfect circles, but my mother's family is from
Guanajuato; they are *provincianos,* country folk. They only know
how to make flour tortillas. My father's family, on the other
hand, is *chilango*[2] from Mexico City. We ate corn tortillas but we
didn't make them. Someone was sent to the corner tortilleria to
20   buy some. I'd never seen anybody make corn tortillas. Ever.

Somehow my Latino hosts had gotten a hold of a packet of
corn flour, and this is what they tossed my way with orders to

---

1. **NEA:** National Endowment for the Arts, a federal agency that grants
   money to selected organizations and individuals so they may engage
   in creative pursuits.
2. *chilango:* variation of "*Shilango,*" name used by people of coastal
   Veracruz for those who live inland, especially the poor people of
   Mexico.

produce tortillas. *Así como sea.* Any ol' way, they said and went back to their cooking.

Why did I feel like the woman in the fairy tale who was locked in a room and ordered to spin straw into gold? I had the same sick feeling when I was required to write my critical essay for the MFA[3] exam—the only piece of noncreative writing necessary in order to get my graduate degree. How was I to start?

30 There were rules involved here, unlike writing a poem or story, which I did **intuitively.** There was a step by step process needed and I had better know it. I felt as if making tortillas—or writing a critical paper, for that matter—were tasks so impossible I wanted to break down into tears.

Somehow though, I managed to make tortillas—crooked and burnt, but **edible** nonetheless. My hosts were absolutely ignorant when it came to Mexican food; they thought my tortillas were delicious. (I'm glad my mama wasn't there.) Thinking back and looking at an old photograph documenting the three

40 of us consuming those lopsided circles I am amazed. Just as I am amazed I could finish my MFA exam.

I've managed to do a lot of things in my life I didn't think I was capable of and which many others didn't think I was capable of either. Especially because I am a woman, a Latina, an only daughter in a family of six men. My father would've liked to have seen me married long ago. In our culture men and women don't leave their father's house except by way of marriage. I crossed my father's threshold with nothing carrying me but my own two feet. A woman whom no one came for and no

50 one chased away.

To make matters worse, I left before any of my six brothers had **ventured** away from home. I broke a terrible **taboo.** Somehow, looking back at photos of myself as a child, I wonder if I was aware of having begun already my own quiet war.

---

3. **MFA:** master of fine arts.

INTERPRET

Cisneros uses an **allusion** from "Rumpelstiltskin" in lines 25–26. How would you explain her allusion? *(Grade 9–10 Review)*

_____

_____

_____

_____

_____

_____

IDENTIFY

Re-read lines 25–29. Circle another situation that made Cisneros feel as if she'd been asked to do the impossible.

VOCABULARY

intuitively (in·tōō'i·tiv·lē) *adv.:* without conscious reasoning.
edible (ed'ə·bəl) *adj.:* capable of being eaten.
ventured (ven'chərd) *v.:* dared or risked going.
taboo (tə·bōō') *n.:* social restriction.

IDENTIFY

Re-read lines 42–54. Underline details that tell you what women of Cisneros's cultural background are expected to do, and what Cisneros did instead.

I like to think that somehow my family, my Mexicanness, my poverty, all had something to do with shaping me into a writer. I like to think my parents were preparing me all along for my life as an artist even though they didn't know it. From my father I inherited a love of wandering. He was born in Mexico

60 City but as a young man he traveled into the U.S. vagabonding. He eventually was drafted and thus became a citizen. Some of the stories he has told about his first months in the U.S. with little or no English surface in my stories in *The House on Mango Street* as well as others I have in mind to write in the future. From him I inherited a sappy heart. (He still cries when he watches Mexican soaps—especially if they deal with children who have forsaken their parents.)

My mother was born like me—in Chicago but of Mexican descent. It would be her tough streetwise voice that would haunt

70 all my stories and poems. An amazing woman who loves to draw and read books and can sing an opera. A smart cookie.

When I was a little girl we traveled to Mexico City so much I thought my grandparents' house on La Fortuna, number 12, was home. It was the only constant in our **nomadic** ramblings from one Chicago flat to another. The house on Destiny Street, number 12, in the colonia Tepeyac would be perhaps the only home I knew, and that **nostalgia** for a home would be a theme that would obsess me.

My brothers also figured greatly in my art. Especially the

80 older two; I grew up in their shadows. Henry, the second oldest and my favorite, appears often in poems I have written and in stories which at times only borrow his nickname, Kiki. He played a major role in my childhood. We were bunk-bed mates. We were co-conspirators. We were pals. Until my oldest brother came back from studying in Mexico and left me odd woman out for always.

What would my teachers say if they knew I was a writer now? Who would've guessed it? I wasn't a very bright student. I didn't much like school because we moved so much and I was

90 always new and funny looking. In my fifth-grade report card I have nothing but an avalanche of C's and D's, but I don't remember being that stupid. I was good at art and I read plenty of library books and Kiki laughed at all my jokes. At home I was fine, but at school I never opened my mouth except when the teacher called on me.

When I think of how I see myself it would have to be at age eleven. I know I'm thirty-two on the outside, but inside I'm eleven. I'm the girl in the picture with skinny arms and a crumpled skirt and crooked hair. I didn't like school because all they
100 saw was the outside me. School was lots of rules and sitting with your hands folded and being very afraid all the time. I liked looking out the window and thinking. I liked staring at the girl across the way writing her name over and over again in red ink. I wondered why the boy with the dirty collar in front of me didn't have a mama who took better care of him.

I think my mama and papa did the best they could to keep us warm and clean and never hungry. We had birthday and graduation parties and things like that, but there was another hunger that had to be fed. There was a hunger I didn't even have
110 a name for. Was this when I began writing?

In 1966 we moved into a house, a real one, our first real home. This meant we didn't have to change schools and be the new kids on the block every couple of years. We could make friends and not be afraid we'd have to say goodbye to them and start all over. My brothers and the flock of boys they brought home would become important characters eventually for my stories—Louie and his cousins, Meme Ortiz and his dog with two names, one in English and one in Spanish.

My mother **flourished** in her own home. She took books
120 out of the library and taught herself to garden—to grow flowers so envied we had to put a lock on the gate to keep out the midnight flower thieves. My mother has never quit gardening.

This was the period in my life, that slippery age when you are both child and woman and neither, I was to record in *The House on Mango Street.* I was still shy. I was a girl who couldn't come out of her shell.

INTERPRET

What does Cisneros mean by saying, "inside I'm eleven" (lines 97–98)?

_____

_____

_____

_____

_____

_____

_____

_____

_____

_____

_____

IDENTIFY CAUSE & EFFECT

Re-read line 111–118. Underline the effects on the Cisneros children of moving into their own house.

VOCABULARY

flourished (flur′isht) v.: thrived; prospered.

CLARIFY

What part of Cisneros's background would she later record in a novel (lines 123–126)? Underline the answer.

VOCABULARY

prestigious (pres·tij′əs)
adj.: impressive; having
distinction.

IDENTIFY

Re-read the details of
Cisneros's many travels and
adventures in lines 131–147.
Why is Texas especially
important to her? Underline
the answer.

INTERPRET

The last two sentences of
the essay contain another
allusion to the Rumpelstiltskin story. What does
Cisneros mean by the
"straw" that she has "spun"
into "gold" in her own life?
(Grade 9–10 Review)

_____

_____

_____

_____

_____

_____

_____

_____

_____

_____

_____

How was I to know I would be recording and documenting
the women who sat their sadness on an elbow and stared out a
window? It would be the city streets of Chicago I would later
130 record, as seen through a child's eyes.

I've done all kinds of things I didn't think I could do since
then. I've gone to a **prestigious** university, studied with famous
writers, and taken an MFA degree. I've taught poetry in schools
in Illinois and Texas. I've gotten an NEA grant and run away
with it as far as my courage would take me. I've seen the
bleached and bitter mountains of the Peloponnesus.[4] I've lived
on an island. I've been to Venice twice. I've lived in Yugoslavia.
I've been to the famous Nice[5] flower market behind the opera
house. I've lived in a village in the pre-Alps and witnessed the
140 daily parade of promenaders.

I've moved since Europe to the strange and wonderful
country of Texas, land of polaroid-blue skies and big bugs. I met
a mayor with my last name. I met famous Chicana and Chicano
artists and writers and *políticos.*

Texas is another chapter in my life. It brought with it the
Dobie-Paisano Fellowship, a six-month residency on a 265-acre
ranch. But most important, Texas brought Mexico back to me.

In the days when I would sit at my favorite people-
watching spot, the snakey Woolworth's counter across the street
150 from the Alamo (the Woolworth's which has since been torn
down to make way for progress), I couldn't think of anything
else I'd rather be than a writer. I've traveled and lectured from
Cape Cod to San Francisco, to Spain, Yugoslavia, Greece,
Mexico, France, Italy, and now today to Texas. Along the way
there has been straw for the taking. With a little imagination, it
can be spun into gold.

---

4. **Peloponnesus** (pel′ə·pə·nē′səs): large peninsula on the mainland of
   Greece.
5. **Nice** (nēs): port city in southern France.

Straw into Gold

Reading Skills: Understanding a Writer's Background   Sandra Cisneros's self-portrait presents some experiences that shaped her as a writer. Use details from "Straw into Gold" to complete the chart below.

Experiences that Shape a Life	Details from Text
Parents and Family Background	
Places	
Education	
Travel	
Brothers and Sisters	

Evaluation   What are some of the influences that shaped Sandra Cisneros as a writer?

_____

_____

_____

_____

_____

Straw into Gold

VOCABULARY IN CONTEXT

DIRECTIONS: Write vocabulary words from the Word Box to complete the
paragraph below. Not all words will be used.

Word Box

- subsisting
- intuitively
- edible
- ventured
- taboo
- nomadic
- nostalgia
- flourished
- prestigious

     No one had to tell Sandra Cisneros that her culture considered it wrong
for a young woman to leave home before her older brothers. She knew her
culture's "rules" (1)_____. However, instead of staying
home until she was married, she broke a cultural (2)_____
and (3)_____ out on her own ahead of her brothers. Even
though she (4)_____ on the travel that filled her life for
many years, she always felt a (5)_____ for her grand-
parents' house in Mexico. It was one place to which the family kept returning.

LITERAL MEANINGS OF WORDS

DIRECTIONS: Read the statements containing the boldface words carefully.
Then, indicate if each statement is true or false by writing "true" or "false"
on the line provided. Be sure to explain your answer.

1. If a guide to mushrooms says that a certain type of mushroom is **edible,**
   that mushroom is pretty poisonous.

   _____

2. **Nomadic** people tend to be homebodies.

   _____

3. The United States Supreme Court is a **prestigious** institution.

   _____

4. Someone who is **subsisting** is probably at risk of dying.

   _____

**Reading
Standard 1.1
(Grade 9–10
Review)**
Identify and use
the literal and
figurative
meanings of
words and
understand
word
derivations.

 Check your Standards Mastery at the back of this book.

The Beautiful Changes by Richard Wilbur

LITERARY FOCUS: AMBIGUITY

The title of Richard Wilbur's poem is **ambiguous**—that is, it suggests at least three different, conflicting meanings. Sometimes ambiguity is accidental, as in this headline:

School Board Denies Youth Band Funds

This headline could either mean (1) that the board denies funds for the formation of a youth band, or (2) that the board won't give a specific youth money to cover band costs.

Unlike headline writers, poets use ambiguity deliberately. Wilbur's title, "The Beautiful Changes," can mean several things: that our *idea* of what is beautiful is subject to change; that the poet has observed some beautiful *changes* or transformations; that beautiful things in the world change. Wilbur wants us to be aware of all those meanings.

Accidental Ambiguity   The chart below presents another ambiguous headline. In the space at the right, identify two different things the headline could mean.

Ambiguous Headline	Two Meanings
Truck Stops Artists	

READING SKILLS: PARAPHRASING

When you **paraphrase** a text, you restate the text using your own words. When you write a paraphrase of a poem, it is especially important that you explain the figures of speech to make clear what is being compared with what. A paraphrase is usually longer than the work itself.

Use the Skill   As you read "The Beautiful Changes," pause every so often to paraphrase the poem.

Reading Standard 3.8 **(Grade 9–10 Review)** Interpret and evaluate the impact of ambiguities, subtleties, contradictions, ironies, and incongruities in a text.

The Beautiful Changes

Richard Wilbur

> ### BACKGROUND
> When the speaker mentions "Lucernes" (line 6), he is referring to the beautiful, glacier-fed Lake Lucerne in Switzerland. The "mantis" (line 9) is a kind of long insect that grasps its prey with its forelegs.

IDENTIFY

Queen Anne's Lace, a weed that has pretty white flowers, is compared to water lilies (line 2). Underline the line in stanza 1 that tells how they transform the meadow.

ANALYZE

The speaker addresses someone in lines 5–6. How does the speaker seem to feel about this person?

_____

INTERPRET

Pause at line 12. How do chameleons and mantises "change"?

_____

_____

WORD STUDY

Sunder in line 16 means "to break apart". Re-read lines 13–18, and underline the reason "the beautiful" wish to separate things from things' selves.

One wading a Fall meadow finds on all sides
The Queen Anne's Lace lying like lilies
On water; it glides
So from the walker, it turns
5   Dry grass to a lake, as the slightest shade of you
Valleys my mind in fabulous blue Lucernes.

The beautiful changes as a forest is changed
By a chameleon's tuning his skin to it;
As a mantis, arranged
10   On a green leaf, grows
Into it, makes the leaf leafier, and proves
Any greenness is deeper than anyone knows.

Your hands hold roses always in a way that says
They are not only yours; the beautiful changes
15   In such kind ways,
Wishing ever to sunder
Things and things' selves for a second finding, to lose
For a moment all that it touches back to wonder.

The Beautiful Changes

Reading Skills: Paraphrasing   A **paraphrase** of a text is a restatement of that text, using your own words. When you paraphrase a poem, you must try to take account of each line. This poem is written in stanzas, which are units of meaning. Your paraphrase of the poem should contain three paragraphs, one paragraph for each stanza.

The first few lines of each stanza have been paraphrased for you. Complete the paraphrase using the chart below. When you discuss your paraphrases in class, be sure to talk about the lines you found ambiguous or difficult to paraphrase. See if the class can agree on the best paraphrase of those lines.

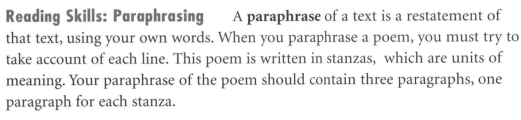

Paraphrase of "The Beautiful Changes"
Stanza I: When you are walking through a meadow in autumn, you find Queen Anne's Lace all around; they seem like lilies lying on water . . .
Stanza 2: Beautiful things in the world change just as a forest is changed when a chameleon changes the color of its skin, . . .
Stanza 3: The speaker talks to the woman he loves again and says that her hands hold roses in ways that change the roses and give them deeper meaning; . . .

Check your Standards Mastery at the back of this book.

The Bells by Anne Sexton

Reading Standard 3.4 Analyze the ways in which poets use imagery, personification, figures of speech, and sounds to evoke readers' emotions.

Reading Standard 3.11 (Grade 9–10 Review) Evaluate the aesthetic qualities of style, including the impact of diction and figurative language on tone, mood, and theme, using the terminology of literary criticism. (Aesthetic approach)

BEFORE YOU READ

REVIEW SKILLS

As you read "The Bells," think about what **theme** it conveys.

THEME
A truth about human experience revealed in a work of literature.

LITERARY FOCUS: IMAGERY

Imagery is language that evokes a picture or a concrete sensation. Most images appeal to the sense of sight, but images may also appeal to the senses of hearing, touch, taste, and smell. A poet might use words such as *clanging* or *whining* to suggest sounds, and *syrupy* or *tangy* to suggest taste and smell. In this poem, Sexton evokes the sense of touch when she says an old circus poster "is scabbing off the concrete wall."

READING SKILLS: IDENTIFYING THEME

The **theme** of a literary work is the insight about human life that it reveals. Most poets expect you to infer theme from the details that appear in the poem. Good poets almost never state their theme directly.

Theme is not the same as the *subject* of a poem. A poem's subject might be anything from broccoli to elephants. A theme is what the poem says *about* a subject. For example: "Eating broccoli gives a child her first taste of bitterness."

Use the Skill   As you read "The Bells," think about what the poem reveals to you about the relationship between a father and a child. Underline or highlight words and images that help you understand what this relationship means to the little girl.

THE BELLS
Anne Sexton

Today the circus poster

is scabbing off the concrete wall

and the children have forgotten

if they knew at all.

5   Father, do you remember?

Only the sound remains,

the distant thump of the good elephants,

the voice of the ancient lions

and how the bells

10   trembled for the flying man.

I, laughing,

lifted to your high shoulder

or small at the rough legs of strangers,

was not afraid.

15   You held my hand

and were instant to explain

the three rings of danger.

Oh see the naughty clown

and the wild parade

20   while love love

love grew rings around me.

This was the sound where it began;

our breath pounding up to see

the flying man breast out

25   across the boarded sky

and climb the air.

I remember the color of music

and how forever

all the trembling bells of you

30   were mine.

IDENTIFY

Stop at line 5. Whom is the speaker talking to? Underline the answer.

INTERPRET

Stop at line 17. What are the "three rings of danger"?

_____

_____

_____

INTERPRET

The image in line 27 is an example of **synesthesia,** meaning it describes one kind of sensory impression in terms of another sensory impression. What are the two sensory impressions?

_____

_____

_____

INTERPRET

Re-read the poem. Underline all the reasons the speaker was happy at the circus.

The Bells

Reading Skills: Identifying Theme   To write a statement of a poem's **theme,** you need to consider its events, imagery, key words, sounds, and the feelings of the speaker. Remember that a theme is the insight into life communicated to you by the poem as a whole.

Identify the images that help you understand the relationship the little girl had with her father and what it meant to her. Write several of these images in the outer circles of the diagram below. Write the subject of the poem in the box at the top. Then, think about what the poem *says* about the subject. Write a statement of the poem's theme in the large center circle.

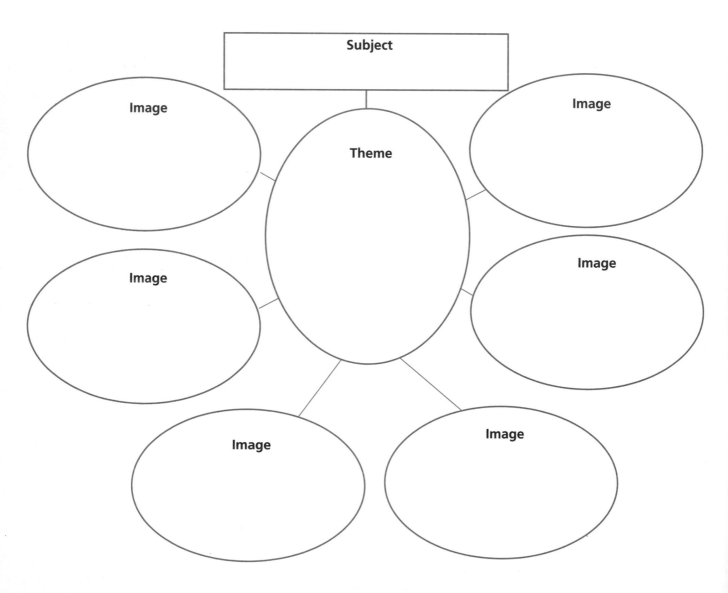

 Check your Standards Mastery at the back of this book.

The Bean Eaters by Gwendolyn Brooks

BEFORE YOU READ

LITERARY FOCUS: THE USES OF RHYME

Before the twentieth century, most poets used rhyme. Establishing a rhyme scheme and sticking to it was part of the poet's discipline. Nowadays, rhyming poetry is uncommon. When you read a poem that rhymes, ask yourself why the poet made that choice. How does the use of rhyme support the ideas or feelings in the poem? How does the rhyme create music in the poem?

READING SKILLS: VISUALIZING

Poets usually want to help you *see* something, or even smell it, feel it, taste it, or hear it. Poets use **images** to help us participate in the poem by using our senses.

When you read a poem, you should allow the images to help you visualize what the poet is describing. Visualizing will help you be certain you understand a text. If you try to visualize something in a poem and you are having trouble, you might find that you need to re-read the poem to clarify its meaning.

Use the Skill   Which details in Brooks's poem help you visualize the Bean Eaters and their setting? As you read, underline details in the poem that help you picture this old pair and the room they live in. When you finish reading, you might like to draw what the poet brings to life with words.

REVIEW SKILLS

As you read "The Bean Eaters," pay attention to the following literary device.

IMAGERY
The use of language that appeals to one or more of the five senses.

Reading Standard 3.4 Analyze the ways in which poets use imagery, personification, figures of speech, and sounds to evoke readers' emotions.

Reading Standard 3.7 (Grade 9–10 Review) Recognize and understand the significance of various literary devices, including figurative language, imagery, allegory, and symbolism, and explain their appeal.

THE BEAN EATERS

Gwendolyn Brooks

They eat beans mostly, this old yellow pair.

Dinner is a casual affair.

Plain chipware on a plain and creaking wood,

Tin flatware.

5   Two who are Mostly Good.

Two who have lived their day,

But keep on putting on their clothes

and putting things away.

And remembering . . .

10   Remembering, with twinklings and twinges,

As they lean over the beans in their rented back room that

      is full of beads and receipts and dolls and cloths,

      tobacco crumbs, vases and fringes.

"The Bean Eaters" from *Blacks* by Gwendolyn Brooks. Copyright © 1991 by Gwendolyn Brooks. Published by Third World Press, Chicago, 1991. Reprinted by permission of **The Estate of Gwendolyn Brooks.**

Waiting Room (1984) by Phoebe Beasley. Collage (36" × 36").
© Phoebe Beasley/Omni–Photo Communications.

INTERPRET

"Chipware" (line 3) is an invented word. (We usually say "dinnerware.") "Flatware" refers to knives, forks, and spoons. What **image** of the couple's dishes does "chipware" call to mind? *(Grade 9–10 Review)*

_____

_____

IDENTIFY

Re-read lines 5–8. Underline the repeated words.

INTERPRET

Pause at line 10. What does the phrase "twinklings and twinges" tell you about the couple's feelings?

_____

_____

_____

_____

IDENTIFY

List the rhyming words in the poem.

_____

_____

The Bean Eaters

Reading Skills: Visualizing   Re-read the poem carefully. Then, fill in the boxes in the chart that follows to indicate what **images** the poet has put in your mind. When you are finished, compare charts with your classmates. You will see that, although you all read the same poem, what you visualized might be very different.

Visualizing "The Bean Eaters"	
They eat beans mostly, this old yellow pair. Dinner is a casual affair. Plain chipware on a plain and creaking wood, Tin flatware.	I picture . . .
Two who are Mostly Good. Two who have lived their day, But keep on putting on their clothes and putting things away.	I picture . . .

And remembering . . .
Remembering, with twinklings and twinges,
As they lean over the beans in their rented back
    room that is full of beads and receipts and
    dolls and cloths, tobacco crumbs, vases and
    fringes.
	I picture . . .

Check your Standards Mastery at the back of this book.

The Latin Deli: An Ars Poetica by Judith Ortiz Cofer

BEFORE YOU READ

LITERARY FOCUS: CONCRETE AND ABSTRACT LANGUAGE

Concrete language is language that uses sensory details to describe a particular subject. Concrete language enables you to participate in a literary work because it helps you to see, hear, touch, smell, and even taste things that a writer describes. The use of concrete language is extremely important in poetry, where it not only evokes sensory impressions but also helps establish mood.

Opposite to concrete language is **abstract language,** language that names categories, qualities, values, and other concepts that cannot be sensed physically. For example, a word like *contentment* is an abstract word. *A cup of hot chocolate on a cold day,* on the other hand, is a concrete description of something that might bring contentment.

READING SKILLS: IDENTIFYING KEY WORDS

As you read this poem, be aware of the specific words the poet uses to evoke the atmosphere of the Latin deli. Also be aware of key words in the poem that seem to suggest the **theme** of the poem—the truth it reveals about our human experience. Write in the "Notes" part of these pages any word or phrase that you think is key to the meaning of the poem. Remember that the poem's subtitle is "ars poetica," and refers to the art of poetry. What words in this poem also refer to language and poetry?

The Latin Deli:

An Ars Poetica

Judith Ortiz Cofer

Presiding over a formica counter,
plastic Mother and Child magnetized
to the top of an ancient register,
the heady mix of smells from the open bins
5   of dried codfish, the green plantains[1]
hanging in stalks like votive offerings,[2]
she is the Patroness of Exiles,
a woman of no-age who was never pretty,
who spends her days selling canned memories
10   while listening to the Puerto Ricans complain
that it would be cheaper to fly to San Juan
than to buy a pound of Bustelo coffee here,
and to Cubans perfecting their speech
of a "glorious return" to Havana—where no one
15   has been allowed to die and nothing to change until then;
to Mexicans who pass through, talking lyrically
of *dólares* to be made in El Norte—
                                    all wanting the comfort
of spoken Spanish, to gaze upon the family portrait
20   of her plain wide face, her ample bosom
resting on her plump arms, her look of maternal interest
as they speak to her and each other
of their dreams and their disillusions—

---

1. **plantains** *n. pl.:* type of banana.
2. **votive offerings:** sacrifices made to fulfill a vow or offered in devotion.

"The Latin Deli: An Ars Poetica" by Judith Ortiz Cofer from *The Americas Review,* vol. 19, no. 1. Copyright © 1991 by Judith Ortiz Cofer. Published by **Arte Público Press-University of Houston, 1991.** Reprinted by permission of the publisher.

PREDICT

"Ars Poetica" in the subtitle is Latin for "the art of poetry." What do you think this poem will be about?

_____

_____

_____

_____

IDENTIFY

Circle the **concrete language** in lines 1–6 that helps you visualize the deli. Underline words that evoke smells.

IDENTIFY

Re-read lines 8–17. Underline the phrase that tells you what the woman behind the counter "sells."

CLARIFY

Re-read lines 18–23. What does everyone who comes into the shop want? Underline the answer.

Un día a la vez (*One Day at a Time*) (1953) by Joe Villareal.

FLUENCY

The boxed passage describes the interactions between the homesick customers and the woman who runs the deli. Read this section of the poem aloud twice. Use the footnotes to help you with Spanish pronunciations, or ask a classmate who knows Spanish to help you. On your second reading, use your voice to evoke the **mood** of the poem. How would you describe its mood? *(Grade 9–10 Review)*

how she smiles understanding,
25 when they walk down the narrow aisles of her store
reading the labels of packages aloud, as if
they were the names of lost lovers: *Suspiros,*[3]
Merengues,[4] the stale candy of everyone's childhood.
                                        She spends her days
30 slicing *jamón y queso*[5] and wrapping it in wax paper
tied with string: plain ham and cheese
that would cost less at the A&P, but it would not satisfy
the hunger of the fragile old man lost in the folds
of his winter coat, who brings her lists of items
35 that he reads to her like poetry, or the others,
whose needs she must divine, conjuring up products
from places that now exist only in their hearts—
closed ports she must trade with.

---

3. *suspiros* (sōōs·pē'rōs): type of small spongecake.
4. *merengues* (mā·rān'gās): candy made of meringue (mixture of egg whites and sugar).
5. *jamón y queso* (khä·mōn' ē kā'sō): Spanish for "ham and cheese."

The Latin Deli: An Ars Poetica

Reading Skills: Identifying Key Words   Use the chart below to analyze the poem and identify its theme—the truth about human experience that the text reveals. Compare your statement of theme with the statements made by your classmates. You should find that each reader of the poem states its theme differently.

"The Latin Deli"	
Subject of poem	
What happens in poem: Lines 1–17	
What happens in poem: Lines 18–38	
Key words/lines in poem; Meaning of poem's subtitle	
Mood of poem	
Theme of poem	

Check your Standards Mastery at the back of this book.

Part Two

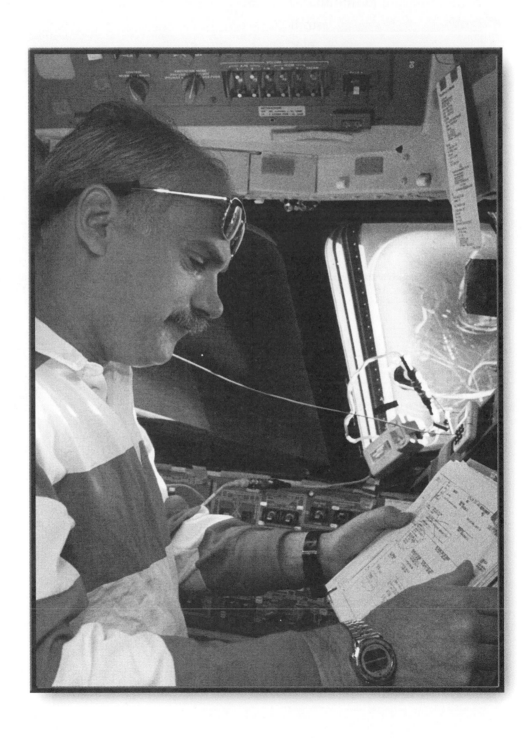

Consumer, Workplace, and Public Documents

Academic Vocabulary

These are the terms you should know
as you read and analyze the selections that follow.

Consumer documents Documents used in the selling and buying of products. Many consumer documents, such as warranties, protect the rights of the purchaser and the seller. Other consumer documents include advertisements, contracts, instruction manuals, and product information.

Public documents Documents that inform the public. Public documents are created by governmental, social, religious, or news-gathering organizations. They include safety information, government regulations, schedules of events, explanations of services, and informational articles.

Workplace documents Documents used in offices, factories, and other work sites to communicate job-related information. These include business letters, contracts, instruction manuals, memorandums, and safety information.

Technical documents Documents used to explain or establish procedures for using technology, such as mechanical, electronic, or digital products or systems. Technical documents include how-to instructions, installation instructions, and instructions on carrying out scientific procedures.

Functional documents Any documents prepared for a specific function, such as consumer, public, workplace, and technical documents.

Grand Canyon Web Site

BEFORE YOU READ

There may be no substitute for actually visiting the Grand Canyon. However, if you have questions about it—from "Can I ride my mountain bike into the Canyon?" to "How far would I fall before I hit the bottom?"—the National Park Web site can answer them.

INFORMATIONAL FOCUS: PUBLIC DOCUMENTS

Public documents are documents that inform the public. They include safety information, government regulations, schedules of events, explanations of services, and newspaper articles. Many public documents appear on Web sites. You can find lots of useful information on the Internet if you know how to navigate a Web site. Here are some important features:

- **Home page.** This page is a Web site's starting point. Most of what a site offers is shown on the site's home page. If you find yourself off track or lost, just return to the home page and start over.

- **Table of contents.** The table of contents lists the site's other pages and often appears on the side of the home page. You can generally reach the other pages of a site by clicking on the items listed.

- **FAQs.** Many Web sites have a page where they answer FAQs, or "frequently asked questions." A FAQs page is a good place to get a quick overview of the Web site's subject.

- **Links.** Also known as hyperlinks or "hot spots," links are text and graphics you can click on that will take you to other locations, whether on the same page, on another page in the same site, or on another site entirely. Hot text is often a different color from the surrounding text. When your cursor passes over a link, it turns into an arrow or a pointing finger.

- **URLs.** Each page of a Web site has its own Internet address, or URL (uniform resource locator). The URL of the Grand Canyon Web site's home page is www.nps.gov/grca. If you copy and save a URL, you'll be able to find the Web site again.

Reading Standard 2.3 (Grade 9–10 Review) Generate relevant questions about readings on issues that can be researched.

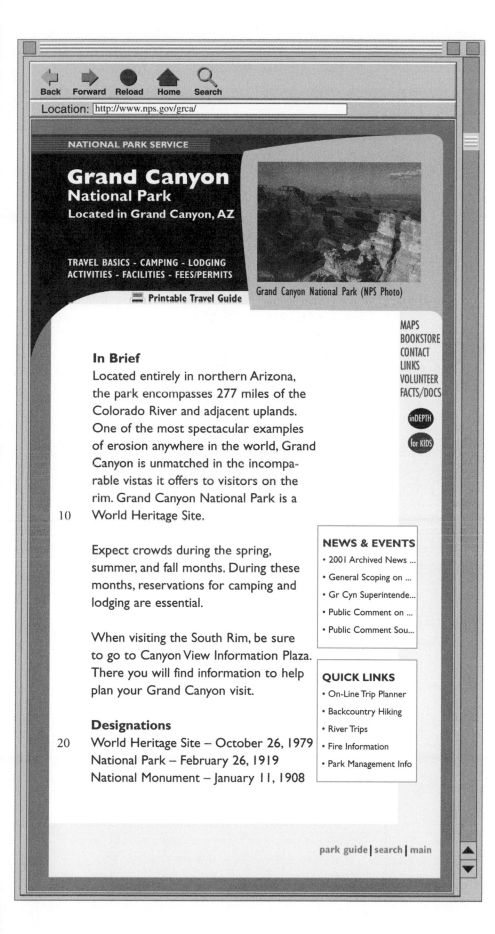

NATIONAL PARK SERVICE

Grand Canyon
National Park
Located in Grand Canyon, AZ

TRAVEL BASICS - CAMPING - LODGING
ACTIVITIES - FACILITIES - FEES/PERMITS

Printable Travel Guide

Grand Canyon National Park (NPS Photo)

MAPS
BOOKSTORE
CONTACT
LINKS
VOLUNTEER
FACTS/DOCS

inDEPTH

for KIDS

In Brief

Located entirely in northern Arizona,
the park encompasses 277 miles of the
Colorado River and adjacent uplands.
One of the most spectacular examples
of erosion anywhere in the world, Grand
Canyon is unmatched in the incompa-
rable vistas it offers to visitors on the
rim. Grand Canyon National Park is a
10 World Heritage Site.

Expect crowds during the spring,
summer, and fall months. During these
months, reservations for camping and
lodging are essential.

When visiting the South Rim, be sure
to go to Canyon View Information Plaza.
There you will find information to help
plan your Grand Canyon visit.

Designations
20 World Heritage Site – October 26, 1979
National Park – February 26, 1919
National Monument – January 11, 1908

NEWS & EVENTS
• 2001 Archived News ...
• General Scoping on ...
• Gr Cyn Superintende...
• Public Comment on ...
• Public Comment Sou...

QUICK LINKS
• On-Line Trip Planner
• Backcountry Hiking
• River Trips
• Fire Information
• Park Management Info

park guide | search | main

Location: http://www.nps.gov/grca/

Back Forward Reload Home Search

IDENTIFY

Each Web site has its own
URL, or Internet address.
Locate and circle this Web
page's URL.

WORD STUDY

In line 3, *encompasses* means
"includes or surrounds."
Literally, it means "to make a
circle around."

WORD STUDY

Vista (line 8) means "view"
in both English and Spanish.
(In Spanish, it also means
"eyesight.")

IDENTIFY

Where would you click if you
wanted to telephone or
email the National Park
Service with a question?

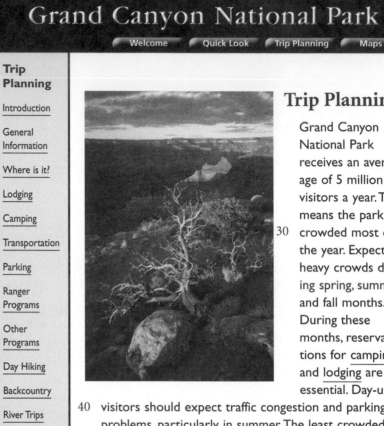

Location: http://www.nps.gov/grca/grandcanyon/trip_planner

Grand Canyon National Park

Welcome   Quick Look   Trip Planning   Maps

Trip Planning

Introduction

General Information

Where is it?

Lodging

Camping

Transportation

Parking

Ranger Programs

Other Programs

Day Hiking

Backcountry

River Trips

Mule Trips

Air Tours

Weather

Accessibility

Entrance Fees

Sunset/Sunrise Times

Medical Services

Pets

Bicycling

Tuweep

FAQs

Print Version

Trip Planning

Grand Canyon National Park receives an average of 5 million visitors a year. This

30 means the park is crowded most of the year. Expect heavy crowds during spring, summer, and fall months. During these months, reservations for camping and lodging are essential. Day-use

40 visitors should expect traffic congestion and parking problems, particularly in summer. The least crowded time is November through February. However, winter weather is a major consideration when planning a trip during these months.

Most visitors come to the South Rim (facilities open all year). The North Rim (services and overnight facilities open mid-May through mid-October) has fewer facilities and is more remote. It is over 200 miles/*322 kilometers* one way by automobile from the South Rim to

50 the North Rim, a 5-hour drive for most. When making reservations for lodging and camping, remember to identify the rim you plan on visiting.

The South Rim of Grand Canyon averages 7000 feet/2134 meters above sea level. The North Rim is over 8000 feet/*2438 meters* above sea level. Visitors with respiratory or heart problems may experience difficulties. All walking at this elevation can be strenuous.

Standards Review

DOCUMENTS

 **Grand Canyon Web Site**

Complete the sample test item below by circling the correct answer. Then, read the explanation to the right.

Sample Test Item	Explanation of the Correct Answer
For help in finding your way around the Grand Canyon, which link would you click on? A Contact B Maps C Volunteer D Links	*B* is the answer. If you wanted to hike through the Grand Canyon, you would probably need to refer to a map. Choices *A*, *C*, and *D* provided useful information but nothing closely related to finding one's way around.

DIRECTIONS: Circle the letter of each correct response.

1. During which months would you need to make reservations for camping and lodging at the Grand Canyon?

   A spring, summer, and fall months

   B winter and spring months

   C spring and summer months

   D none of the above

2. If you were interested in a rafting excursion, which of the Quick Links would you click on?

   F Park Management Info

   G On-Line Trip Planner

   H Fire Information

   J River Trips

3. When making reservations for camping and lodging, what information would you need to provide?

   A whether you have been to the Grand Canyon before

   B whether you want to visit the North or South Rim

   C whether you want an air tour

   D whether you need a parking space

4. Like all Web sites, this site has a—

   F bulleted list

   G marvelous photograph

   H URL

   J warning label

Reading Standard 2.3 (Grade 9–10 Review) Generate relevant questions about readings on issues that can be researched.

 Check your Standards Mastery at the back of this book.

NASA Frequently Asked Questions

An enormous asteroid hurtles on its unstoppable destruction course toward Earth. Big-eyed, green-skinned aliens step down from their ships, ready to make contact. Somewhere in the future, humans with advanced technology explore distant galaxies that hold unimaginable secrets.

TV shows, movies, video games, books—Americans are fascinated by outer space. Our questions are endless. And NASA (National Aeronautics and Space Administration) has some of the answers.

INFORMATIONAL FOCUS: FUNCTIONAL DOCUMENTS

Functional documents have a function, or purpose—to communicate information. One common type of functional document is a **FAQ** (frequently asked questions) **sheet.** It presents basic information about its topic in a **Q & A** (question and answer) **format,** answering the questions people most often ask.

Functional documents present their information in the following ways:

- **Expert Answers.** Functional documents are written by people who have authoritative knowledge about the subject. In the case of FAQ sheets, general questions are immediately followed by expert answers. Sometimes questions are preceded by the letter "Q," while answers are proceeded by an "A." Other times, either the question or answer will be **boldface,** so that you can easily tell one from the other.

- **Facts and Statistics.** Functional documents supply information that is true and can be supported by facts. FAQ sheets often bolster their information with statistics, percentages, numbers, or other relevant data.

- **Visual Cues.** All functional documents should be easy to skim. One way to simplify functional documents is to break up the text with spaces and to include **heads.** Heads are printed titles that appear at the top of a page or above a new section of text. Each head tips you off to the fact that you're about to encounter a new block of information. Similarly, spaces and **bulleted lists** are intended as visual cues that prepare you for new information or invite you to pay attention.

- **Links.** Because a functional document is sometimes short, additional sources of information are referenced for those who'd like to know more. For instance, a FAQ sheet might provide a URL for a companion Web site or the name of an article relating to the topic.

Reading Standard 2.5 (Grade 9–10 Review) Extend ideas presented in primary or secondary sources through original analysis, evaluation, and elaboration.

NASA

Frequently Asked Questions

Why NASA?

Why explore space?

Space research and exploration generate a wide range of direct and indirect benefits:

Knowledge—Space science missions produce basic knowledge about our environment, our solar system and the universe, which then gives us a deeper understanding of the history and the state of our world. With this new information, we can make better decisions about how to sustain and improve life on
10   Earth in the future.

Applications—Orbiting spacecraft transmit information like phone and television signals around the globe with extreme speed and precision. Other satellites monitor the weather and the health of the atmosphere, the dynamics of the oceans and the vitality of the land. Satellite-based navigation systems aboard airplanes and boats enable people to determine their geographic position and heading with greater accuracy than ever before. This improves safety and makes travel more efficient.

The unique conditions of space-weightlessness, temperature
20   extremes, vacuum, and radiation create the opportunity for laboratory experiments and industrial processes that are impossible or impractical to perform on Earth.

Technology—Technology created to prepare systems and people to operate in the harsh conditions of space contributes to advances in composite materials, electronics, robotics, medicine, energy production, manufacturing, transportation and many other areas of human activity.

In many cases, these advances would occur much more slowly or not at all without the challenge of space exploration.

30   **Inspiration**—The urge to explore the unknown is part of human nature and has led to many of the most profound changes in our standard of living. It enriches our spirits and reminds us of the

"NASA: Frequently Asked Questions" by Elvia Thompson from NASA Web site at http://www.nasa.gov/qanda/why_nasa. html#SAREX. Reprinted by permission of **NASA**.

IDENTIFY

Pause at line 3. This article appears in question and answer format. To follow the Q & A format, write *Q* in the margin by each question and *A* next to each answer.

ANALYZE

Skim the article from line 5 to line 30. What do the bold-face heads tell you?

_____

_____

_____

_____

_____

_____

_____

_____

_____

_____

_____

_____

_____

_____

Notes _____

_____
_____
_____
_____
_____
_____
_____
_____
_____
_____
_____
_____
_____
_____
_____
_____

great potential for achievement within us all. The drive to develop the next frontier also has been a fundamental part of the heritage of the people of the United States.

Why not reduce the amount of money spent on space exploration and increase spending on social programs?

NASA's funding represents about one penny out of every dollar in the U.S. federal budget (down from a peak of four cents per
40   dollar at the height of the Apollo program in the late 1960s). Diverting this money into social programs would provide a very minimal increase for those immediate funding needs, while eliminating resources for one of the few federal agencies devoted to the future. Such a move could forfeit new solutions to our social and economic problems in favor of the limited means that we already know.

Can I become a member of a NASA club or have my name put on a mailing list?

NASA does not maintain public mailing lists, nor does it spon-
50   sor a space club. However, there are numerous private groups and professional organizations throughout the country that support the space program. There also are many weekly and monthly magazines and newsletters that report on space and aeronautics activities.

Your local school or community library should be a good source of information on these groups and publications, as well as one of the best places to find books about NASA, its history, and its future plans.

NASA press releases can be obtained automatically by sending
60   an Internet electronic mail message to domo@hq.nasa.gov. In the body of the message (not the subject line) users should type the words "subscribe press-release" (don't use quotes and note the hyphen). The system will reply with a confirmation via e-mail of each subscription. A second automatic message will include additional information on the service. The NASA Public Affairs Web site is located at: http://www.nasa.gov/ under "News and Information." Informational materials are also available via anonymous FTP (File Transfer Protocol) server at ftp.pao.hq.nasa.gov/pub/pao. Within the /pub/pao directory
70   there will be a "readme.txt" file explaining the directory structure.

IDENTIFY

NASA believes that federal money used to support the space program is money well spent (lines 38–46). Underline the reasons they give.

IDENTIFY

Re-read lines 59–65. Underline the e-mail address you would use to request a press release. Circle the words that you should include within the body of your message.

The NASA Headquarters Newsroom contains NASA news releases, mission press kits, fact sheets and other publications.

Can I apply to take a ride on the Space Shuttle?

NASA has no immediate plans to send members of the public into space. For the near future at least, space flight remains too risky and too expensive for anyone but highly trained astronauts and payload specialists to take part in it. However, one of our goals is to help industry develop new rocket systems that would make space flight much more simple and routine, so that many more people could go into orbit in the future.

80

How can my school talk to a Space Shuttle crew over ham radio?

Teachers should send e-mail to the Amateur Radio Relay League at ead@arrl.org.

WORD STUDY

In line 78, payload refers to anything a spacecraft carries that relates directly to the purpose of the flight (for example, scientific instruments to measure and record information), as opposed to items that are necessary for the spacecraft's operation (such as fuel or food for the astronauts).

_____

_____

_____

_____

_____

_____

_____

_____

_____

_____

_____

_____

_____

_____

_____

_____

_____

_____

_____

_____

Standards Review

NASA Frequently Asked Questions

Complete the sample test item below by circling the correct answer. Then, read the explanation to the right.

Sample Test Item	Explanation of the Correct Answer
This NASA article follows which of the following formats? A point-counterpoint B question and answer C true or false D least important to most important details	*B* is the answer. This article is arranged in question-and-answer format; therefore, *A*, *C*, and *D* are incorrect.

DIRECTIONS: Circle the letter of each correct response.

1. Which of the following is *not* listed as an area that space research has advanced?

   A robotics   C mathematics

   B medicine   D manufacturing

2. What explanation does NASA give for not sending members of the general public into space?

   F There is not enough public interest.

   G It's too risky and too expensive.

   H More spacecraft would need to be built in order to accommodate requests.

   J NASA needs to do more research before sending the public there.

3. Where would you find the NASA Public Affairs Web site?

   A under "News and Information"

   B in the File Transfer Protocol

   C in an e-mail

   D in the NASA Headquarters Newsroom

4. The NASA Frequently Asked Questions sheet contains all of the following features of a functional document *except*—

   F bulleted items in a list

   G boldface type

   H charts

   J headings

Reading Standard 2.5 (Grade 9–10 Review) Extend ideas presented in primary or secondary sources through original analysis, evaluation, and elaboration.

 Check your Standards Mastery at the back of this book.

Smithsonian Institution Internship Application

The Smithsonian Institution includes sixteen museums in two cities, from the Air and Space Museum (where you can touch a moon rock and see the original Wright Brothers' 1903 Flyer) to the National Museum of American History. The Smithsonian also maintains the National Zoo as well as research centers here and abroad.

An *intern* is an apprentice—someone who learns by working with experienced professionals. The Smithsonian Institution offers dozens of paid and unpaid internships for high school and college students.

INFORMATIONAL FOCUS: WORKPLACE DOCUMENTS

Workplace documents are used in offices, factories, and other work sites to communicate information. Workplace documents may take many forms, including business letters, applications, contracts, instruction manuals, memorandums, and safety information. On the following pages, you'll find an information sheet and an application for internships at the Freer Gallery of Art and Arthur M. Sackler Gallery, which together make up the National Museum of Asian Art.

Information sheet. This is where the museum tells you what you need to know to apply for an internship. Read carefully—each paragraph contains a lot of information.

Application. This is where you tell the museum about yourself. Applications should be filled in carefully. Here are some tips for filling one out:

- Read the instructions before you start filling out the application.

- When you fill out an application, print neatly and clearly. It's a good idea to make an extra copy to practice on first.

- Don't leave any lines blank. If a question doesn't apply to you, write *n/a*, which means "not applicable."

- If the form requires a signature, be sure to sign and date it.

- After you fill out the application, read through it carefully to make sure you didn't miss anything.

Terms to Know

Format—the design of the document.

Header—a label or heading that begins a section of a document.

Boldface—dark, heavy type.

Italic—type that slants to the right.

Reading Standard 2.1 (Grade 9–10 Review) Analyze the structure and format of functional workplace documents, including the graphics and headers, and explain how authors use the features to achieve their purposes.

Smithsonian
*Freer Gallery of Art and
Arthur M. Sackler Gallery*

Education Department

RE: Internships

Thank you for inquiring about internships at the Freer and Sackler Galleries. The Freer Gallery of Art and the Arthur M. Sackler Gallery are the national museum of Asian art of the Smithsonian Institution and are jointly administered. Interns are selected by each of the museum's thirteen departments: Administration, Conservation and Scientific Research, Collections Management (Registrar), Curatorial, Design and Installation, Development, Education, Exhibition Management, Library

10 and Archives, Photography, Public Affairs, Publications, and Shops. Approximately 20 percent of applicants are accepted for internships during any one year. Internships range from one month to one year. The duration is based on arrangements made between the department and the intern. The postmark deadlines for applications are: November 15 (for winter/spring), March 15 (for summer), July 15 (for fall). The Dick Louie Internship for Americans of Asian descent is open to Washington-area high school students who are of Asian descent and are entering or completing their senior year of high school. The stipend is $1,500, and the application postmark deadline is March 15. For informa-

20 tion, call 202-357-4880, ext. 246.

To apply exclusively and directly to the Freer and Sackler Galleries for unpaid internships, please complete and send the enclosed application form along with a letter indicating your reasons for applying, a resume and/or high school or college transcript (it does not need to be official), and two letters of recommendation to: Intern Coordinator, Freer and Sackler Galleries, 1050 Independence Ave., SW, Washington, DC 20560. Please send all items together.

For information about paid internships, contact the Office of Fellowships and Grants, 955 L'Enfant Plaza, Suite 7000, Smithsonian

30 Institution, MRC 902, Washington, DC 20560 [202-287-3271; siofg@ofg.si.edu]. Their Web site provides descriptive information on other Smithsonian internships as well: www.si.edu/research+study.

Thank you for your interest in the Freer and Sackler Galleries, and good luck in your internship endeavors.

Smithsonian
Freer Gallery of Art and
Arthur M. Sackler Gallery

Education Department

Application for Unpaid Internships:

1. Name: Last _____

   First _____ Middle _____

2. Current Address:

   _____

   _____

3. Current phone number(s): (____) _____ - _____

4. Permanent Address (if different):

   _____

   _____

5. Permanent phone number(s) (if different): (____) _____ - _____

   (____) _____ - _____

6. Date of Birth: _____ / _____ / _____

7. Current (or most recent) college or university: _____

   _____

8. Current degree sought: _____

   Current major: _____ Date expected: ___ / ___ / ___

9. Degrees already held (if any), college or university, and date conferred:

   _____ ___ / ___ / ___

   _____ ___ / ___ / ___

10. Languages and fluency (including English): _____

    Native fluency: _____

    Fluent second language: _____

    Basic conversation and reading: _____

    Reading only: _____

–Over–

IDENTIFY

Circle the numbers of the items that ask for the applicant's name and date of birth.

IDENTIFY

Bracket the items that ask about the applicant's education.

CONNECT

If you had earned no degrees as of yet, how would you fill item 9?

_____

_____

_____

DRAW CONCLUSIONS

Why would an intern's ability to speak or read more than one language be of value to the museum (item 10)?

_____

_____

_____

_____

_____

_____

_____

_____

_____

_____

Item 11: Go over the list of departments in which internships are available. (You may need help from a dictionary to figure out what each department does.) Which three sound most appealing to you? List them on the lines provided in order from 1 to 3, with your favorite being 1.

_____

_____

_____

_____

_____

_____

_____

_____

_____

_____

_____

_____

_____

In item 16, *affiliation* means "connection with an organization." For example, if your English teacher wrote you a letter of recommendation, his or her affiliation would be the name of your school.

11. Specific departments within the Freer and Sackler Galleries in which you have interest in interning (list in order of preference no more than three from the following thirteen departments): Administration, Conservation and Scientific Research, Collections Management (Registrar), Curatorial, Design and Installation, Development, Education, Exhibition Management, Library and Archives, Photography, Public Affairs, Publications, and Shops.

1. _____

2. _____

3. _____

12. Internship term applying for (circle):   winter/spring   summer   fall

13. Citizenship (if not U.S. citizen, indicate visa type): _____

14. Social Security Number: _____ - _____ - _____

15. List any other Smithsonian museums to which you are applying for internships: _____
_____

16. Names and affiliation of those from whom we will receive letters of recommendation:

1. _____

2. _____

17. Institution(s) from which academic transcripts will be sent:

1. _____

2. _____

18. Are you covered by health insurance (if so, list the insurance company and policy number):

Insurance company: _____

Policy number: _____

19. The information provided above is correct to the best of my knowledge:

Signature: _____ Date: _____

Standards Review

TestPractice

Smithsonian Institution Internship Application

Complete the sample test item below by circling the correct answer. Then, read the explanation to the right.

Sample Test Item	Explanation of the Correct Answer
According to the information sheet, which of the following students would be eligible for the Dick Louie Internship? A a high school senior of Asian descent living in San Francisco B a high school senior of Asian descent living in a suburb of Washington, D.C. C a high school sophomore of Asian descent living in Washington, D.C. D a high school senior of Spanish descent living in Washington, D.C.	The correct answer is *B*. The internship is open to Washington-area high school students who are of Asian descent and are entering or completing their senior year of high school. *A* does not live in the Washington area. *C* is not entering or completing the senior year. *D* is not of Asian descent. Only *B* meets all the criteria for eligibility.

DIRECTIONS: Circle the letter of each correct response.

1. If you want to help create exhibits, you might apply to any of these departments *except*—

    A   Public Affairs

    B   Exhibition Management

    C   Curatorial

    D   Design and Installation

2. Which of the following is *not* required from internship applicants?

    F   letter explaining why you are applying

    G   letters of recommendation

    H   completed application form

    J   official high school transcript

3. If you want to start an internship on April 15, apply by—

    A   March 15   C   November 15

    B   July 15   D   April 1

4. The application form on pages 363–364 can be used to apply for—

    F   paid and unpaid internships at the Freer and Sackler Galleries

    G   unpaid internships at the Freer and Sackler Galleries

    H   unpaid internships at any museum of the Smithsonian

    J   the Dick Louie Internship for Americans of Asian Descent

Reading Standard 2.1 (Grade 9–10 Review) Analyze the structure and format of functional workplace documents, including the graphics and headers, and explain how authors use the features to achieve their purposes.

 Check your Standards Mastery at the back of this book.

Armed Forces Enlisted Rank and Insignia

BEFORE YOU READ

The Revolutionary Army wasn't really very revolutionary, at least when it came to rank. The American colonists adapted their system from the British military (who in turn had based theirs on the Roman army). Enlisted soldiers in 1776 were privates, corporals, and sergeants, just like today—except back then they also had a rank just for musicians.

INFORMATIONAL FOCUS: CHARTS AND DIAGRAMS

The chart on the following pages communicates a great deal of information about U.S. military rank—not just through its words and pictures, but by the way those words and pictures are organized into a logical **pattern of organization.** Here's what you'll see:

- **Columns** (vertical, or up-and-down). There are four columns: Army, Navy/Coast Guard (both branches use the same ranking system), Air Force, and Marine Corps.

- **Rows** (horizontal, or side-to-side). There are ten rows, one for each enlisted pay grade from E-1 (lowest) to E-9 and Special Pay Grade (highest). Pay grades are used to standardize pay across the different branches of the military. (*E* stands for *enlisted.*)

- **Rank.** The location of each rank in the chart reveals its branch, pay grade, and equivalence to other branches ranks. For example, Airman Basic is the lowest rank in the Air Force, paid at E-1. It is equivalent to the rank of Private in the Army or Marine Corps, or Seaman Recruit in the Navy or Coast Guard. The ranks are arranged in a **hierarchical order,** going from the lowest rank to the highest.

- **Insignia.** The picture above each rank is its *insignia*—the badge worn (usually on the sleeve) to indicate rank. These insignia are examples of **graphics**—visual elements that convey information.

Reading Standard 2.2
Analyze the way in which clarity of meaning is affected by the patterns of organization, hierarchical structures, repetition of the main ideas, syntax, and word choice in the text.

Reading Standard 2.7 (Grade 9–10 Review)
Critique the logic of functional documents by examining the sequence of information and procedures in anticipation of possible reader misunderstandings.

Armed Forces
Enlisted Rank and Insignia

	Army	Navy/Coast Guard	Air Force	Marine Corps
E-1	No insignia Private (PV1)	 Seaman Recruit (SR)	No insignia Airman Basic (AB)	No insignia Private (PVT)
E-2	Private (PV2)	Seaman Apprentice (SA)	Airman (Amn)	Private First Class (PFC)
E-3	Private First Class (PV2)	Seaman (SN)	Airman First Class (A1C)	Lance Corporal (Lcpl)

IDENTIFY

The lowest rank and the lowest pay is shown in row E-1. Circle the second lowest rank in the Air Force. Circle the equivalent rank in the Army.

SEQUENCE

Are the rows and columns of the chart arranged in any particular order? Explain.

_____

_____

_____

_____

_____

_____

_____

DRAW CONCLUSIONS

Who would you expect to earn more, a private or a sergeant? Check your answer against the chart.

_____

_____

COMPARE & CONTRAST

What is the Marine Corps equivalent of a Navy Seaman (E-3)?

_____

_____

Have you ever seen a Hollywood drill sergeant screaming at new recruits and making them do push-ups? If so, you might be surprised to know that *sergeant* (E-5) comes from the Latin word for "servant." That's because a sergeant served the officers—not the privates.

IDENTIFY

Take a moment to scan the insignias in the chart. In general, how do the insignias change as rank increases?

_____
_____
_____
_____
_____
_____
_____
_____
_____
_____
_____
_____
_____
_____

	Army	Navy/Coast Guard	Air Force	Marine Corps
E-4	Corporal (CPL) 1 / Corporal (CPL) 1	Petty Officer Third Class (PO3)	Senior Airman (SrA)	Corporal (Cpl)
E-5	Sergeant (SGT)	Petty Officer Second Class (PO2)	Staff Sergeant (SSgt)	Sergeant (Sgt)
E-6	Staff Sergeant (SSG)	Petty Officer First Class (PO1)	Technical Sergeant (TSgt)	Staff Sergeant (SSgt)

	Army	Navy/Coast Guard	Air Force	Marine Corps
E-7	Sergeant First Class (SFC)	Chief Petty Officer (CPO) (Collar & Cap)	Master Sergeant First Sergeant (Master Sergeant)	Gunnery Sergeant (GySgt)
E-8	Master Sergeant (MSG) First Sergeant (1SG)	Senior Chief Petty Officer (SCPO) (Collar & Cap)	Senior Master Sergeant (SMSgt) First Sergeant (Senior Master Sergeant)	Master Sergeant (MSgt) First Sergeant (1stSgt)
E-9	Sergeant Major (SGM) Command Sergeant Major (CSM)	Master Chief Petty Officer (MCPO) (Collar & Cap)	First Sergeant (Chief Master (Sergeant) Command Chief Master Sergeant	Master Gunnery Sergeant (MGySgt) Sergeant Major (SgtMaj)
Sp Pay Gd	Sgt. Major of the Army (SMA)	Master Chief Petty Officer of the Navy (MCPON) (Collar & Cap)	Chief Master Sergeant of the Air Force (CMAF)	Sgt. Major of the Marine Corps (SgtMajMC)

ANALYZE

Each row in the chart indicates a change in pay scale. According to the chart, does every promotion to a higher rank come with higher pay?

_____

_____

_____

_____

_____

_____

_____

EVALUATE

Does the information on the chart follow a logical pattern of organization? Why or why not? *(Grade 9–10 Review)*

_____

_____

_____

_____

_____

_____

_____

_____

_____

_____

_____

DOCUMENTS

Armed Forces Enlisted Rank and Insignia

Complete the sample test item below by circling the correct answer. Then, read the explanation to the right.

Sample Test Item	Explanation of the Correct Answer
According to the chart, which of the following ranks are equivalent? **A** Seaman (Navy/Coast Guard) and Airman (Air Force) **B** Sergeant First Class (Army) and Petty Officer First Class (Navy/Coast Guard) **C** Sergeant First Class (Army) and Chief Petty Officer (Navy/Coast Guard) **D** Private First Class (Marine Corps) and Private First Class (Army)	*C* is the answer. Sergeant First Class and Chief Petty Officer are shown on the chart as equivalent ranks. Here's why the other choices are incorrect: Seaman outranks Airman (*A*). Sergeant First Class outranks Petty Officer First Class (*B*). Army Private First Class outranks Marine Corps Private First Class (*D*).

DIRECTIONS: Circle the letter of each correct response.

Reading Standard 2.2
Analyze the way in which clarity of meaning is affected by the patterns of organization, hierarchical structures, repetition of the main ideas, syntax, and word choice in the text.

1. According to the chart, which of the following has the highest rank in the Army?

   A Sergeant Major

   B Sergeant First Class

   C Master Sergeant

   D Staff Sergeant

2. Which of the following ranks is *not* equivalent to the others?

   F Private First Class (Army)

   G Seaman Apprentice (Navy/Coast Guard)

   H Airman First Class (Air Force)

   J Lance Corporal (Marine Corps)

3. The lowest enlisted rank in the Navy is—

   A Seaman

   B Petty Officer Third Class

   C Seaman Apprentice

   D Seaman Recruit

4. The chart is organized by—

   F alphabetical order

   G chronological order

   H hierarchical order

   J order of easiest to find

 Check your Standards Mastery at the back of this book.

How to Apply a Car Decal

If you like the idea of having your car "make a statement," you'll enjoy the next selection. Vinyl decals are a relatively inexpensive way to individualize a car (or any other item with a smooth, flat surface).

INFORMATIONAL FOCUS: TECHNICAL DIRECTIONS

Technical directions are step-by-step instructions that explain how to perform some specialized task. Effective directions are—

- **Complete.** Everything you need to do Is spelled out and explained.

- **Clear.** Sentences are straightforward and understandable. Vocabulary is appropriate for the intended audience.

- **Sequential.** Directions are given step by step, in the order they are to be followed. (These may appear in a numbered or bulleted list.)

- **Accurate.** If you do exactly what they say, you should achieve the promised results.

    Always read directions through before you start.

INFORMATIONAL FOCUS: GRAPHIC FEATURES

Effective directions often contain certain **graphic features** to help readers. As you look through the following set of directions, look for these graphic features—

- Boldface headers that clearly identify steps in the process

- A bulleted list that describes the parts of a decal

- A numbered list that presents directions in a step-by-step sequence

- Drawings and photos that illustrate the text

Terms to Know

Bullets: dots, diamonds, squares, or other shapes used to introduce lists in point-by-point order.

Caption: text that labels, explains, or describes an illustration, diagram, or photograph.

Graphic: any visual device used to illustrate, demonstrate, or highlight a text.

Point-by-point sequence: a sequence that states each point in no particular order.

Step-by-step sequence: a sequence that tells what to do first, second, third, etc.

Reading Standard 2.6 (Grade 9–10 Review) Demonstrate use of sophisticated learning tools by following technical directions (e.g., those found with graphic calculators and specialized software programs and in access guides to World Wide Web sites on the Internet).

"How to Apply a Car Decal" from Decalzone Web site at http://www.decalzone.com/decfacts.shtml. Copyright 2001 by **Decalzone.** Reprinted by permission of the publisher.

How to Apply a Car Decal

Measuring for Decals

Measuring for decals is not difficult, but it does take a bit of common sense. When we refer to overall area, this refers to the imaginary rectangular area that surrounds the particular group of letters you are measuring for. Here are some examples of measurements of overall area:

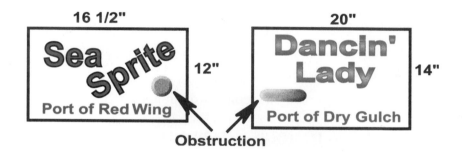

Sometimes, you might need to include a minor obstruction within the overall area, but make sure it
10   will fall in a spot that won't interfere with the lettering. Please be aware that doing so might require the decal to be modified before installation. For instance, you can always separate lines or individual letters of a decal before application, if you wish.

The Three Parts of a Decal

- **Application paper** is the paper or plastic mask that makes multiple letters stay together.
- **Backing** is the wax paper that is applied to the sticky side of the decal. The backing keeps the decal
20   from sticking to anything prior to installation.
- The actual **decal** is sandwiched between the application paper and the backing at the time of purchase. The decal is what ends up installed to the surface.

Before You Start, Check:

Surface compatibility. The surface must be hard, flat, and nonporous. Special skills are needed to deal with major bodylines, complex curves, corrugated surfaces, etc.

30 **Surface Temperature and Weather Conditions**

- Surface temperature must be between 60°F and 90°F, with 70°F to 80°F being the ideal range.

- It can't be raining or even drizzling. Decals must be kept absolutely dry until installed.

- Try to avoid installing decals in direct sunlight. Surface temperatures in direct sunlight often change rapidly and are difficult to judge.

- Make sure there is no wind. Wind or gusts will cause a problem.

40 **Cleaning and Prepping Surface**

- If surface is at all dirty, wash with soap and water. Rinse with water until there is no more soap or soap residue. Make sure surface is absolutely dry before proceeding to next step.

- Thoroughly wipe down the area of the surface where decal is to be applied, using a commercial "surface prep" fluid or alcohol. Glass cleaners and other ammonia-based products are not recom-
50 mended for this purpose, even with glass installations.

- Once the surface is clean, installation may begin. A clean surface will help to ensure that your decal will stay in place for both the short and long run.

Installing Decals Using the Simple Method (Smaller Decals)

1. Decide where you want your decal to go. Tape it into position with small pieces of masking tape along the top of the decal.

ANALYZE

Water soluble means "able to be dissolved in water." Why is it important to use a pencil that is water soluble (lines 59–62)?

_____

_____

_____

_____

_____

CLARIFY

Line 84 says to "apply moderate heat," but does not explain where the heat should come from. Reading ahead to the next paragraph (*Decal Removal*), what heat source might be used to flatten bubbles?

_____

_____

EVALUATE

Based on the criteria given on page 371, does "How to Apply a Car Decal" seem to be an effective set of directions? Explain.

_____

_____

_____

_____

_____

_____

60 2. Make a mark on each end of the decal (see right) with a water soluble pencil. Start the mark on the application paper of the decal, and end the mark on the surface that you are installing to.

3. Remove the decal, leaving the marks on the installation surface. Remove and discard the masking tape and backing at this time.

70 4. Keeping the decal taut, line up marks and adhere decal. (The help of another person makes positioning much easier.)

5. With the application paper still intact, take a squeegee and apply the lettering by pressing on the surface of the application paper. Using even strokes, start at the middle of the letters, and work your way out. Carefully remove application paper.

The job is done!

Dealing with Bubbles

80 You will probably end up with some bubbles in your decal job. Small bubbles will go away in time. (The film breathes and will flatten out after a few weeks at an appropriate temperature.) If you want to work on the bubbles immediately, apply moderate heat, then poke them with a pin, pressing the film down with your thumb immediately afterward.

Decal Removal

Decal removal can vary in difficulty, depending on a few things: the quality of the film to be removed, 90 how long it's been on, if it's weather-beaten, etc. Move along the decal with a hair dryer or a heat gun, picking the letters or stripping off as you go. If there is glue left behind, clean it up with some petroleum naphtha (available at your local hardware store) applied to a rag.

Standards Review

DOCUMENTS

## How to Apply a Car Decal

Complete the sample test item below by circling the correct answer. Then, read the explanation to the right.

Sample Test Item	Explanation of the Correct Answer
Which of the following features provided in the directions helps you measure for decals? A sample measurements B a definition of what a decal is C a numbered list of steps for installing a decal D an illustration of a decal	The correct answer is *A*. The definition (*B*) does not help you measure; the numbered list (*C*) is useful but also provides no measuring help; the photograph (*D*) is interesting, but not useful for measuring itself.

DIRECTIONS: Circle the letter of each correct response.

1. Which of the following set of conditions is best for decal application?

   A drizzling, no wind

   B windy and hot

   C shady and warm

   D bright sunshine

2. Which of the following application steps should be done *last*?

   F Remove the masking tape and backing.

   G Remove the application paper.

   H Tape the decal into position.

   J Mark each end of the decal with a pencil.

3. Which of the following is not listed as a difficulty factor in decal removal?

   A how long the decal has been on

   B quality of the decal

   C whether the decal is weather-beaten

   D whether the decal was installed properly

4. In what order are the items presented in the bulleted list on surface temperature and weather conditions?

   F point-by-point

   G step-by-step

   H chronological

   J order of importance

Reading Standard 2.6 (Grade 9–10 Review) Demonstrate use of sophisticated learning tools by following technical directions (e.g., those found with graphic calculators and specialized software programs and in access guides to World Wide Web sites on the Internet).

 Check your Standards Mastery at the back of this book.

Checklist for Standards Mastery

Each time you read, you learn something new. Track your growth as a reader and your progress toward success by checking off skills you have acquired. If you read all the selections in this book and complete the sidenote questions and activities, you will be able to check off, at least once, all the standards for success listed below.

✓	California Reading Standard (Grade 9–10 Review)	Selection/Author
☐	**1.1** Identify and use the literal and figurative meanings of words and understand word derivations.	
☐	**1.2** Distinguish between the denotative and connotative meanings of words and interpret the connotative power of words.	
☐	**1.3** Identify Greek, Roman, and Norse mythology and use the knowledge to understand the origin and meaning of new words (e.g., the word *narcissistic* drawn from the myth of Narcissus and Echo).	
☐	**2.1** Analyze the structure and format of functional workplace documents, including the graphics and headers, and explain how authors use the features to achieve their purposes.	
☐	**2.3** Generate relevant questions about readings on issues that can be researched.	
☐	**2.5** Extend ideas presented in primary or secondary sources through original analysis, evaluation, and elaboration.	
☐	**2.6** Demonstrate use of sophisticated learning tools by following technical directions (e.g., those found with graphic calculators and specialized software programs and in access guides to World Wide Web sites on the Internet).	

✓	California Reading Standard (Grade 9–10 Review)	Selection/Author
☐	**2.7** Critique the logic of functional documents by examining the sequence of information and procedures in anticipation of possible reader misunderstandings.	
☐	**2.8** Evaluate the credibility of an author's argument or defense of a claim by critiquing the relationship between generalizations and evidence, the comprehensiveness of evidence, and the way in which the author's intent affects the structure and tone of the text (e.g., in professional journals, editorials, political speeches, primary source material).	
☐	**3.3** Analyze interactions between main and subordinate characters in a literary text (e.g., internal and external conflicts, motivations, relationships, influences) and explain the way those interactions affect the plot.	
☐	**3.4** Determine characters' traits by what the characters say about themselves in narration, dialogue, dramatic monologue, and soliloquy.	
☐	**3.5** Compare works that express a universal theme and provide evidence to support the ideas expressed in each work.	
☐	**3.6** Analyze and trace an author's development of time and sequence, including the use of complex literary devices (e.g., foreshadowing, flashbacks).	
☐	**3.7** Recognize and understand the significance of various literary devices, including figurative language, imagery, allegory, and symbolism, and explain their appeal.	
☐	**3.8** Interpret and evaluate the impact of ambiguities, subtleties, contradictions, ironies, and incongruities in a text.	

✓	California Reading Standard (Grade 9–10 Review)	Selection/Author
☐	**3.9** Explain how voice, persona, and the choice of a narrator affect characterization and the tone, plot, and credibility of a text.	
☐	**3.11** Evaluate the aesthetic qualities of style, including the impact of figurative language on tone, mood, and theme, using the terminology of literary criticism. (Aesthetic approach)	
☐	**3.12** Analyze the way in which a work of literature is related to the themes and issues of its historical period. (Historical approach)	

✓	California Grades 11–12 Reading Standard	Selection/Author
☐	**1.0** Students apply their knowledge of word origins to determine the meaning of new words encountered in reading materials and use those words accurately.	
☐	**1.1** Trace the etymology of significant terms used in political science and history.	
☐	**1.2** Apply knowledge of Greek, Latin, and Anglo-Saxon roots and affixes to draw inferences concerning the meaning of scientific and mathematical terminology.	
☐	**1.3** Discern the meaning of analogies encountered, analyzing specific comparisons as well as relationships and inferences.	
☐	**2.1** Analyze both the features and the rhetorical devices of different types of public documents (e.g., policy statements, speeches, debates, platforms) and the way in which authors use those features and devices.	
☐	**2.2** Analyze the way in which clarity of meaning is affected by the patterns of organization, hierarchical structures, repetition of the main ideas, syntax, and word choice in the text.	

✓	California Grades 11–12 Reading Standard	Selection/Author
☐	**2.4** Make warranted and reasonable assertions about the author's arguments by using elements of the text to defend and clarify interpretations.	
☐	**2.5** Analyze an author's implicit and explicit philosophical assumptions and beliefs about a subject.	
☐	**2.6** Critique the power, validity, and truthfulness of arguments set forth in public documents; their appeal to both friendly and hostile audiences; and the extent to which the arguments anticipate and address reader concerns and counterclaims (e.g., appeal to reason, to authority, to pathos and emotion).	
☐	**3.1** Analyze characteristics of subgenres (e.g., satire, parody, allegory, pastoral) that are used in poetry, prose, plays, novels, short stories, essays, and other basic genres.	
☐	**3.2** Analyze the way in which the theme or meaning of a selection represents a view or comment on life, using textual evidence to support the claim.	
☐	**3.3** Analyze the ways in which irony, tone, mood, the author's style, and the "sound" of language achieve specific rhetorical or aesthetic purposes or both.	
☐	**3.4** Analyze ways in which poets use imagery, personification, figures of speech, and sounds to evoke readers' emotions.	
☐	**3.5** Analyze recognized works of American literature representing a variety of genres and traditions: **a.** Trace the development of American literature from the colonial period forward. **b.** Contrast the major periods, themes, styles, and trends and describe how works by members of different cultures relate to one another in each period. **c.** Evaluate the philosophical, political, religious, ethical, and social influences of the historical period that shaped the characters, plots, and settings.	

✓	California Grades 11–12 Reading Standard	Selection/Author
☐	**3.6** Analyze the way in which authors through the centuries have used archetypes drawn from myth and tradition in literature, film, political speeches, and religious writings (e.g., how the archetypes of banishment from an ideal world may be used to interpret Shakespeare's tragedy *Macbeth*).	
☐	**3.7** Analyze recognized works of world literature from a variety of authors: **a.** Contrast the major literary forms, techniques, and characteristics of the major literary periods (e.g., Homeric Greece, medieval, romantic, neoclassic, modern). **b.** Relate literary works and authors to the major themes and issues of their eras. **c.** Evaluate the philosophical, political, religious, ethical, and social influences of the historical period that shaped the characters, plots, and settings.	
☐	**3.8** Analyze the clarity and consistency of political assumptions in a selection of literary works or essays on a topic (e.g., suffrage, women's role in organized labor). (Political approach)	
☐	**3.9** Analyze the philosophical arguments presented in literary works to determine whether the authors' positions have contributed to the quality of each work and the credibility of the characters. (Philosophical approach)	

Index of Authors and Titles

Vocabulary Development

Pronunciation guides, in parentheses, are provided for the vocabulary words in this book. The following key will help you use those pronunciation guides.

As a practice in using a pronunciation guide, sound out the words used as examples in the list that follows. See if you can hear the way the same vowel might be sounded in different words. For example, say "at" and "ate" aloud. Can you hear the difference in the way "a" sounds?

The symbol ə is called a **schwa.** A schwa is used by many dictionaries to indicate a sort of weak sound like the "a" in "ago." Some people say the schwa sounds like "eh." A vowel sounded like a schwa is never accented.

The vocabulary words in this book are also provided with a part of speech. The parts of speech are *n.* (noun), *v.* (verb), *pro.* (pronoun), *adj.* (adjective), *adv.* (adverb), *prep.* (preposition), *conj.* (conjunction), and *interj.* (interjection). To learn about the parts of speech, consult the *Holt Handbook.*

To learn more about the vocabulary words, consult your dictionary. You will find that many of the words defined here have several other meanings.

---

at, āte, cär; ten, ēve; is, īce; gō, hôrn, lŏŏk, tōōl; oil, out; up, fur, ə *for unstressed vowels, as* a *in ago,* u *in* focus; ' *as in* Latin (lat''n); chin; she; zh *as in* azure (azh'ər); thin, *the;* ŋ *as in* ring (riŋ)

Picture Credits